P9-DIB-617

THE

CITY OF

FLORENCE

THE

CITY OF

FLORENCE

Historical Vistas and

Personal Sightings

R . W . B . LEWIS

Farrar, Straus and Giroux

NEW YORK

351 p. ; ill. ; 24cm

Copyright © 1995 by R.W.B. Lewis
All rights reserved
Printed in the United States of America
Published simultaneously in Canada by HarperCollinsCanadaLtd
First edition, 1995

Library of Congress Cataloging-in-Publication Data
Lewis, R.W.B. (Richard Warrington Baldwin)
The city of Florence : historical vistas and personal sightings /
R.W.B. Lewis.—1st ed.
p.   cm.
Includes bibliographical references and index.
1. Florence (Italy)—History.   I. Title.
DG736.L49   1995   945'.51—dc20   94–20160   CIP

FRONTISPIECE
View of Florence from Via della Fornace

FOR NANCY

*Tanto gentile e tanto
onesta pare
La donna mia . . .*

Contents

Prologue: The Belated Florentine / *3*

I. DESIGNS AND DESIGNERS

1. Along the Arno / *21*

2. Stories of the Casentino / *57*

3. The Real City of Arnolfo di Cambio / *81*

   The Public Thing / *81*

   The Works of Arnolfo / *94*

   A Knowable City / *108*

4. Medici Country / *119*

   Florence Becomes a Work of Art / *119*

   Brunelleschi's Vision / *134*

   The Dominion of Cosimo / *158*

   The Day of the Palazzi / *165*

5. The Making and Unmaking of Modern Florence / *171*

   The Interval: 1500–1850 / *171*

   Poggi and the City Shape: The 1860s / *182*

   Destruction at the Center: The 1880s / *189*

II. POINTS OF VIEW

6. *Roman Gate and Beautiful Outlook: The 1970s* / *199*
    Down in the City / *199*
    Up at the Villa / *213*
7. *Vespucci Territory: 1987* / *245*
    Summertime / *245*
    L'idea di Firenze / *260*
8. *The Santa Croce Neighborhood: 1992–93* / *273*
    The Piazza / *273*
    The Quartiere / *286*
    The Neighborhood / *297*
    E pòi: Last Words / *311*

Acknowledgments / *323*
Notes on Maps and Illustrations / *327*
Some Scholarly and Literary Sources / *335*
Contemporary Guidances / *341*
General Index / *343*
Index of Florentine Place-names / *349*

THE

CITY OF

FLORENCE

Prologue

The Belated Florentine

"Why do you live in that dusty backwater?" asked Ignazio Silone. It was the spring of 1958, and we were sitting with the Italian novelist in the Stazione Termini in Rome, waiting for our train to Florence. We had just returned, Nancy Lewis and I, from a visit with Silone to his native Abruzzi (where I had spent the war-winter of 1944 and had first come upon Silone's writings, *Fontamara*, *Bread and Wine*, and the others). Like many non-Roman-born residents of Rome, Silone was never able to understand why anyone would want to spend more than a weekend anywhere else in Italy. A few years earlier, when I was writing a long essay about him, Silone braced himself to come up to Florence for an American Thanksgiving dinner in our Costa dei Magnoli apartment, across the river from the Uffizi. This visit, announced by telegram with customary succinctness—ARRIVO POMERIGGIO GIOVEDI SILONE—threw us into something of a turmoil; it was uncertain that our oven was big enough for a turkey. In any event, the stay evidently did nothing to change Silone's mind—that quizzical, darkly amused Abruzzese mind—about the huge disparity of stimulus between the city on the Tiber and the city on the Arno.

Silone's question tantalized me for a long time afterwards. In a ruthlessly contemporary perspective, Florence *is* something of a backwater. The lives of arts and letters are mostly concentrated elsewhere; and, at least until recently, the harried dramas of Italy, both political and criminal, have taken place on other urban stages—Rome, Milan, Turin, Naples. The bomb that exploded outside the Uffizi in April 1993 may signal a new stage of things terroristic: an attempt to stir agitation and disruption by destroying works of art instead of political or financial figures. What seemed to be follow-up bombings a couple of months later in Rome and Milan, where churches and an art gallery were the targets, intensify that sense of threat. One can only pray that these will turn out to be isolated events. And the fact is, meantime, that over the decades the relative calm of Florence has been one source of its appeal.

For anyone, like myself, who usually comes abroad (until recently, on academic leaves of absence) seeking a quiet place for work, Florence seems to provide an environment at once attractive and undemanding. But for peace and quiet there are other places an American might choose, beginning with some little corner of New England and following with sheltered nooks across the land through New Mexico to northern California.

The university folk I have known, if they come to Italy at all, tend to head for Rome; we have grown used to kindly letters from friends who tell us how they envy our being in Florence, they were there for several days ten years ago and have never forgotten it. Nor have I had any professional involvement with the city and its history, but have customarily arrived in Florence with half a dozen boxes of books and chapter notes relating to American literature and history. For *work*, that New England corner would be much more sensible.

Why Florence? This book is an attempt to answer that question, Silone's question. The inquiry must perforce be both inward and outward; it must dip into the past, both the historical and personal; and it must explore the present.

In the great division between Italophiles, my father was a Roman rather than a Florentine (devoted Venetians must also, now, be numbered among visiting Americans, but the older division was the one traditionally described). This was natural enough: he was an Anglican clergyman with a scholarly interest in church history, and lost no opportunity to pursue his researches in the Vatican library, in the Catacombs, in St. Paul-Outside-the-Walls. One such occasion, in 1920, brought the entire family, including my older four-year-old brother and me, to Rome for a stay of several months. So, as it happened, my earliest Italian memory came from well south of the Tuscan border—a memory of a side trip to Naples and of being carried up Mount Vesuvius on the back of a good-natured guide. A decade later I came down from the little English-run school in the Bernese Oberland, where I had been convalescing from tuberculosis with the help of the Swiss air, to join the family for Easter in Rome. My enthusiasm for the city, where my father piloted us knowingly through the Forum and onto the Spanish Steps, was unrestrained. "It beats everything else all hollow," I wrote a school friend back home.

It was the fortunes of war that next brought me back to Italy, and for the first time into Tuscany. After a long season in and out of Cairo and the Western Desert as liaison officer with a British intelligence unit, I was assigned to a headquarters in southeastern Italy in September 1943. We moved north to a site on the Adriatic coast in the fall, below Pescara; and it was from here, trying to carry out a mission on a November night, that I got myself trapped behind enemy lines. A more detailed account of the misadventure will be offered in a later chapter. Suffice it for now that, after I managed to make my way back to Allied territory, I was given my own mobile command with the same intelligence outfit. Following the liberation of Rome in 1944, with the front lines advancing rapidly northward, I shifted base from a villa below the walls of Assisi to a farmhouse outside Arezzo, in the upper Arno valley. In mid-August, I drove a heavily laden Jeep across the Ponte Vecchio into Florence, so recently and ferociously shattered by German dynamite; and there or thereabouts, with a stint in the South Tyrol, I was to remain for almost two years.

But for some time before the war my intellectual interests had been drifting almost insensibly toward Tuscany. As an undergraduate at Harvard, I had majored in the history and literature of the Renaissance; and though my honors essay was on Marguerite de Navarre—the sister of King Henri IV of France and the author of an elegantly bawdy imitation of Boccaccio—I had devoted a fair amount of study as well to medieval and Renaissance Florence. Under the gracious and winning tutelage of Theodore Spencer, I worked my way through the *Divine Comedy*, one of the two most unforgettable reading experiences of my life. I also audited a course on Florentine painting given by an irascible professor named Chandler Post, a man who detested and feared Leonardo da Vinci as though the latter were still alive, still exercising a malign influence on the development of Italian art, still ruining his canvases by headstrong experimentations with pigments. I attended a series of richly learned lectures on Florentine history by Gaetano Salvemini, the embattled, aggressively bearded, and heroic exile from Fascist Italy, who was one of the most humane scholars of his time. The ignorance I brought to this course was immeasurable, but by the end of it I had acquired some grasp of the political and economic vicissitudes of Florence from the twelfth century onward, and its gradual ascendancy over the domain of Tuscany.

During two years of graduate work at the University of Chicago, I continued my study of the later Middle Ages and the Renaissance in Europe, though without any clear sense of direction or commitment. I wrote a master's essay (for the life of me, I cannot remember or imagine why) on an obscure fifteenth-century German logician; but I felt much more at home in courses on Italian culture. There was the extravagantly histrionic Giuseppe Borgese lecturing brilliantly on Ariosto's comic epic, *Orlando Furioso*, staring out the window when he came to the delightful figure of Angelica and saying, as though speaking to himself of a former mistress, "She . . . was . . . ADD-orable!" There were the fast-moving slide-lectures on Tuscan art and architecture by a young German-born art historian, Ulrich Middledorf. (Thirty-five years later, I reencountered Professor Middledorf as the enormously helpful director of the German Institute in Florence, possibly the greatest center in the world for Renaissance studies.) And there was an unexpectedly enjoyable seminar on Renaissance Latin, in which the scholarly instructor pointed with some excitement, in one of Petrarch's letters, to the first use of the informal *tibi* since Cicero. He also introduced us to the elegant writings of the fifteenth-century Italian humanists, from Leonardo Bruni to Angelo Poliziano.

So as I made my way through the rubble of Florence and into the comparatively untouched sections of the city in 1944, I had reason to bless whatever precomputer apparatus it was that had dispatched me to the Italian war zone.

And yet the immediate effect of the long period in Tuscany during the latter part of the war and for a year afterwards was not to solidify my involvement with Florentine history, art, and literature. On the contrary. Toward the end of my stay I read *Moby-Dick*; it was the second of my most mind-consuming reading experiences, and on the spot I became dedicated to the study of American literature. Indeed, though the process was slow and unsystematic, the experience of wartime Italy was leading me to question—in a way that had never before occurred to me to do—just what being an American was all about.* I received a lively shock of recognition, a few years later, when I read the first sentence of the travel journal *From the Heart of Europe*, by my former and revered teacher F. O. Matthiessen: "I came to Europe to discover what it means to be an American." Gradually, it seemed, everything began to serve—by contrast—to illuminate the matter: language, manners, sense of humor, women; the lethal political deviousness of the French authorities in Italy (before which the innocent American stood aghast and bewildered); the British reluctance to dispose of even the most decrepit equipment (before which the wasteful American stood seething with impatience). Most of all, there was the felt inescapable presence of the past at every turn. It extended to the root matter of identity. I was struck, examining the identification card of an Abruzzese

---

* I rehearsed this bit of personal history, to somewhat different purpose, in the preface to my collection of literary essays, *Literary Reflections: A Shoring of Images* (1993).

peasant who had befriended me, by the fact that he was described in it as *Sciotti Berardino di fu Lorenzo*—Berardino Sciotti [son] of the late Lorenzo. The man's very identity included his father and the fact that his father was no longer alive.

When I returned to graduate study at the University of Chicago in the fall of 1946, I began a strenuous course of study of American literary and intellectual history, with special attention to the age of Melville and Emerson—jumping, as Matthiessen remarked on a visit to the university, from the European to the American Renaissance. For my doctoral dissertation, I addressed myself to a phenomenon that Berardino's identity card had prepared me to recognize: the continuing image in nineteenth-century writing of the characteristic American as a man *without* a past, a sort of newborn Adam inhabiting a country evasive of the forces and lessons of history.

In 1950–51, when I was Dean of Studies at the Salzburg Seminar in American Studies (an intercultural entity founded by F. O. Matthiessen and others after the end of the Second World War), my duties involved traveling about the Continent recruiting European applicants. More than once I managed to include Florence in my itinerary. Nancy Lindau and I had gotten married at the start of the Salzburg year, in June 1950, and we traveled together on these recruiting trips. Our shared love affair with Florence began with several three-week sojourns in the city. Since 1950, we have stayed in Florence more than a dozen times, for a total period of something like six years.

These occasions were not "visits," properly speaking, for on every one we were *living* in the city; we were (increasingly) at home in it—in this or that apartment or converted farmhouse or portion of a villa. When, in the spring of 1963, we occupied a penthouse high above Via Lamarmora overlooking the Duomo— at night, a motionless, majestic red-and-white bowl within the larger bowl of the dark-blue Tuscan sky—I began to understand Ghirlandaio's remark, that whenever he was away from Florence for any length of time he suffered from the "Duomo-sickness." And I came to understand what was meant by Lorenzo Magalotti, the seventeenth-century man of many artistic and intellectual trades, when, abruptly abandoning his diplomatic post in Vienna and hurrying back to his native city, he remarked to a friend that it was unreasonable that "we Florentines be asked to stay for more than six months beyond the reach of the shadow of the Cupola." Even today, Florentines are almost harder to dislodge from their *città* than are the Romans.

But these understandings were for many years no more than a general engagement of the heart. There was a not unfamiliar paradox in our relationship to Florence: exactly because we were living in it, because we were residents rather than curiosity-driven visitors, we did not seek to know it in depth. We became familiar soon enough with the best-known sites and monuments: the Piazza della Signoria and the Palazzo Vecchio; the Duomo (the cathedral of Santa Maria del Fiori) and the Baptistery, with its bronze doors. Santa Maria Novella, its exquisite facade vivid in my mind from the moment I saw it on a slide in Ulrich Middledorf's graduate course; Santa Croce and its illustrious dead; San Lorenzo and the Medici tombs; San Marco and, in the adjoining convent, the *Annunciation* of Fra Angelico that leaps out at you, breathtakingly, from the head of the stairs. Orsanmichele, with its progression of statues in niches outside, taking part in the very life of the busy streets around it; inside, the glittering tabernacle of Andrea Orcagna. The Bargello, with its infinitely friendly cortile and the statuary of Donatello; the Accademia and Michelangelo's *David*; the galleries in the Uffizi and the Palazzo Pitti. Ponte Santa Trinità and Ponte Vecchio; Palazzo Strozzi and Palazzo Medici. Via Tornabuoni, Via della Vigna Nuova, Via dei Calzaiuoli, Borgo San Jacopo. To these we returned time and again, as to old friends always there to be looked up and, as it were, chatted with after a period of absence. But we did not set out on planned explorations of the city. All we knew was that we helplessly loved the place, and did not pause to ask why.

To make the point, at the risk of sounding even more comatose than perhaps I was, let me offer an example. In the fall of 1957, we were living in a small apartment on the first floor of a narrow-fronted palazzo in Piazza Santa Trinità (I was Fulbright Lecturer at Munich that year, but classes didn't start until November). We were quite aware that ours was a superb location: the river and the graceful Trinità bridge visible from our drawing-room window; across the way, the church of Santa Trinità, which we ducked into of an afternoon to catch a glimpse of the Ghirlandaio frescoes; stretching away to our right, Via Tornabuoni and its stately old palaces, its bookstores and music stores, its inviting cafés. Three minutes away was Piazza della Signoria and, squeezed hulkingly into one corner, Palazzo Vecchio, beneath whose battlements and gaunt thrusting tower we would sit for an hour at a time, sipping *cappucini* and staring upward.

Yet we made little attempt to pin down, to particularize, these surroundings, or to take in new aspects of the city at large. Florence was where we were most contentedly living, and where I was working—on something entirely unrelated to Tuscany: in fact, on a full-scale essay about the writings of Graham Greene, which was to provide the next-to-last part of a book dealing with a group of modern novelists and called *The Picaresque Saint*. To this I devoted my mornings and late afternoons; in between, I would go out, if so inclined, to look at the Botticellis in the Uffizi or the tombs of Michelangelo and Machiavelli in Santa Croce.

One of the phases of Florentine life that we most enjoyed at this time (as at any other time) and that pleasantly occupied our attention had to do with meals. At one o'clock every Sunday, Leo Vadorini, the high-spirited waiter from Harry's Bar, came hastening up Via Parione to Piazza Santa Trinità bringing us a large tray that held a beaker of Bloody Marys and a pile of fresh, tasty chicken sandwiches. And on the ground floor of the rugged old building that stood up square-shouldered and battlemented between us and the river was a small "Tea Room" run by the ageless and lively Leland. He was a Florentine by birth, who had adopted his American name, so he used to say, after serving as a houseboy in the California home of Leland Stanford. He offered the best dry martinis in town (concocted by his daughter Clara); but for the knowing few, and working in a space not much bigger than a telephone booth, with an electric burner and a saucepan, Leland would also perform miracles of superlative and original cooking. When we dropped by of a late morning to ask what was on the menu that day, Leland would invariably fling up his hands and exclaim that it was something *fan-TAS-tico!*

It was more than a decade before we began to give an artistic and historical identity to these several places. The palazzo we lived in during the fall of 1957 turned out to be that of Bartolini-Salimbene, one of the handsomest and ultimately one of the most influential private buildings of the early cinquecento. It was begun in 1520 by the forward-looking Florentine architect Baccio d'Agnolo* for the arrogantly independent Giovanni Bartolini, whose family had moved to Florence from Siena two centuries before. The palazzo reflected Baccio d'Agnolo's architectural studies in Rome and the attractive examples of Raphael and Bramante—enough, at the outset, to arouse derision and animosity among the artistically patriotic Florentines. The firmly delineated facade facing the piazza—the ground-floor columns standing out in bold relief, the several stories clearly distinguished one from another, the square windows alternating with niches on the first and second floors, and the whole a delicate play of light and shadow—caused something of an uproar. It was said that the windows, each divided by a stone cross and topped by a triangular pediment, were more suitable to a church (or perhaps to any public building) than to a private home; and, indeed, they do resemble the windows of the church of Santa Trinità across the way. After listening to the complaints, Baccio d'Agnolo came back and cut an inscription above the door: *Carpere promptius quam imitare*—It is easier to criticize than to imitate. Imitation followed in due course, most notably in the modest and charming Palazzo Larderel (1580) further along Via Tornabuoni; and the Duc de Retz had an exact copy built for him in Paris.

The construction of no other Renaissance building in Florence is as thoroughly documented as that of Palazzo Bartolini. We know that Giovanni Bartolini paid almost 2,000 florins for the houses and shops in Piazza Santa Trinità which he bought and tore down to make way for his new home. Baccio d'Agnolo

---

* Sometimes spelled d'Angelo. On the erratic spelling of Florentine names, of both persons and places, see p. 339.

worked exactly thirty-six of the thirty-nine months between February 1520 and May 1523 at two florins a month: miserable pay, incidentally, especially as against the 10,000 florins which the far from liberal Bartolini spent on the entire enterprise.

Palazzo Bartolini remained a family residence until 1839. It was then rented out to a young foreign couple who converted it into the Hôtel du Nord, for many years the most cosmopolitan hotel in the city. James Russell Lowell passed the winter of 1870 there; a plaque commemorating his visit is on the Via delle Terme side of the building. Ralph Waldo Emerson stayed in the hotel throughout the autumn of 1873 with his daughter Ellen. Thomas Babington Macaulay was among its other guests. In late March 1857, on his way back from the Holy Land and en route from Naples and Rome to Venice, Herman Melville arrived for a few days.

Though Melville based a number of poems on his Italian journey (among them the powerful and twisting lyric "In a Bye-Canal") and though he faithfully made notes for a lecture on "Statuary in Rome," he was, to judge from his journal jottings, a rather conventional traveler—a phenomenon observable elsewhere with writers of genius groping about on unfamiliar ground. There is a certain cheeriness of tone, an effort, so to speak, to domesticate the alien. About a crowded thoroughfare in Rome, he wrote: "Could hardly tell it from Broadway. Thought I was there." And after inspecting a portrait of Lucrezia Borgia in Rome, he remarked: "No wicked look about her. Good looking dame— rather fleshy." In Florence, Melville spent a good many hours at Doney's Cafe, a few doors down from the Hôtel du Nord; it had opened in 1822 and by now was a main gathering point for foreign visitors. He even thought that "something good might be written on the 'Caffe Doney,' " the young men who gathered there, and the "flower-girls," pretty young Florentine women who pressed bouquets of flowers upon the cafe's clientele in the hope of securing their patronage. For the rest, Melville was "amazed" by the "magnificence" of the Duomo and the bell tower, and the view from the cupola was "noble." The Uffizi simply wore him down, as it has many others; he quoted with sympathy the com-

Ponte Santa Trinità, 1744

Lungarno, with palazzi, 1744

ment of a lady coming out of the gallery, exhausted (as he said) by "an excess of pleasure": "It's as bad as too much pain; it gets to be pain at last." But it was, for me and in lengthy retrospect, a stirring little experience to think that the author of *Moby-Dick* had stayed in the same building—perhaps the same rooms?— almost precisely a century ahead of us.

The fortresslike edifice that contained Leland's Tea Room, we discovered, was Palazzo Spini. It was built after the flood of 1288, which half destroyed the tower house then existing, for Geri degli Spini, a man of many outstanding abilities—political, mercantile, and military—who performed valiantly in the crucial battle between the Florentines and the forces of Arezzo at Campaldino in 1289 (see Chapter Two). The Spini palace may well have been based on a design of Arnolfo di Cambio; it is certainly Arnolfian in its robust, clifflike, and concentrated character. It is the oldest surviving example in Florence of the grandiose medieval private home; and for a long time the river road, Lungarno, ran right through a ground-level opening in the tower on the palace's southern flank. (The tower was demolished in 1824 to make carriage traffic easier.)

At Harry's Bar,* we would sometimes sit late in the twilight of a Sunday afternoon—Harry's was accommodatingly open on Sundays at this time. We would look across the narrow street into the Via Parione entrance to Palazzo Corsini. Originally built in the late-sixteenth century, the palazzo came into the hands of the Corsini family around 1650, and they transformed and enlarged it, adding a roof terrace with statuary overlooking the Arno and, below it, a much broader *terrazza* for social extravagances. Gardens pushed out to the riverbank. Palazzo Corsini, with its two

---

* Harry's Bar opened at Via Parione 5or in December 1953. It was the creation of Enrico (Henry, or Harry) Mariotti and Raffaello Sabatini, whom I had come to know as the skillful and courteous bartenders at the Hotel Excelsior in Florence during the last winter of the war. It had no formal relation with the more famous Harry's Bar in Venice, which entered American literature in the pages of Hemingway's *Across the River and Into the Trees*; but the Venetian restaurateurs gave a good deal of friendly advice. The Florentine Harry's Bar moved to its present address on Lungarno, fronting the river not far from the Carraia bridge, in 1964. It is now owned and managed by the greatly skilled and outgoing Leo Vadorini.

immense wings rearing up on either side of the big terrace, is another imposingly large building, yet not massive like Palazzo Spini but full of movement and vivacity—its whole being, one feels, an ample gesture of welcome to the convivialities of social life. (Its infrequently visitable gallery holds paintings by Botticelli, Signorelli, Giovanni Bellini, and Bronzino, among others.)

In that autumn of 1957, accordingly, we were in immediate touch with a rapid or exemplary survey of Florentine architectural and social history—medieval, Renaissance, and post-Renaissance. These three palazzi—rugged Spini, severely graceful Bartolini, festive and ornate Corsini—are as unlike one another as buildings can be. Yet looked at from across the river—from where a single glance can take in all three—they appear oddly conscious of one another. They have a living relationship; they stand juxtaposed without jostling, respectful and self-respectful. Much of old Florence, in its private life, is implicit in the pattern they form.

In *Rome and a Villa*, one of the fine pieces of imaginative travel writing of our time in English, Eleanor Clark, almost in an aside, sums up this sense of Florence. She is talking about the first and the last great impression made upon one by Rome—its visible layers of time, dislocated, unconnected. The impression is most striking in the piazza adjacent to Piazza Venezia, from which, peering up, you can see the early medieval church of Aracoeli, with its alarmingly long, steep flight of steps; to the right, the broader and gentler stone ramp, designed by Michelangelo in 1536 and leading up to the Capitol (*Campidoglio*), its splendid piazza, and surrounding palaces, likewise the creation of Michelangelo; to the left, the huge, garish, and somehow endearing monument of 1913 to King Vittorio Emmanuele. And behind it all, one is aware, lies the ancient Roman forum with its temples, statues, and sacred ways. These various buildings, Ms. Clark comments, ignore one another in present fact, as their architects did at the creative moment. They exist in self-affirming independence; they are antisocial. She continues:

The city has its own language in time, its own vocabulary for the eye, for which nothing else was any preparation; no other place was so difficult, performed under the slow action of your eyes such transformation. So the ordinary traveler runs off in relief to Florence, to the single statement, the single moment of time, the charming unity of somewhat prisonlike architecture.

"The single statement, the single moment." Ms. Clark would be the first to agree that anyone who spends any length of time in Florence soon discovers, within the statement and the moment, an astonishing variety and complexity; and although "prisonlike architecture" is what first besieges the eye—Palazzo Vecchio, the Bargello (which *was* a prison for a time), Palazzo Spini—this impression is soon modulated by buildings like Palazzo Corsini and its neighbor, the gracious and vernal Palazzo Ricasoli, begun in 1480. But the remark goes to the heart of things; and it was when I began, all so late, to grasp its cogency that I made a start at answering the question: why Florence?

The question itself arose with particular force some years back, in the mid-1970s, after I had completed an eight-year task of literary biography, an enterprise sufficiently exacting to make me want to take stock, to reconsider past and future. It was then that the persistence of Florence in my life began to come home to me, so much so that I determined to come back to the city with my family (we were five in all by this stage), to meditate the question, and perhaps to write a book about it. We had scarcely settled—in a spacious apartment occupying the entire second floor (American) of a small villa on a slope above the south bank of the Arno—before several things began to edge their way into my consciousness.

One was this: if there is not much new cultural energy in the Florentine atmosphere—there is some, but not a lot—this only makes one alert to a different kind of energy, which I am tempted to call the energy of life itself. I thought of the response of Clarissa Dalloway to the sights and sounds of Westminster, in the Virginia Woolf novel I had discussed in class the previous spring: "In people's eyes, in the swing, tramp and trudge; in the bellow and the uproar . . . In the triumph and the jingle and the strong high singing of some aeroplane over head was what she loved: life; London; this moment in June." Remembering the passage, I was inclined to rewrite the last words and phrases: "life; Florence; this moment in autumn." But the "life" of Mrs. Dalloway's London was made up of fascinating discords and incongruities, and this was another realization. The life and look of Florence were composed of strikingly different elements—differing shapes and styles from historical periods over many centuries—that nonetheless fitted together, lived together, spoke to each other.

And it was this, so I found myself reasoning, that beckons us back: not any particular building or painting or statue or piazza or bridge; not even the whole unrivaled array of works of art. It is the city itself—the city understood *as* a self; as a whole, a miraculously developed design. It is the city as what Italians call an *insieme*, an all-of-it-together. For a late-twentieth-century American, accustomed to the battering if sometimes exhilarating incoherence of the American city, the effect was extraordinary. The belatedly acquired sense gave me the outline of what it was that I had to look into and try to find words for, though it would require a good many years and five more extensive visits before the undertaking was completed.

PART I

DESIGNS AND

DESIGNERS

[1]

Along the Arno

Florence, wrote the chronicler Dino Campagni early in the fourteenth century, is a noble city with a temperate climate; and though poor in subject territory, it is blessed with a "broad and majestic river, of sweet water, that divides the city almost in the middle." The Arno in fact had a more intimate as well as a more troubled relation to Florence, in Campagni's time and later, than his words suggest; but he was right to identify Florence, at the opening of his *Cronaca*, by reference to the river that flows through it. One good way to begin taking the measure of Florence is to consider the role of the Arno in the shaping and the historical life of the city—a role that has been variously cooperative and inimical, enhancing and disruptive; part of an ongoing urban drama. The story is far from over.

Dante Alighieri, a contemporary of Dino Campagni, appears to have been the first to offer a summary account of the Arno's entire shifting course, and he did so in no friendly terms. On the second terrace of Purgatory, the poet encounters two noblemen, Guido del Duca and Rinier da Calboli. They ask Dante about his origins, and (in John Ciardi's translation) he replies:

> In Falterona lies the source
> of a brook that grows and winds through Tuscany
> till a hundred miles will not contain its course.
>
> From its banks I bring this flesh.*

Guido remarks that Dante is obviously speaking of the Arno, and his friend wonders why Dante shies away from naming the river, as though merely to utter it would be to invoke a horror. Into Guido's mouth, the exiled and embittered poet then puts a full-scale indictment. "It would be a mercy," Guido begins, "if even the name of such a valley dies." From its source all the way to the sea, he continues,

> Men run from virtue as if from a foe
> or poisonous snake. Either the land is cursed,
> or long corrupted custom drives them so.
>
> And curse or custom so transforms all men
> who live there in that miserable valley
> one would believe they fed in Circe's pen.
>
> It sets its first weak course among sour swine,
> indecent beasts more fit to grub and grunt
> for acorns than to sit at bread and wine.
>
> It finds next, as it flows down and fills out,
> a pack of curs, their snarl worse than their bite,
> and in contempt it turns away its snout.
>
> Down, down it flows, and as the dogs grow fewer,
> the wolves grow thicker on the widening banks
> of that accursed and God-forsaken sewer.

* On the choice of an English translation of Dante, see "On Translations of Dante," p. 338.

[22]

It drops through darkened gorges, then, to find
the foxes in their lairs so full of fraud
they fear no trap set by a mortal mind.

In this furious bestiary, the sour swine are the dwellers in the Casentino eastward of Florence (where Dante had been the ungrateful guest of many a lord of the castle). The snarling curs are the citizens of Arezzo to the south. The wolves are the Florentines, and the fraudulent foxes are the Pisans. Dante's visionary understanding of what it means to be a complete human being, the essential subject of the *Purgatorio*, here expresses itself in the imagery of large clusters of humans, a goodly portion of the Tuscan population, behaving like savage or filthy beasts.

The passage remains a most accurate account of the river's windings. It takes its rise on the southern slope of Monte Falterona, one of the highest peaks (5,000 feet) in the Apennines. It flows almost due south through the Casentino, filling out a little, past the towns of Poppi and Bibbiena toward Arezzo. Just above Arezzo it makes a sharp turn westward, as though, Dante suggests, veering away contemptuously from Florence's old rival. The river then follows a northerly course through the upper Arno valley to Pontassieve ("Bridge over the Sieve"), where the river Sieve joins it. Here it makes another nearly right-angle turn to flow west through "darkened gorges" (in particular, the haggardly beautiful Gonfolina), past Empoli and the walled town of San Miniato Tedesco. It curves through Pisa and flows on to the sea a little way beyond. Dante gives the river's length as one hundred miles (he uses the Italian word *miglia*), but taking into account the many twists and turns, it runs closer to a hundred and fifty miles. After the Tiber, it is the longest and widest river in central Italy. It was along the Arno that Florence did much of the fighting and bargaining and conniving that led to its preeminence in the region of Tuscany; until, with the conquest of Pisa and the purchase of Livorno in the early-fifteenth century, the city and its river finally had unimpeded access to the sea.

Yet the Arno entered Florentine history relatively late. When the Romans founded the tiny *urbs* of Fiorentia by consular decree of Julius Caesar (and perhaps under his supervision) in the spring of 59 B.C., they paid little attention to the river and the surrounding countryside. The site may have been chosen because the Arno, flowing below it, suddenly narrowed there to the point where it was most easily fordable. But the Romans were both militant and traditional, and they built according to their needs and anxieties rather than to the environment. Fiorentia, in its Roman days, was an extremely stiff affair, four-square and fortified, and keeping a wary eye on Fiesole in the hills to the north. It contained a forum, capitol, temple, baths, and aqueduct; and, eventually (by about 150 A.D.), a theater, an amphitheater, and more baths outside the walls. The turreted gates, set precisely in the middle of each wall, faced due north, due east, due south, and due west—the directions, in those compassless days, being probably taken from the North Star. The terrain itself, however, curves gently northeast from the river and southwest from the Fiesole hills. And the architects and city planners who created medieval and Renaissance Florence managed to tilt the whole structure sideways a matter of forty-five degrees to the right, even while greatly expanding it, and so to bring the city at last into harmonious relation with nature. River, hills, and *pianura* participated from that moment forward in the evolving character of Florence.

The Arno was a useful waterway from the outset, when lumber from the heavily wooded Casentino was carried along it on rafts as far as Pisa. The Romans even seem to have had a sort of quirky reverence for the Arno as a beneficent source of fertility, along with a sense of its potential menace: such is the testimony of a first-century-A.D. bas relief representing the Arno as a squat male figure, brawny and threatening, yet slightly clownish, and brandishing a sheaf of wheat. But they did almost nothing to engage the river in the life of Fiorentia; and it was not for well over a thousand years, until about 1175, that the Arno can be said to have become an organic part of Florence itself. Reawakening trade, a considerable increase in population (Florence, having dwindled to a relative handful in the Dark Ages, was by this time the second largest city in Europe after Paris and counted some 30,000 inhabitants), a desire to incorporate the exurban groups of

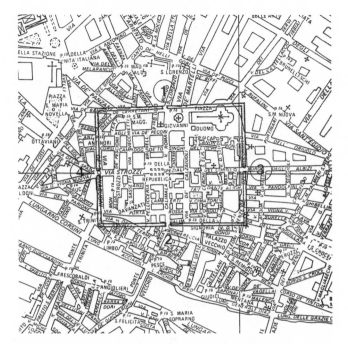

The Roman city, outline

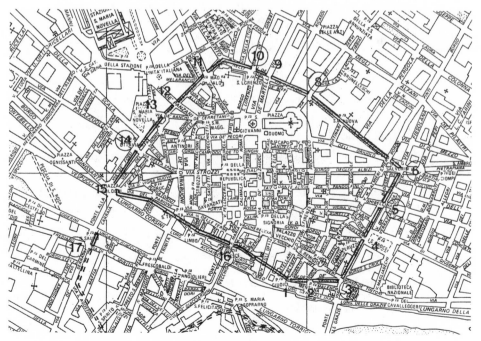

The 1175 wall-circuit

borghi that had been forming over the decades: all this led the authorities in 1173 to order a new circuit of walls. It was triple the size of the old Roman wall; and, not less importantly, it contained within it a stretch of the river and a small jagged semicircle of houses, shops, churches, narrow, twisting streets, and unoccupied spaces on the south bank—roughly the section that now lies between Via de' Bardi and Piazza Santo Spirito, with the lowest or southernmost point at the foot of Via Maggio. The part of Florence known as Oltrarno, "beyond the Arno," came into existence.

The Arno thereafter played a major role in the city's life for a very long time. Little ships plied it steadily, bringing wool, minerals, timber, hides from outlying districts.* Wool, for long the chief element of Florentine commerce, was washed in the riverbed and then spread out on the banks to dry and be gaudily colored by the dyer's hand; next, it was hung on the rafter of a wooden building overlooking the river called a *tiratoio*, or stretcher, there to be pulled into the desired size and shape. River water kept the mills turning on both banks, and the coin-minting apparatus operating on the north side. The scene was alive with activity. In the course of time, strongly built women could be seen doing their daily laundry down by the river, slapping the garments on the rocks to drain them and, we are told, cursing cheerfully the while. Nearby *renaioli*, sand diggers, worked in a steady, slow-paced manner; sand produced by the erosion of stone in houses along the banks during the periodic floods was invaluable for new Florentine buildings. There was always a little fleet of fishing boats, while individual fishermen made their casts from stone crossways (*pescaie*) especially set up for them. From fairly early times—and despite the pollution caused by soap, dyestuffs, and garbage: the Arno, in Dante's word, was the city's sewer, and its

---

* Partly because it is so high above sea level in the Florentine area, and partly because of its changeability—nearly dry in the summer, swollen and dangerous in the winter—the Arno was never as navigable as the Florentines would have liked. Various schemes were proposed and abandoned for increasing the flow during the summer months, the last of these, apparently, by Leonardo da Vinci with the backing of Machiavelli.

water was never quite as sweet as Campagni would have us believe—there were public baths in the river, carefully divided by social class. It was a favorite sport for a nobleman to swim under the partition to consort with his lower-class mistress.

The river has usually been said to be the scene of working-class life, but the Arno inside-the-walls also became a desirable site for big private homes of the wealthy and influential. By the end of the thirteenth century, the great fortresslike Palazzo Spini was built along it, next to Ponte Santa Trinità; and to this there were added others equally resplendent, if a good deal more gracious, with gardens pushing down to the very edge of the river. Urban celebrations took place on the Arno in a series of spectacles and theatrical displays. In 1304, a bad year in general for the Florentines, a pageant was given on barges between the little islands that then dotted the river, showing the mode of life in the next world. So many spectators crowded onto Ponte alla Carraia that the bridge collapsed and great numbers were dashed into the water and drowned.

Such was the periodic fate of the Florentine bridges. The 1175 circuit of walls had barely been completed before the Arno flooded and swept away the city's only bridge. The latter had been a narrow wooden structure, set up in the ninth century to replace the walled bridge that, it is believed, had been erected seven centuries earlier by the Emperor Hadrian and that had disappeared during the Dark Ages. (Earlier, when Fiorentia was founded, there had been a ferry to connect the riverbanks and, soon after, an original wooden bridge.) It was succeeded in short order after 1175 by another wooden crossway that spanned the river at the exact place where Ponte Vecchio does today. But for several decades this remained the sole convenient way of getting across to the left bank and the Oltrarno—places that, in any event, were then held in contempt.

The story of Florence is deeply implicated in the story of its bridges. On the right, or north, bank of the river at the head of Ponte Vecchio, to give it its later name, there was set a damaged statue thought to be of Mars—it was probably that of a barbarian king, but the pugnacious Florentines liked to think of themselves as descending from a race protected by the old war god; and here, in 1215, there occurred an event that changed the course of medieval Florentine history. A young nobleman named Buondelmonte de' Buondelmonti was engaged to marry a girl of the Amidei clan. But one day as he was passing the palazzo of the Donati family, he was espied by Madonna Donati, who came onto the balcony with one of her daughters and called out: "Whom have you chosen for your wife? I was saving this one for you." Buondelmonte was instantly smitten and agreed to abandon his Amidei *fidanzata*. The Amidei, whose fortified tower house abutted Ponte Vecchio, were joined in vengeful outrage by their powerful Uberti relatives. At a clan council, one of them, according to Dante and others, declared: *"Capo ha cosa fatta,"* a thing done is finished; in other words, let's get it over with. A group lay in wait, and when on Easter morning Buondelmonte came riding across the bridge on his white horse, the avengers fell upon him in front of the old statue and cut him to pieces.

Dante's ancestor Caccaguida, in *Paradiso* XVI, has this to say about the act and its consequences:

> *Ma conveniesi a quella pietra scema*
> *che guarda il ponte, che Fiorenza fesse*
> *vittima nella sua pace postrema.*

You find the words inscribed at the northern end of Ponte Vecchio: "But it was fitting that to the broken stone / that guards the bridge, Florence should offer a victim / to mark the last day's peace she has ever known."

The passage records the historical fact that the murder of Buondelmonte gave rise to the sometimes ferocious factionalism that kept the city in a state of turbulence, with monstrous physical wreckage on both sides, for almost a century. The Buondelmonti and their allies made part of the local Guelph party, the Amidei and Uberti of the Ghibelline party. It was all part, of course—and in a hopelessly confused and changing way—of the larger struggle between Pope and Emperor. There were rapid alliances between each of the Florentine factions and the Guelph and the Ghibelline groups elsewhere in Tuscany; but for Florentines, it was mainly an interfamily war for power in the city. And Dante finds it harshly fitting that the act which shattered the city's peace should have taken place near, as though in ritual sacrifice to, the god of war. Still, the medieval Florentines had a talent for hostility and rarely needed a precise occasion for erupting into violence against one another. After the Ghibelline forces, in 1289, had been pretty much crushed once and for all, the Guelph Florentines promptly divided into bitterly antagonistic Blacks and Whites and, in 1304, took to burning down one another's houses, setting off the worst conflagration in the city's history and razing most of the area between Ponte Vecchio and Orsanmichele.

Yet the Florentines, in their quarrelsome and ironic way, always loved their city, and they came to cherish the river along which it lay. Over the first half of the thirteenth century, they saw to the erection of three more bridges at thoughtfully selected points. The location of bridges, the great architect and theorist Leon Battista Alberti would say two hundred years later, eyeing the Florentine accomplishment with approval, was one of the most important decisions a town planner had to make; a bridge ought not to be "in a remote corner of town where it can be of use to but a few" but, rather, "in the very heart of town, to lie at hand for everybody." By 1220, a bridge was built in the heart of town some little distance below the one that was now given the name Ponte Vecchio to distinguish it from the Ponte Nuovo. The latter, a few decades later, was renamed Ponte alla Carraia—a word that means "cart road"; carts heavily laden with wool crossed the bridge in unending succession from the parish of Ognissanti on the right bank to the wool workers in Borgo San Frediano on the left. For it was in the area around Ponte alla Carraia that Florentine wool manufacture was now flourishing, under a monkish order from Lombardy known as the Umiliati. This gentry, who were anything but humble (or "humiliated"), built the church and convent of Ognissanti and oversaw a sort of laboratory for wool working; they also controlled the tolls on the Carraia bridge.

The bridge itself has followed a history so characteristic as to be worth rehearsing, though we shall be coming back to bits of it. Solid as it was, it was destroyed in the big flood of 1269 and rebuilt at once by the Umiliati; it partly collapsed during the previously mentioned evening spectacle in 1304, and was wholly demolished in the deluge of 1333. The bridge was reconstructed this time under the general supervision of Giotto. The torrential rains of September 1557 virtually destroyed it once again, and it was put back together, as was, by Bartolomeo Ammannati. The Giotto-Ammannati version endured for almost four centuries, until it was blown to pieces by the Germans in August of 1944. It now exists as a somewhat heavy-hipped bridge of medieval style.

By 1237, traffic between the right bank and Oltrarno was busy enough to require yet another bridge, and the place chosen was about as far up river from Ponte Vecchio as Carraia was on the downriver side. The new bridge was a sturdy stone structure that crossed the river at its broadest Florentine point, requiring nine arches of over two hundred yards in total length to do so. It was originally named Ponte Rubaconte, in honor of the current *podestà*. For some time the chief authority in Florence had been given to a secular figure called the *podestà* ("authority" is perhaps as close as one can come to this word, which literally means "power"), following a long period when it had been exercised by consuls. Since 1207, the *podestà* had been a "foreign individual"—"a nobleman from another city," in the definition of the fourteenth-century Florentine chronicler Giovanni Villani—the notion being that such a person might deal impartially with the city's combative elements, the nobles and the developing guilds. In 1237, the *podestà* was a Milanese named Rubaconte, the fourth member of his family to serve the commune. Even Dante had a kind word for the administration of Rubaconte, and the Florentines rejoiced in him for, among other things, having paved most of the city's streets and so (Villani wrote) having made Florence "cleaner, more beautiful, and healthier." Rubaconte endeared himself by laying the first stone of the bridge which the Florentines, honoring the man and expressing their own civic pride, named after him. The bridge was given its present attractive name, Ponte alle Grazie, in the fourteenth century, from a tabernacle on one of the

Ponte alla Carraia

Ponte alle Grazie, pre-1876

Ponte Santa Trinità, fifteenth century

Ponte Santa Trinità, today

bridge's flanks which contained a deeply revered image of the Madonna delle Grazie.

The start of anything remotely approaching a genuine republic in Florence can be dated in the 1250s, during the important but short-lived institution known as the *Primo Popolo*, and it was this that ordered a fourth—and, until the mid-nineteenth century, a final—bridge on the Florentine Arno. It stood midway between Ponte Vecchio and Ponte alla Carraia, and took its name from the adjacent church of Santa Trinità—more exactly from the monks in the Vallombrosan order of that church, who joined the wealthy merchant banker Lamberto Frescobaldi in underwriting its creation. (The splendid Palazzo Frescobaldi, though much altered, still stands at the south end of the bridge, directly across from Palazzo Spini.) Ponte Santa Trinità was made of wood and designed chiefly for strolling pedestrians; it was not much traveled at this time, but it was a fine vantage point from which to observe river spectacles. The bridge led from a main arterial street on the north side over to the newly created Via Maggiore—"larger," because notably broader than the nearby streets; later foreshortened to Via Maggio; first mentioned in a document of 1257, and angling its way through the heart of Oltrarno toward Porta Romana.

By this stage the bridges of Florence had brought into being a new city, or at least the potential shape of one. It was a city, now, of 85,000 inhabitants (population statistics for medieval cities are notoriously erratic, but the figure cited gives some sense of the relative size of Florence, still about half as big as Paris); yet large numbers of citizens lived and worked outside the 1175 walls, and their situation was hazardous. Besides, to live *outside* the walls—whose gates closed tight each night until seven in the morning—was not fully to belong to the city. For the medieval Florentine, a city was walled or it was not a city; to put it differently, a citizen, properly speaking, was someone who resided within the city walls. So in 1284, the officials commissioned a new and dimensionally larger circuit of walls. Chosen for the great task was Arnolfo di Cambio, a forty-year-old architect and sculptor who had been born in a village near Siena and who had trained in the Pisan workshop of Nicola di Pisano. Giorgio Vasari has left us a painting—it can be seen among Vasari's other historical tableaus in the ceiling of the great hall in Palazzo Vecchio—that shows Arnolfo down on one knee, presenting the city authorities with his design for the new circuit, to the accompaniment of festive drums, trumpets, and cymbals. If the sixteenth-century painting has its basis in fact (and Vasari, one discovers, is more often than not to be trusted in historical matters of this kind), those designs may constitute the most significant of Arnolfo's immense achievements in Florentine urban planning.

The circuit embraced all four bridges, and where the walls were interrupted by the river, at the eastern and western extremities, defense was provided by the diagonal damlike *pescaie* (fishing places). The river, with its bridges, was more clearly than ever a crucial and lively component of the city: in the words of one analyst, an infrastructure within the larger structure. Filippo Brunelleschi caught the idea perfectly one hundred and thirty years later, when, invited to remodel the church of Santo Spirito on the south side, he sought to have the church's facade face a large piazza which was to extend all the way to the water, the whole ensemble thus participating in the life of the river and presenting to visitors arriving in town by boat a beautiful vista that characterized at a stroke the relation between the city and the Arno. The proposal was thwarted by the understandably indignant *signori*, the wealthy owners of the houses which Brunelleschi's plan would have required demolishing.

Oltrarno, meanwhile, vastly widened by Arnolfo's circuit and coming to a point at Porta Romana, now became the conspicuous lower third of the city of Florence. To articulate the emergent urban design still further, the first *circonvallazione*, or ring road, was laid out: not a single road but a series of connecting streets leading northeast from the river at Ponte alla Carraia, curving through Piazza San Lorenzo, and eventually turning southwest down Via de' Benci to return to the river at Ponte Rubaconte. The process of tilting the contour of the city forty-five degrees eastward, begun in 1175, was now completed; and the shape decisively given to Florence by Arnolfo and his colleagues would

Arnolfo presents his plans for a wall-circuit

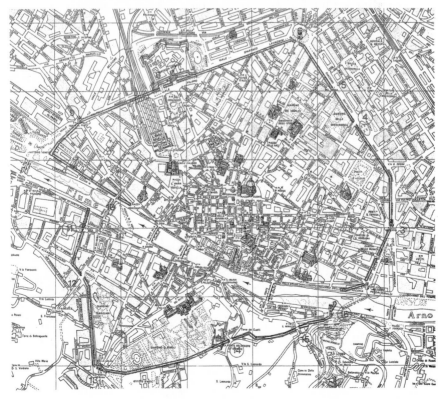

The 1284 circuit of walls

endure until the walls were ruthlessly torn down in the 1860s. Yet from certain vantage points—for example, from Piazzale Michelangelo high above the river on the south bank—the Arnolfian urban outline is unmistakably clear even today. The city it contains is what most of us mean when we say "Florence"; what is known as "the historic center."

The varied uses to which the bridges were put reflected the special Florentine capacity to convert a technical function into a vital one. Bridges were not merely ways of getting back and forth across the river; they were scenes of diversified activity, like the great piazzas. Ponte Vecchio, in fact, may be said to have contained a piazza at its midpoint. Vasari attributes its creation to Taddeo Gaddi, better known as a painter and disciple of Giotto; modern scholarship has advanced other possible names, but someone, anyhow, was commissioned to build a new Ponte Vecchio after the original one had been wrecked in the disastrous flood of 1333. Gaddi succeeded nobly, and the result was the one medieval Florentine bridge that has survived to the present day. He erected two stout towers at either end (one of these is still detectable on the left bank at Via de' Bardi) and along each side two pairs of porticos, with battlemented terraces above them. The porticos moved toward and away from the bridge's center, where the architect left a space open for citizens to gather and argue and gaze up and down the river. One could climb up to the terraces and there, on seats provided by authorities curiously called the "Officials of the Five Things," observe the water spectacles below. The porticos became divided into dozens of little shops of all kinds: forty-eight at one moment, and including general provision stores, fruit stands, tanners' and pursemakers' and shoemakers' shops, and an array of butchers ("filthy butchers very ill-suited to that place," grumbled one lordly Florentine). There was even a little inn bearing the sign of the dragon tucked in among the shops. For a spell in 1378, all the shops were rented out to Salvestro de' Medici, the great-uncle of Cosimo the Elder.

Ponte Vecchio, combining as it did a piazza for mingling, a bustling marketplace, and, at one end, a hospital of the Knights of the Holy Sepulchre—where pilgrims on their way to Rome were invited to spend the night—could be regarded as a concentrated version of the city itself. This was perhaps the most striking aspect of medieval and Renaissance Florence: its constant and ubiquitous bodying forth of the civic idea; its habit of reenacting its urban self in small—in tiny particular sections of town where all human services were available; in the piazzas enclosing church, preaching spaces, stores, bars, taverns, palaces, parks, and fountains; and even in the grandiose interiors of some of the churches (the interior of the Duomo, one commentator has remarked, was in some ways the greatest of the city's public piazzas). These entities were socially and urbanistically as well as artistically conceived; they were places where varieties of human business could be transacted, places for the exercise of the civic virtues. Of none of the public buildings of Florence was this truer than of the bridges.

In 1565 Giorgio Vasari added another dimension to Ponte Vecchio and its civic role. Some years earlier Duke Cosimo I had moved the ducal household across the river to the outsized palazzo near the left bank that his wife, Eleonora of Toledo, had bought from the deteriorating Pitti family; and Cosimo wanted an avenue to connect Palazzo Pitti with the administrative offices in Palazzo Vecchio, without having to push his way past the evil-smelling tanners' establishments on the old bridge. He took the occasion of his son's marriage to Giovanna (Joan) of Austria, an extraordinarily sumptuous event, to commission Vasari to create such an avenue. Vasari, an uneven painter but a brilliant architect, built a long, raised, and closed corridor, about ten feet wide, with many small and large windows. It began in Palazzo Pitti and, forming a second story as it went, passed over the church of San Felicita and above the entire length of Ponte Vecchio. At the north end of the bridge, the corridor swung to the right over the loggia that runs along the Uffizi, through which the Duke could proceed to the adjacent Palazzo Vecchio over a little bridge. To support the corridor above the open space between the porticos on the east side of Ponte Vecchio, Vasari built an elegant small loggia, thus enhancing the piazzalike atmosphere of the bridge. As the piazza is the chief ornament of the city, Leon Battista Alberti had declared, so the loggia is the chief ornament of the piazza.

At the end of the sixteenth century, another Medici duke tidied up Ponte Vecchio and diminished its vitality by abolishing the marketplace and decreeing that all the shops be given to jewelers and goldsmiths. Ponte Vecchio remains highly picturesque, and it is one of the world's most famous landmarks; looked at from a certain distance, it retains its culturally laden fascination. Some of its shopkeepers continue to do skilled and inviting (and expensive) business in silver and jewelry. But the bridge is rather disfigured and discolored from the Gaddi-Vasari construct, and by early May nowadays the diminutive old piazza can be obliterated by crowds. From time to time, until moved on by the police, there are little clusters of persons (from the locale-shifting drug community) strumming tunelessly on makeshift instruments and staring vacant-eyed; while other groups spread out their wares on carpets that impede passage.

If the life of republican Florence, meanwhile, was permeated by the civic idea, the civic element itself was always engaged in an ongoing dialogue with the religious, and to this too the bridges bear primary testimony. Ponte Vecchio catered to almost all imaginable human needs; but the adjacent Ponte alle Grazie (formerly Rubaconte) developed into something like a religious center. Places of worship were set up along its flanks: tabernacles, with chapel attached, dedicated to a saint or to the Madonna; oratories, each with its own rector; little houses for periods of solitary penance. Perched on the struts that overhung the river at the ends of the arches there were, for a time, a number of dwelling places that served as solitary or group hermitages (*romitori*). The devout Florentine women who chose to pass their lives in these places were known as *le murate* (the walled-up ones); never setting foot outside, they were served food through little windows reached by ladder from the riverbed, and Holy Communion was delivered in the same way every Sunday morning. *Le murate* were later transferred to a convent on Via Ghibellina, and the religious buildings gave way to shops and family homes. But Ponte alle Grazie

Ponte Vecchio

Ponte Vecchio, August 1944

carried its charming burden of tiny houses, strung out along it in pairs, until 1876, when all were removed to allow heavier carriage traffic; and so was destroyed, the historian Piero Bargellini has said, the most poetic of the Florentine bridges.

Having united the right bank of the Arno with the expanding Oltrarno, and having grown into major settings for the city's human and spiritual life, the bridges also brought into view new Florentine spaces, destined to become some of the city's most beguiling aspects. These were the Lungarni—"Along the Arno" —roadways that run along each bank of the river. The word Lungarno first appeared in a document of 1246, soon after the completion of the Carraia and Rubiconte bridges, which, between them, made the new east-west stretch of unused space visible. The earliest portion of Lungarno, finished by the end of the thirteenth century, connected all four bridges on the north bank, while the entire south bank continued to consist of fortified houses standing at the river's edge (as the part nearest Ponte Vecchio still does). The other Lungarni—Vespucci, Guicciardini, Soderini, and so on—were constructed in the nineteenth century, most of them with the large-scale transformations wrought by the architect Giuseppe Poggi when Florence was established as the capital of the new Kingdom of Italy. By this time, the 1860s, Lungarno had long been a favorite area for the Sunday display of the carriages of the aristocracy and the leisurely stroll of less glittering folk. Lungarno today is that part of Florence where the one-way traffic gets peculiarly congested. But to walk along it on the river side on an early spring evening, while the waters flow slowly, slowly, in drifts and pools toward Pisa, is one of the true remaining pleasures in life.

But it is a pleasure obscurely modified by a lurking sad awareness. For the fact is that something long ago began to go subtly wrong in the relation between river and city. It is true that Giotto, Taddeo Gaddi maybe, Michelangelo, Ammannati, Vasari, and others before and after performed some of their most inspired architectural feats building, rebuilding, and embellishing the four great bridges. But the consequence was unexpected: the bridges became more important than the river. As early perhaps as the mid-fourteenth century, the river was primarily something that citizens walked or drove across over handsome bridges on their way to work or some other human encounter; and if they lingered to buy meat or say a prayer or dispute with friends, they were engaging in the bridge life rather than the river life. A few years ago one Florentine commentator suggested that the time had come to write the story of the Arno—from the point of view of the Arno; and in that perspective, he remarked, it has been a story of attempted subjugation. He has a case. The Florentines exploited the river, drew on its power, dug in it for their own purposes; but too rarely, historically speaking, have they sought to understand it, to study how best the city might act in partnership with it. Hart Crane, in the "Cape Hatteras" section of his modernist epic *The Bridge*, would say that the aviators who explored planetary space made the fatal error of seeking to conquer it: in Crane's idiom, to *sub*jugate space rather than to *con*jugate it. The outcome is imaged in an airplane plunging to its destruction and ending up as "mashed and shapeless debris." The Florentines may be charged with an analogous mistake vis-a-vis the Arno's water space; and here, too, the result, from epoch to epoch, has been a good deal of mashed and shapeless debris.

The river's response—to what its imagined biographer might describe as the city's continuing assault upon it—has been the recurring act of flooding, sometimes rising up to destroy or seriously to damage the four bridges. There has been a river flood about every fifteen years since 1175; and it has been calculated that Florence has been visited by a medium-sized or a large flood every twenty-five years and a catastrophic flood on an average of once a century. Between 1490 and 1557 alone there were no less than twelve inundations, the last of them being described by a contemporary as "the flood of the millennium." In earlier epochs, the worst of the floods were attributed by commentators to divine wrath: the one that erupted on November 4, 1177, according to Villani, was a "judgement of God"; the Florentines had become overly proud of their military victories, had shown themselves "ungrateful towards God, and were full of other wicked sins." The alleged statue of Mars was tumbled into the river by the high waters of 1177; this was regarded as a dreadful augury, and the statue was hurriedly recovered and put back in place on the reconstructed Ponte Vecchio. More recent observers, especially after 1966, while continuing to manifest the inveterate Florentine habit of reading history allegorically, have (as we shall see) added some sound scientific fact—mainly about the long-standing failure to institute a system of flood control—to their interpretations of the Arno's behavior.

Before 1966, the most disastrous of the visitations had been the flood of 1333. For four days and four nights it rained torrentially across the whole of Tuscany—"as though," Villani wrote, "the very cataracts of the sky had been opened." Flowing westward, the swollen Arno waters submerged the Casentino plain and the entire upper Valdarno. Joined there by the flooding river Sieve some miles east of Florence, the river poured down upon the city, arriving there on the morning of November 4. All the bells in the city's churches had been ringing uninterruptedly, beseeching God's help to divert the horror, and now there were desperate cries of *"Misericordia, misericordia!"* as citizens fled from house to house and scrambled from roof to roof. Villani reckons that in places the water rose to nearly twenty feet; this may have been an exaggeration, but Villani was an eyewitness—"I who saw these things"—and the scope of the damage is incontestable. In the cathedral and again in Santa Croce the surging waters struck above the high altar; in Palazzo Vecchio, halfway up the main staircase. Ponte alla Carraia went, then Ponte Santa Trinità and Ponte Vecchio; the long-limbed, muscular Ponte Rubiconte was battered but managed to stand firm. The statue of Mars disappeared once and for all under the first waves, and Villani darkly recalled the ancient saying that the fall of the statue would mean an evil change in the city's fortunes. There was chaos on Lungarno, and every well in the city was polluted. The Arno then swept on through the lower valley, devastating the area around Pisa, and so onward to the sea.

In Florence and its environs, some three hundred persons were killed, as well as an untold number of livestock. The loss of goods was enormous: merchandise, wool, wine, furniture, tools, grain, and vast acreages of vineyards and plowed fields. Villani declares himself incapable of estimating the financial cost; but the commune of Florence alone spent 150,000 florins (a staggering sum) on the repairs. The aging Giotto, even then supervising the construction of the Campanile, was asked to take charge of the whole process of urban restoration. Meanwhile, a sharp-tongued Augustinian friar named Simone da Cascia went about asserting loudly that the whole business had been a divine rebuke to the vices of certain Florentine nobles, whom he was careful to name—among them the Guidi counts, who, in an offense against the city's poor folk, had had the audacity to enclose the windows of their palaces with glass.

The flood of 1465 is memorable chiefly as providing the setting of one of Leon Battista Alberti's most engaging Italian dialogues—the speakers, who have been holding forth on Ponte alle Grazie, observe the rising waters and sensibly decide to take shelter. That was only a minor calamity, but the inundation of 1557 took a frightful toll. Ponte Santa Trinità was completely smashed, and Ponte alla Carraia and Ponte alle Grazie were grievously shaken; for several years, Ponte Vecchio was the only safe means of crossing the river. Duke Cosimo I assigned to Bartolomeo Ammannati the task of designing a new Ponte Santa Trinità.

A decade went by before the physical work of building actually began. During this time Ammannati was constantly in touch with Michelangelo, as he was proud to announce; and he promised to bear witness, once the bridge was done, to those writings and designs of Michelangelo which had served to shape it. He neglected to do so, however; Ammannati was acclaimed then and later as the sole creator of Ponte Santa Trinità—one of the marvels of Europe, as a contemporary justly exulted—and Michelangelo's contribution, though undoubtedly central, will never precisely be known. Construction finally began in April 1567, after the Ave Maria had been sounded from a nearby chapel while the workmen knelt in prayer; and much is to be forgiven Ammannati, too often an overreaching artist, for the architectural masterpiece that resulted: Ponte Santa Trinità as we see it and cross it today (the best view, if you are lucky enough to gain admission, is from the big window in Vasari's corridor above Ponte Vecchio). With its three exquisite oval arches and its lithe abutments, it is at once elegant, weightless, and firm, a miracle of delicate tensions. In Ammannati's time, the bridge rose somewhat higher than its neighbors—Lungarno visibly elevates a little at the approaches—and it gave the citizen in transit an inspiriting vista north along Via Tornabuoni, south along Via Maggiore, east and west to the other bridges and the far encircling hills. Duke Cosimo, enchanted by the structure, used to meet there with other nobles to sing madrigals, and it provided the city's most beautiful setting for ducal festivals and processions.

The flood of 1844 was another bad one (a Florence-loving American friend of mine has noticed with a faint *brivido*, or tremor, how often the big floods occur in years ending in duplicate digits—1333, 1844, 1966). An anonymous painter of the time has left us a colorful sketch of the event—of Via dei Benci, near Ponte alle Grazie, at nighttime; the street itself a churning river under a somber sky, with citizens manipulating buckets, up to their waists in the water or moving along on rafts, the whole scene illuminated by torches. But then, as the decades passed, it seemed to the self-congratulatory Florentines that the long epoch of disaster was finally over. One can read in a learned commentary of the 1950s, for example, that because of fine technical improvements in the system of flood control, no further catastrophe need be apprehended. And then, of course, at nine on the morning of November 4, 1966, again after a tremendous rainfall, the Arno once more hurtled down upon the city.

As it overflowed the banks and coursed along the streets and into the piazzas, the torrent of 1966 at some moments reached a velocity of thirty-five miles an hour. Houses, shops, little hotels were ripped apart, not only near the river but far into the interior of the city on both sides; the wanderer in Florence today can find inscriptions or drawn lines—often above eye level—on buildings

The Florence Flood of 1844

several miles from the Arno, indicating how high the waters had sprung there on that November morning. Ten thousand auto-mobiles were sunk and buried in the mud, their frantic automatic horning stilled at last. Compared with the disaster of 1333, there was relatively little loss of life, mostly elderly folk like the 71-year-old Armido Peruzzi, who drowned in his sleep in the mud of his own basement; though to such melancholy but limited statistics there should be added a number of old persons who were driven out of their wits by the terror.

The 1966 flood was catastrophic chiefly for the city's works of art and its archives; and as to that the Florentines immediately began to indulge in vociferous debate. "Why can we only find money to restore works of art?" the Florentine workingman could be heard demanding. "When there are 20,000 people without roofs, and thousands of homes and shops destroyed, when there are so many who have lost everything, it's not the time to talk about Cimabue. We can talk about him later." Figures like these were not inaccurate; and fully aware of the city's temper, Piero Bargellini, the scholarly, art-loving mayor of Florence, quickly set up two committees, one for art and one for human needs, giving them equal authority and support.

Calculations vary about the artistic losses, but probably about nine hundred items were damaged or destroyed, including five hundred paintings, eleven fresco cycles, seventy individual fres-coes and one hundred fifty pieces of statuary. Among the most famous of these was indeed the much lamented *Crucifixion* of Cimabue, though even before the flood that stupendous work of the late-thirteenth century was not in the best condition. It had long stood in the Uffizi, as many visitors will remember, but legally it belonged to the church of Santa Croce; and after much litigation the Franciscans had succeeded in having it returned to them. It was an unlucky victory, for in any Florentine flood the depressed Santa Croce area, so near the river, invariably gets the worst of it. The *Crucifixion* is ruined beyond repair. Next in im-portance were the frescoes of Giotto in Santa Croce and those of Paolo Uccello (the latter already fading) in the Green Cloister of Santa Maria Novella. Oil splashes did harm to the walls of Brunelleschi's Pazzi Chapel, around the side of the heavily victimized Santa Croce. The superlative Etruscan section of the Archaeological Museum at midtown was nearly wrecked and for long remained in abysmal disorder; some of the panels of Andrea Pisano and of Ghiberti's Gates of Paradise outside the Baptistery were torn off. Geographically speaking, the savage floodwaters played no favorites.

Yet in retrospect it seems that the amount of serious damage to truly great works of art was less than at first feared, and the amount of irrecoverable loss not nearly so great. In some instances, it has been argued, artworks were positively improved by the experience—Donatello's wooden Mary Magdalene in the Baptistery, for example, was revealed to be covered with gilt. The fact was that much of the more appalling damage lay elsewhere, and if the scope of artistic disaster was somewhat exaggerated by the Florentine authorities, it was because it was much easier to raise money for paintings and sculpture than for soaked archives and smashed historic scientific instruments. The archival damage was literally incalculable; it runs to scores of millions of documents and many hundreds of thousands of volumes dating from the thirteenth century onward. The science museum in the Palazzo Giudici, behind the Uffizi, was particularly badly hit. Its heroic curator swam through the water to retrieve Galileo's parchment-paper telescope and some eighteenth-century surgical instruments, but many items in its distinguished collection were destroyed.

The government in Rome waited the better part of a week before coming gingerly to the aid of the devastated city. The Florentines themselves pitched in at once with the same abrupt and untypical unity of spirit they had shown on earlier occasions (genuine disaster has almost always, even if briefly, strengthened the Florentine feeling for community). They worked with dedication and energy, and with little else—spades, hammers, scythes—hacking away the mountains of mud; laboring on in a sort of violent silence, interrupted by curses and ironic commentary.

After the Florentines came the volunteers, people from England and Germany skilled in the techniques of restoration: art historians, students, lovers of Florence, lovers of civilization; the generous and compassionate ones. Hundreds of students from many nations (and this, it is recalled, in the very midst of the rebellious sixties) set themselves to work, under guidance, polishing the superb collection of bronzes in the Bargello, the national museum, and assembling torn documents and dispersed folders in the libraries. Art historians, several of them from America, gave special help by establishing priorities of aesthetic importance—as among the frescoes, for example—and digging up information on how canvases were originally painted. Large sums of money were obtained by an international organization to assist Florence, by the American-sponsored Center for the Advancement of Restoration, by the Volkswagen industry, and by a Scandinavian outfit. UNESCO contributed its share. This all added up to a splendid effort, though as is likely to be the case with charitable undertakings the results were slow and sporadic, with considerable bickering among the Florentines in charge. It is claimed by the Florentine archival office that, two dozen years or so after the great flood, most of the precious documents have been attended to.

While the flood had its natural origins in the almost unprecedented rainfall, arguments go on as to what failure of judgment or of technical functioning served to enlarge the catastrophe. The best explanation seems to be that the keeper of a dam near Pontassieve opened the floodgates there to reduce the pressure of the waters, and that land masses then fell into the river and tree trunks jammed the opening, making it impossible to close the gates again. Nor could the keeper get through to Florence by telephone. But the event was of such magnitude as to traumatize the Florentine imagination; and several observers have been reconsidering the entire long history of the relation between river and city—and have seen in the *diluvio* of 1966 the river's most cataclysmic act of revenge against the city that had first sought to dominate and then had betrayed it. There is nothing unduly fanciful in the concept of nature retaliating against man's mistreatment of it, but in the case of Florence there are also more graspable considerations.

During the last century or so—the point should be made but not overstated; exceptional persons and exceptional moments are shortly to be noted—the Florentines have lost something of their feeling about the river's place in the urban scheme. Lungarno, however attractive, began by wiping out the palace gardens that once so handsomely adorned the riverbanks; and it ended by encasing the river, setting it apart, in such a way that the Arno seems less obviously than before to flow through the heart of Florence, a vital element in its life and its reality. And as the city itself has bulged outward in all directions—to the northwest, especially, in a remarkably ugly and cluttered manner—the Arno's role in the larger urban pattern has become further blurred. The most important consequence has been the lack of serious attention given to flood control; so there is a definite scientific underpinning to the older "mythic" image of the river turning in fury on its negligent ancient partner. There seems no reason why the flood of 1966 will not be repeated, though probably not until around 2088; parapets have been raised on Lungarno, and there have been some other rudimentary precautions taken or talked about; nothing more. And in Florence each year, one approaches November 4, the Italian Armed Forces Day, with deepening anxiety, scanning the skies for the first signs of rain.*

With their tendency to the exclamatory and histrionic, and their curious zest for apocalypse, the Florentines, during and after the flood of 1966, declared that it was "worse than the war." But with regard to pure physical destruction, it really was not. The worst thing that ever happened to the river area and the bridges of Florence took place on the night of August 3, 1944. The Allied forces were encamped on the slopes above the south bank of the Arno, cautiously preparing to make their assault upon the city. Their mission was the plan called Diadem: which had the Amer-

---

* 1993 note: The uninterrupted sixty-day rainfall in the autumn of 1992, which reached its greatest intensity in early November, caused the Florentine Arno to swell and rise to near-flood proportions. Florentines were expressively aware that this was just twenty-six years after the great flood of 1966: almost exactly on time, so it was observed. See Ch. 8 below.

ican and British divisions bursting through Florence, and then on, immediately, under overwhelming air cover, up through the Apennines to Bologna; thence across the flatlands of the Po valley to the final destruction of the German armies in Italy. In fairness to the Allied commanders, Sir Harold Alexander and Mark Clark, it should be recalled that they were faced not only with an enormous strategic challenge (never in history had the Italian peninsula and its mountain ranges been conquered from the south) but also with an unexpected logistical problem. At the last minute they were forced to relinquish seven of their divisions, including crack American troops, for Operation Anvil, the pointless invasion of southern France which was to be launched on August 15. The battle chiefs were left with twenty divisions, several less than the Germans, and they did not enter Bologna in fact until eight months later.

On July 29, the German command in Florence issued an order requiring all persons living along the Arno, on either side, to clear out at once because of "expected enemy attacks upon the bridges." One hundred fifty thousand people, among them large numbers of the elderly and infirm and of the very young, packed such belongings and food as they could into hand-drawn carts and moved out, many of them to huddle together wretchedly in Palazzo Pitti. On August 3, a state of emergency was announced; from two o'clock in the afternoon, no one was permitted to leave his house or "to walk in the streets and squares of Florence." Patrols of German paratroopers roamed the city, firing on any native who stirred or any open window, and there was a good deal of casual looting. That same evening, bands of Italian partisans, sensing what was in store, attacked the teams of German engineers at work around the bridges, and were beaten back. At 10:30 p.m., the Florentines, shut up in their homes, heard tremendous rumblings from the vicinity of the river. Half an hour later there was a colossal explosion, and this was followed by periodic earthshocks until 5 a.m.

Except for Ponte Vecchio, all the bridges of Florence had been dynamited and reduced to rubble, including two of more recent vintage, Ponte San Niccolò east of Ponte alle Grazie, and Ponte della Vittoria to the far west. Ponte Vecchio appears to have been spared by a direct order of Adolph Hitler. The Führer had made two visits to Florence. On May 9, 1938, with Heinrich Himmler and Joachim von Ribbentrop, he had enjoyed a meal at Doney's Cafe on Via Tornabuoni and had signed the guest book; on the second and wartime occasion, he had been well, even tumultuously, received by a mass of citizens in Piazza della Signoria and had formed an attachment to the city and its symbolic landmark. But if the Germans left the old bridge standing, they sought to make it useless by blowing up the approaches to it on either bank. On the left bank, the ancient Via de' Bardi, with its magnificent facade on the river, lay in ruins; mines destroyed the buildings between Ponte Vecchio and Palazzo Pitti down the length of Via Guicciardini; and Borgo San Jacopo, parallel to the river, was a pile of debris. On the right bank, Por Santa Maria (which leads directly north from the bridge) was smashed, and the popular parish priest of the church of Santo Stefano died of a heart attack during the dynamiting.

Altogether, the Germans destroyed five bridges, 267 shops, 71 workshops, 123 houses containing four hundred living quarters, about a dozen medieval towers, and some twenty old palazzi. Among the human casualties were a number killed by land mines left in the ruins.

It is difficult to compare gigantic national barbarities with one another—Coventry, Florence, Dresden, Hiroshima. What is certain is that there was virtually no military justification for the destruction of the Florentine bridges and of Lungarno; it was a grotesquely useless act, entirely unworthy of the great German commander Albert Kesselring (if indeed he was the one to give the order). The river had pretty well dried up in the August heat, as it often does, and the British and the Americans had little difficulty making their way down one bank, across the riverbed, and up the other side. The allied divisions delayed making their move on Florence not because the bridges had gone but because they had lost a quarter of their strength. They crossed the Arno on August 13, ten days after the night of demolition.

The wholesale disaster of August 1944 was not, unhappily,

taken as the occasion for grand new creative efforts, as the floods of 1333 and 1557 had been; and this is perhaps a measure of modern Florence. It almost was. Giovanni Michelucci, the most gifted Florentine architect of this century, drew up a series of designs intended—in his own phrase and in the great tradition —to reestablish Florence as "the city on the river."* In full consciousness of the achievements and ambitions of Arnolfo di Cambio and Filippo Brunelleschi, Michelucci wanted to make the city take part again in the re-created life along the Arno and on its bridges. His friend Bernard Berenson urged him to rebuild the destroyed area "where it was and as it was," but Michelucci envisioned rather a fusion of ancient and modern. Two of the older elements in particular were to be exploited. In the spaces suddenly emptied of the crowding edifices that had hidden them for centuries, the medieval towers that survived the blasts (which is to say, most of them) now stood out, not only in all their grim and angular beauty but as clearly integral to the old coherent layout of the city. Michelucci proposed drawing them into a larger pattern by raising additional towers on both sides of the river, streamlined and even futuristic but in general harmony with their predecessors. He had been fascinated, too, by Vasari's corridor as a model of the elevated street or passageway and as one too little appreciated, he thought, in its urban significance. Each of the huge bridges designed by Michelucci was to have its own upper and lower "corridor," one for automobiles and one for human traffic. The littered approaches to the bridges were to be cleaned out and converted into spacious piazzas. Flights of steps were to lead down from bridge to river, and upon the bridges there was planned a teeming life of shops, chapels, restaurants, and theaters.

The conservative Florentine authorities rejected Michelucci's

---

* Michelucci, born in Pistoia in 1891, was the creator of the great Florence railroad station of Santa Maria Novella (1931), as well as many palazzi and gardens and public buildings in and around Florence and in Tuscany. He was a professor of architecture, on and off, and for some years head of the Architecture Faculty at the University of Florence. In his late years, he built the Cassa di Risparmio on Via San Egidio and the post office at the end of Via Verdi. He died in 1991 at the age of one hundred.

ideas (as they would reject his very similar proposals after the flood of 1966); they seem but dimly to have understood them and their exhilarating dialogue with the Florentine past. But it should also be admitted that Michelucci's plans were too grandiose, and the urban construct he would have created would have been decidedly out of keeping with the intimate spirit of the old— essentially the medieval—city. Nor was Michelucci much given to compromise and negotiation: in no way was he more markedly the heir of Brunelleschi than in his combination of obstinacy and genius. So between the two parties to the debate, a major opportunity for exemplary urban renewal was lost. River residents were simply told that they could rebuild up to the size of the demolished structures; the towers disappeared once more into a thicket of hotels and shops.

The bridges were rebuilt after the war, with differing artistic success. It was the question of Ponte Santa Trinità (the story has been told more than once) that caused the greatest commotion, a heated running debate in the press and thunderous public meetings. The "harangue site" in front of Palazzo Vecchio, where Florentine citizens had shouted at each other for six centuries, was the scene of protracted argument. Some felt strongly that an altogether new and modern bridge should be put up, a view shared by Michelucci, who was no more disposed to duplicate a destroyed work of architectural art than he was to tear down one that was still standing. The great majority, however, were vehemently in favor of rebuilding the bridge of Ammannati, and so it was decided. The Florentines then fell to quarreling about the materials to be used. Ponte Santa Trinità was finally reconstructed from the original designs, with the same stone (from the Boboli Gardens), the same techniques for cutting, and even the same tools used by Ammannati in 1567.

A noisy hue and cry was next raised against the decision of the Belle Arti people not to replace the figures of the four seasons, a group of overripe statues carved in the early-seventeenth century (on the occasion of a ducal marriage) by two local artists and a sculptor from France, and set on Ponte Santa Trinità, two at either end. They had been rescued more or less intact—except for the head of one of them—after the dynamiting; and when a poll was taken, the popular note was overwhelmingly in favor of replacement. The authorities dawdled as long as they could and then yielded. "In no other city in the world," Mary McCarthy has written, "could a controversy of this kind have embroiled all classes and generated such heat and bitterness." This is well said, though Ms. McCarthy somewhat spoils the effect by adding that Florentines "are not sentimental about their past" and have no taste for ruins. Florentines, of course, are not sentimental about anything; but Florence has spawned a more continuous series of persons—chroniclers and historians from Dino Campagni to Piero Bargellini—dedicated to recording its past than any city in my knowledge; and digging for fragments of the ancient Roman city has been a favorite enterprise from Villani's day to our own. McCarthy is in better form when she goes on to suggest that the intense civic concern over Ponte Santa Trinità and its statuary reflects a feeling, originating far back in time, that the welfare of the city's public buildings is somehow associated with the freedom of its citizens. And indeed, recalling Villani, one almost expects a new statue of Mars-on-horseback to be carved and placed at the north end of Ponte Vecchio. The whole undertaking was completed, anyhow, when the head of the statue of Primavera was discovered by a dredging crew in 1961. It was displayed for a week on a red velvet cushion in the Palazzo Vecchio courtyard and then carried in procession back to Ponte Santa Trinità.

The newest addition to the river life—Ponte Verrazzano, completed in 1971—is a modestly encouraging sign that the Arno can still stir the imagination of individual Florentine artists and even some of those responsible for Florentine urban affairs. Not that its immediate modern predecessors failed to provide comparable signs. The two bridges built in the course of the nineteenth century, Ponte San Niccolò and Ponte della Vittoria, established new and more distant eastern and western extremities to the city-river relationship; and they did so by punctuating the vast modern *circonvallazione* designed by Giuseppe Poggi and consisting of the broad *viali* (boulevards) that encircle the city both north and south of the Arno. Even Ponte Amerigo Vespucci, inaugurated in 1957 and lying between the Vittoria and the Carraia bridges, makes a certain urban sense in easing the flow of traffic to and from Borgo San Frediano. But Ponte Verrazzano, more than the others, was conceived in the spirit of the four medieval bridges, as a true piece of the city on the river and, as it were, an inhabitable entity. The work chiefly of Leopardo Savioli, perhaps the best of the native urban architects in the generation after Michelucci, it is located a good ways upriver from Ponte San Niccolò. It has a single shapely span, and on each side flights of steps lead down to balconies with stone benches. Seated there, you have the sense of belonging for that moment to the river-city, and you can enjoy the inviting prospect of one of the most pleasing and peaceful stretches of the Florentine Arno.

The Florence that I first drove into, by jeep over Ponte Vecchio in mid-August 1944, was a mass of multicolored rubble; the smashed bridges formed a series of inert piles on the riverbed, and there was heaped-up debris all along the banks. The Florentines were exhausted, stunned by the violence done to the bridges and their surroundings, and desperate for water. I watched them, women mostly, queuing up on Lungarno for water supplied by American pumps; their heads drooped, they seemed unable to raise their eyes from the ground. I thought of *The Waste Land* and the images (drawn from two passages by the Florentine Dante) of the crowd moving over London Bridge:

> So many—
> I had not thought death had undone so many.
> Sighs, short and infrequent, were exhaled,
> And each man fixed his eyes before his feet.

But the Florentines, as I was soon to discover, were not the death-in-life figures of Eliot's poem. Within a relatively few days the old resiliency began to assert itself; the old energy, even the old combativeness were regained. Florentine workmen helped Allied engineers fling up Bailey bridges over the wreckage of Ponte della Vittoria and Ponte San Niccolò. Even while the occasional German patrol could still be spotted scarcely ten blocks away in Piazza del Duomo, looking as if it had gotten lost, groups of Florentines were gathering on the riverbanks, quarreling with each other about the process of rebuilding, about recovering the Arno for their urban life. One likes to imagine that they argued the more intensely and with larger gesticulations because of some buried guilt toward the river they had too long taken for granted.

[2]

Stories of the Casentino

The first great age of Florence as a city—the age presided over, architecturally, by Arnolfo di Cambio—was ushered in by the battle of Campaldino in 1289. The Florentine victory at Campaldino ensured the sheer continuance of the city, and it helped determine the form, both the political form and by extension the urban design, that Florence would rapidly grow into.

Campaldino lies some fifty miles due east of Florence at the center of the Casentino valley. The region displays a striking, far-reaching, somewhat untamed beauty; and its history sheds a special light—through conflict and involvement, by example and by contrast—on the development of Florence through the thirteenth century and beyond. Certain key qualities that characterized medieval Florence could here be seen in pure or extreme forms. And as it happened, my own experience of Florence and environs led at an early stage to forays into this relatively little-known and little-visited terrain. Those forays in turn spurred several visits, memorable in their ways, several decades later. As a consequence, the Casentino has come to be an integral part of "Florence" for me, more so than any other neighboring district, and I would like here to explore it a little.

The name Casentino comes from the Roman word *clusentium*, an enclosed valley. Such the Casentino very nearly is, a broad

valley twenty-five miles long, almost entirely surrounded by towering ranges of mountains, the highest of which, Monte Falterona,
was where Dante saw the river Arno taking its start. Driving into
it from Florence these days, you begin to ascend the moment you
cross the Sieve river, climbing, twisting, descending only to climb
again, until you reach the Consuma Pass, ten strenuous miles
beyond Pontassieve. Here, at the Consuma, you are at the head
of the Casentino, and with clear skies (it is a section often heavily
shrouded in mist) the views are staggering: immense, wild, self-
distancing; not without touches of Tuscan softness, but an unexpected change even so from the gentle, hovering dark-green
hills and ridges around Florence. From the Consuma, you wind
down into the valley itself; and soon, far off and commanding
the plain, the old fortified hilltown of Poppi rising like some
gigantic mound alongside the Arno, and above it the high piercing
tower of the castle that was once the seat of the counts of Guidi.

The Guidis played significant and arrestingly varied roles in
Tuscan and central Italian history from the early-tenth century
through the mid-fourteenth; some of the contradictions—violence
mixed with piety, for example—that would beset and energize
the Florentine personality were given early and individual man-
ifestation by them. The first member of this prolific, toughly du-
rable clan to reside in Italy (direct descendants still thrive, so one
is told, in or near the town of Volterra) seems to have come down
from Germany with Emperor Otto I around 965. He was a romantic fellow, according to report, and won as his bride the lovely
and virtuous daughter of the Duke of Ravenna; but the offspring
of this marriage, who set himself up as lord of Ravenna, caused
such outrage by debauching the wives of Ravenna's leading citizens that the latter rose up and massacred the entire family—
with the exception of the infant named Guido, who was off in
the charge of a wet nurse. This Guido, upon reaching his majority,
wreaked a ferocious revenge upon the people of Ravenna, and
became known as Bevisangue (Drinkblood) because of his habit
of licking the blood of his victims off his sword.

Guido Bevisangue founded an abbey or two between acts of
horror, nor should such pious gestures be dismissed as mere self-

serving calculations; and if his son was said by his contemporaries to be literally diabolical, so appalling were his deeds, his grandson exercised yet another element in the family pattern. This one was the first of half a dozen Guidi counts to be called Guidoguerra (Man of War). He earned, indeed, great prowess as a warrior, but he was also a shrewd and friendly man who became political counselor to Matilda, the *gran contessa* of Tuscany (she died in 1115), "the most politically engaged woman that the Middle Ages has to show," in the words of a recent historian.* For almost half a century, beginning in 1069, this adventurous figure ruled over a vast state in central Italy and pitted her considerable strength on the side of the Church and the papacy against the imperial powers.† Matilda adopted the second Guidoguerra as her son.

It was Guidoguerra IV, nicknamed by Villani *il vecchio*, who led the most active life of the medieval Guidis. He dominated the Tuscan scene from about 1160—here and elsewhere in the Guidi story the dates tend to be hazy—till 1220. He was an arrant and skillful opportunist, siding now with the Emperor (first Frederick Barbarossa, and then Otto IV), and now with the Florentine Guelphs. With the aim of expanding and consolidating the family's power, Guidoguerra IV stirred up town after town throughout Tuscany; he failed to cajole the Aretines into making an effort to humiliate their Florentine rivals, but he ably set Lucca, Pisa, Siena, and Florence at one another's throats. A document of 1191 declared him the owner of two hundred castles, mostly in Tuscany; upon his death thirty years later the number had more than doubled.

Around 1180, Guidoguerra IV married the lady Guadralda, the daughter of a Florentine noble named Bellincione Berti de' Ravignana. Villani has passed down to us an account of their meet-

* Marcello Vannucci, *Storia di Firenze* (2nd ed., 1986), p. 24.

† It was to Countess Matilda's castle at Canossa, in the mountains below Reggio Emilia, that Emperor Henry IV, barefooted and in his shirt, came through the snow in November 1077 to seek absolution from Pope Gregory VII, a guest of the castle. The Pope kept the Emperor waiting three days below the snow-swept castle before admitting him. To this day, the phrase "to go to Canossa" in Italian means to humble one's self in a dispute.

Guadralda Refuses to Kiss the Emperor

ing, which is almost certainly apocryphal (Villani is too far off in his dates, for one thing) but which testifies to the capacity of both husband and wife to attract legends to themselves. In the Florentine church of San Reparata (the precursor of the Duomo), Villani writes, the Emperor Otto IV observed and was drawn to a beautiful maiden. The girl's father obsequiously remarked that he was ready to demand of his daughter that she kiss the Emperor; whereupon the maiden replied that "there was no man living who should kiss her save he were her husband." Otto was much impressed by this, and at once arranged a marriage between Guadralda and his henchman Guidoguerra IV, who had been standing by watching the encounter and was no less taken by the damsel's "beauty and her fair speech."

Dante was to add his testimony to the reputation of Guadralda. In the seventh circle of hell (*Inferno* XVI), Dante has pointed out to him an individual, with two others, running about in circles:

> Guido Guerra was the name he bore,
> The good Guadralda's grandson. In his life
> He won great fame in counsel and in war.*

Guadralda undoubtedly was good (*buona*) in the sense of chaste; but the same can hardly be said of her husband. Guidoguerra IV not only made looting raids upon the monastery of Camaldoli, in the mountains across from Poppi; he showed a talent for desecration unusual even in those times, by making the holy place the scene of orgiastic assignations with a series of young women, actresses and singers among them. This behavior earned him a letter of reprimand from Pope Innocent III, demanding that he immediately mend his ways. Whether he did or not, Guidoguerra IV attained a certain political maturity in his final years. He threw in his lot with the Florentine Guelphs in the factional strife that broke out after the murder of Buondelmonte—an event, it will be recalled, that occurred in 1215, and he saw to it that all his five sons became Florentine citizens.

Guido Simone di Battifolle, two generations after that, sided initially with the Ghibellines. Here is another lurid Guidi count, a person who stands accused of wanton murder and other brutalities—and who also diligently, even reverently, supervised the construction of the little Chapel of the Stigmata at the monastery of La Verna in the Casentino, enshrining the spot where Saint Francis of Assisi received the divine scars. Before his death in 1250, Simone too had come to terms with Florence, and his son Guido Salviatico was in the thick of things on the Florentine side, and much honored there, at Campaldino.

The battle—the Florentine Guelphs and their allies against the Ghibelline forces of Tuscany, led this time by Arezzo—took place on the banks of the Arno, almost directly below the town of Poppi, in the second week of June 1289. On the Florentine side, as best we can tell, there were ten thousand foot soldiers and one thousand men on horseback. The Aretines, in Villani's seem-

---

* The description of this later Guidoguerra—literally, as achieving "as much by his wisdom as by his sword"—is fair enough, but no one seems to know on what evidence Dante placed him in the circle of hell reserved for the sodomites.

ingly accurate figuring, numbered "800 horse and 8,000 foot." Florence's standing in Tuscany is suggested by the towns that sent reinforcements: Lucca, Prato, Pistoia, Siena, Volterra, Bologna, San Gemignano. On the other side were

very fine men; and many wise captains of war, . . . for they were the flower of the Ghibellines of Tuscany, of the Marches, of the Duchy, of Romagna.

The Aretines, Villani remarks, held the Florentines in contempt as being overcivilized, even effeminate:

They desired to give battle to the Florentines, having no fear, albeit the Florentines were two horses to one [sic] against them; but they despised them, saying that they adorned themselves like women and combed their tresses.

The Florentines reeled under the first furious Aretine attack; but the two infantry wings on either side held firm. Corso Donati, commanding the men from Lucca and Pistoia, then struck from the flank, and on short order the Aretines were "routed and discomfited." Seventeen hundred of them were killed, and two thousand taken prisoners, among them "many captains and valiant men of the Ghibelline party and enemies of the commonwealth of Florence."

Some modern historians have sought to discount the importance of Campaldino, arguing that it did little to change the basic power structure of Tuscany. Had the Ghibellines won, however, the firebrands might this time have had their way, as they were not allowed to do after Montaperti, and have overseen the abolition of Florence.* Villani himself had no doubt that the battle was a major turning point for the commonwealth: "And there were brought low the arrogance and pride, not only of the Are-

* On the battle of Montaperti (1260), see Ch. 3.

tines, but of the whole Ghibelline party and of the Empire."* Campaldino, it is really not too much to say, dates the beginning for Florence of two centuries of virtually uninterrupted (we will note an exception or two) republican rule and urban self-fulfillment.

The pro-Ghibelline Guidonovello, much despised by the Florentines, stayed on the outskirts of the fighting and, when he saw how matters were faring, fled up the hill to the Guidi castle in Poppi. The Florentines later pursued him there and burned the castle down around him, though he managed to escape. The republic then rewarded his kinsman Guido Salviatico by helping him rebuild the castle in the form in which it now exists. There is no reason not to accept the tradition that the architect called in was Arnolfo di Cambio, and that the castle and tower of Poppi were Arnolfo's own model, on a smaller scale, for the Palazzo Vecchio in Florence.

The twenty-four-year-old Dante Alighieri was one of the thousand Florentine "horse" that rode up to the Consuma Pass, ahead of the foot soldiers, and down into the Casentino valley in that June of 1289. Years later, after his banishment from Florence and the loss of all his property in 1302, on trumped-up charges of bribery and defiance of a papal decree, Dante cited his participation in the battle of Campaldino as evidence of his loyalty and noteworthy service to the Florentine republic. Memories of the battle and metaphors from it are sprinkled through the *Commedia*; and Dante observed in a letter that he had felt "great fear" in the early stages of the battle, but "great happiness" at the outcome.

Dante of course never returned to Florence, though he was invited in 1316, and he spent an indeterminate amount of his time-in-exile in the Casentino. Boccaccio even suggests that the poet put in several years as the guest of Guido Saviatico, which seems unlikely. However it may be, Dante developed a genuine love for the Casentino countryside and its rivers—as we feel when

---

* These words are echoed in the most learned current guide to Tuscany, that of the Touring Club Italiano.

the agonizedly parched forger named Adamo, in the eighth circle of hell, speaks longingly of

> The rivulets that ran from the green flanks
>   of Casentino to the Arno's flood,
>   spreading their cool sweet moisture through their banks.

About the inhabitants, Dante had almost nothing good to say. "Dante," Emerson tells us, "was very bad company and was rarely invited to dinner." Certainly, looking back on this period, when (apparently) he moved from castle to castle across the valley, he found little cause for gratitude in the dinners and lodgings he was forced to accept, and more than a little cause for dislike. *Brutti porci* was the phrase he used for his several hosts and their neighbors: "ugly pigs."

My own knowledge of the Casentino began in the autumn of 1944. The first stay in Florence had, after all, been a short one, and during it I housed our little headquarters—two American officers, two British sergeants, and half a dozen Italian agents—in a luxurious apartment on Lungarno Vespucci (it had belonged to the former Fascist mayor of Florence, who had fled with the Germans and was later brought back and tried). It was a time of curious contrast, for while German shells whistled about the Bailey bridge being thrown up below our windows, we inside, having for the moment nothing to do, indulged in a mild and continuing orgy. In early September, the front line had sufficiently established itself across the Apennines to permit us to go back to work, and we moved to a farmhouse just beyond the village of Rufina, about fifteen miles northeast of Florence and a few miles into the hills above Pontassieve. From here we could dispatch agents through the relatively unguarded mountain areas north toward Imola and Forlì and east into the Casentino.

We were part of an Anglo-American intelligence outfit known in Washington as MIS-X and in London as MI-9; in Italy, we had various cover titles. Our section of it had to do with what was known as "escape and evasion": that is, with prisoners of war who had escaped from enemy camps and were roaming the countryside; or with individuals—members of air crews, for example —who were at large behind the lines but had evaded being taken prisoner. The principal operation prior to Italy had been the exclusively British raid to collect escapees on the island of Crete. The mission in Italy had begun in September 1943, when in the wake of the Italian surrender a great many POW camps were abandoned and scores of thousands of prisoners—mostly English, who had been captured in the Western Desert and, especially, at Tobruk—were wandering the peninsula, a hundred miles and more north of the hastily re-formed German front line.

Shifting our advance headquarters periodically up the Ligurian coast, we dispatched small, carefully briefed missions daily and nightly. Our agents were for the most part Italian, themselves former prisoners of war recruited from Allied camps; they were accompanied by a British or American officer or NCO. Agents went in by parachute, or were taken in by boat, at night, and dropped off at strategic points. An obvious early requirement was to establish radio contact with these agents, once they had found the best place from which to operate. It was in one of our efforts to do so that, on November 1, the night of my twenty-sixth birthday, I went along on a coastal expedition and ran into trouble.

We were aboard an Italian version of an American PT boat: a British officer and myself, and about a dozen Italians, sailors and radio men. We had reached the rendezvous point, and were lying quietly in the darkness, flashing out signals and looking for a response. I was sitting below, talking with an Italian youth who was developing into one of our best and most quick-witted agents, when there came an abrupt but continuing crackle of sound. Peering up the gangway, I could see tracer bullets flying and could hear shouts of consternation and rapid orders from above. My young Italian friend, in the midst of a sentence, fell forward from the bunk to lie dead on the floor; a bullet had penetrated the side of the boat and entered his back.

When all sounds had ceased, I made my way cautiously up on deck, where I found half a dozen bodies strewn around, the boat otherwise deserted. Flames were licking along the railing; from out in the blackness I could hear the desperate appeal of the Italian sailors who had jumped overboard with their life belts and were floating about crying for help: "*Aiuto! Aiuto!*" Stowing my spectacles in the pocket of my battle jacket, wrapping my trousers around my waist, and tying the laces of my boots together so I could hold the boots by my teeth, I slipped into the water and began to swim ashore. The distance may not have been more than half a mile, but I kept losing direction and swimming unnecessary hundreds of yards before I finally made it to the beach and sat, spent and shivering, with my back against a little sand hill. As I watched, exhaustedly, the fire on board reached the torpedo and the boat blew up.

A mobile German patrol, it appears, driving along the coast road, had spotted us and opened fire, putting the boat out of commission with the first round. The patrol had then captured all the surviving Italians and had departed. The British officer, I learned eventually, had swum to the beach safely, walked adroitly south along the shore, and passed the lines two evenings later. He reported me dead, and my family was so informed.

I was about seventy miles north of the British Eighth Army, I discovered, and within forty-eight hours had reduced the gap to less than fifteen, being sheltered and fed along the way by a series of kind and unquestioning Italian peasants (my Italian was still very skimpy). One of these gave me a usefully shabby suit to wear. Technically, this meant that I was now in disguise and, if seized by the Germans, could have been treated as a spy; but it seemed safer than to march along in uniform, even if my regulation boots could give me away. I was almost within sight of the British lookout posts when I got stuck: the long, drawn-out battle of the Sangro River had begun, and the front lines were far too lively for me to attempt to cross. For nearly six weeks, I lay up in the little stone house of a peasant family headed by a shrewd and gutsy man named Sciotti Berardino near the tiny village of Crecchio—while both armies surged forward and fell back in what, from my fretful vantage point, seemed sheer tactical messiness. I made useless little forays toward making my way to safety, only to retreat each time to the welcoming Sciotti household; during these efforts, I had a series of adventures and misadventures with which, decades afterwards, I would regale our young children (in one of them I was taken prisoner by a German soldier on foot patrol, deposited inside a barn, and told to stay there; I slid out a back window and scurried away).

Finally, around mid-December, I took off impatiently and huddled for two nights with a horde of refugees in a barn just this side of the lines; then, having swallowed enough raw red wine to give me the requisite courage, I stumbled through the vineyards, passing within a few feet of a German sentry in the darkness, and fell into a foxhole commanded by a Sikh, a member of the British First Indian Division. His immediate response—until quelled by his elegantly English-speaking, turbaned commanding officer, who was mercifully nearby—was to want to cut off my head.

Shortly before Christmas, I met up with my brother, who was head of CIC in the American II corps on the other side of the peninsula. It was he who told me that our parents had received a cable saying that I was "missing and believed killed over Italy," the authorities having evidently assumed that, since I belonged to the Army Air Corps, I must have been shot down during a bombing raid. My message home, that I was alive and well, arrived as the family was sitting down, not very cheerfully, to Christmas dinner.

After an interval, I was given my own command, and for the next six months we operated out of a small Abruzzese village called Lanciano (this was the time when I came upon the work of the Abruzzese novelist Ignazio Silone). After the fall of Rome to the Allies in June 1944, we moved base into Umbria, taking a villa in the valley below the "open city" of Assisi; and after a few weeks there, we again took to the road, driving north into Tuscany and through the hills to Arezzo (reaching a farmhouse outside of town just after a German patrol had made off with some chickens). So it was, in July, that I entered Florence, leading two other jeeps and a British lorry.

Before the month was over, as I have said, we were established at Rufina, above Pontassieve. Through the summer and autumn, we dispatched agents to the north and east, the operations becoming easygoing and almost routine as the days went by. Our targets were mostly in the direction of Forlì, but we had considerable business as well in the rugged area beyond the Consuma Pass—the Casentino, which was a spacious no-man's-land, rendered useless by its topography for large-scale military maneuvering. Air crew "evaders" made their way down into it and got word to us; several times, I drove up to the Consuma Pass to spy out the valley and the mountainscape with binoculars. We were also asked by the American OSS (with whom we had no formal relation) and the local British Corps headquarters to send intelligence-collecting missions into the area. It was from the reports of our returning agents, and by close scrutiny of the maps, that I became acquainted with the Casentino, and the names of Poppi, Bibbiena, and La Verna.

I first entered the enclosed valley in the 1970s on an entirely different kind of mission—on the trail of Edith Wharton, who on one noteworthy occasion drove across the valley and up to the old monastery of La Verna. We too were headed for La Verna on that early spring day in 1973. But our plan called for a prior visit to the monastery of Camaldoli; and whatever your ultimate goal in the Casentino, your first stop is inevitably the village of Poppi.

Few places in Tuscany occupy as commanding a position as Poppi, standing clear and resolute atop its hill, 1,500 feet above the plain, and culminating in the Guidi castle and its slender tower. The village itself—perhaps 6,000 inhabitants, many of whom commute daily, by bus or car, as far as Florence—is quiet and friendly; nothing more inviting than to stroll its porticoed streets, to pause for a cappuccino, to buy a string of particularly tasty and locally famous *salciccie* from the spotlessly clean shop of the affable butcher. Then you are making your way up to the level plateau of the ancient *castello*, now the Palazzo Pretorio, or hall of the town magistrates.

The castle, as we have seen, was built for Guido Salviatico in 1291 by (presumably) Arnolfo di Cambio. The charming, roofless cortile, with outdoor stairway, was created or improved by the same architect; its walls are adorned by the family arms of the Florentine commissioners, who had their station there after Florence took over the Casentino in 1440. On the second floor there is a life-size statue of Guido Simone di Battifolle, that ever-active man of many contradictions: an extremely good-looking and graceful figure (in armor), if the sculptor is to be believed.

The great attraction of these upper stories is the view, from the windows, of the Arno river: flowing down from the first freshets on Monte Falterona, far off; and immediately below, as you look, taking its course serenely through vineyards and cornfields south toward Arezzo. One should descend and walk around the castle to study the panorama over the parapets on three sides. On the plain beneath is the early medieval stone bridge (or a postwar copy thereof) put up by one of the Guidoguerras. Far to the north is the hermitage of Camaldoli; and away to the east, against the high horizon, you can just make out the craggy thrust of the monastery of La Verna.

The juxtaposition of Camaldoli, La Verna, and the castle at Poppi—others have remarked on it—is the most compelling instance anywhere in Tuscany of the historical coexistence of radical opposites: savagery and religious devotion; ruthless aggression and spiritual withdrawal; depravity and saintliness. Camaldoli is much the older of the two monastic communities, having been founded in 1012 by San Remualdo, a member of a noble Ravenna family. It lies in a huge tract of thick, dark forest land. (The woods were for long a major source of timber for Florence: fir mostly, but also chestnut, oak, larch, and other varieties.) San Remualdo found even the reformed Benedictine order of his day too lenient and permissive, and with five spiritually and physically hardy companions he sought out a place in the Casentino mountains as remote as could be from the temptations of everyday life. Count Maldoli of Arezzo bequeathed the group several thousand acres of forest: hence the name Ca' (Campo) Maldoli.

A hermitage was constructed 3,000 feet above the valley (it can be buried in snow when almond trees are flowering along the Arno below). There is an open space with fountains, and beyond it a high wall encloses a kind of hermits' village. Twenty compact cell houses are spread out in five rows divided by a grid of well-tended pathways. Each unit is or has been the permanent home of a Camaldoli hermit. They are solitary dwellings which yet give an impression of at least minimal comfort. Each has a living room, with a couch in an alcove; a study, with a little library and a tiny wooden dining table; a vestibule; a portico outside, with a bench; a woodshed; and a garden.

The hermits are committed to silence except on special occasions and at the many religious services, the first of which is matins at 1:30 in the morning. They keep two long Lenten seasons each year, and they are not allowed to eat meat. Yet, for the visitor, the atmosphere is anything but dreary. As you observe them today, the hermits, clad in white robes, appear a contented, even cheerful breed—healthy, very much alive, skillful with their hands. Edward Hutton, after calling at the hermitage more than sixty years ago, came away with the memory of something "light-hearted and full of delight." The air is hushed rather than utterly silent, for a few workmen are likely to be conversing in low tones. One has the sense of being not an intruder but a stranger quietly welcomed; and it is not surprising that the unoccupied cells are used occasionally as a retreat for harried men of public affairs from Florence and other parts of Italy. It seems appropriate, too, that the water from the wells outside the hermitage should be the purest and most potable in the region; on this and later visits, we came away with two big containers of it.

A couple of miles below the hermitage, in a narrow pass, is the monastery of Camaldoli, built on a site that had originally held a castle belonging to Count Maldoli. The monks here live a less rigid existence than the hermits up above. In the course of time the order has gathered or was given enough treasure to make the place worth periodic looting—from the raids of Guidoguerra IV in the twelfth century through wholesale plundering by the Venetians in 1498 and a sacking by the French in 1810.

On the inevitable other side of the cultural coin, it was here, in 1468, that the nineteen-year-old Lorenzo de' Medici, with his younger brother Giuliano, Leon Battista Alberti, and others, came, with the humanist Marsilio Ficino in charge and as guests of the Abbot, to spend what has become known as "the four days of Camaldoli." They engaged in leisurely and rambling philosophical discourse of the kind recorded by one of them, the scholarly Cristoforo Landino, in his *Camaldoli Disputations* (*Disputationes Camaldulenses*). This was the beginning of the loosely organized Florentine assembly that, because of its dedication to the recently recovered dialogues of Plato, became known overformally as the Platonic Academy, and which later tended to meet in Fiesole. Whatever the merits of the speculative work emanating from the group (it was a very queer mixture of Plato, neo-Platonism, and Christian mysticism), the art of debate—the greatest feature of quattrocento Florentine culture—reached its highest peak at the Academy; and it seems no more than fitting that it took its start in the inspiring quiet of Camaldoli.

We came to La Verna, as I said, in pursuit of Edith Wharton, who visited the monastery under dire conditions in June 1912, with her old friend, literary conscience, and traveling companion, Walter Berry. The trip was a series of comic and alarming mishaps. Berry was suffering from enteritis to begin with, and was both sulky and in pain. Abandoning a more ambitious plan, the two of them decided to drive up from Rome to Venice for a few days. Berry and Wharton were studious as well as indefatigable travelers, and their researches had brought their attention to the monasteries at La Verna and Camaldoli—both virtually unknown at this time to foreign visitors, few of whom had even penetrated the Casentino. They determined to take in the two shrines on their way north. Here is Edith Wharton's account of the journey, in a letter to Bernard Berenson:

We started [from Arezzo] about 10 o'c, and were to "do" La Verna and dine at Camaldoli. Ye Gods! At 11 P.M. we were hanging over dizzy precipices in the Apennines, unable to turn back and almost unable (but for Cook's coolness and skill) to go on. Our luggage was all taken off and hauled behind us on a cart by a wild peasant, others escorting us with big stones to put behind the wheel at the proper moment, and thus, at 11.30, *fourbus* [exhausted], we reached the gates of La Verna, where it took a good half hour to rouse the Frati, and Walter, under their relentless eyes, had to sup on oil soup and anchovies and cheese before they'd let us go to bed.

La Verna rises from the edge of very steep chalk cliffs—more like one vast rock, itself jutting up from the mountains to a point 4,000 feet above sea level, and topped with a mass of boulders. Paul Sabatier, the biographer of Saint Francis, has compared the monastery to Noah's Ark petrified upon Mount Ararat; and the saint himself is said to have had it revealed to him that the apocalyptic landscape was created by the earthquake that reverberated through the world when Christ died upon the cross. Even today it is no small undertaking to reach La Verna in daylight on the narrow, upward-winding road. For Charles Cook, Edith Wharton's chauffeur, to find his way up to it in pitch darkness along what—despite the map—was no more than a mule track was an astonishing feat.

Next morning Walter Berry, his intestines further inflamed by his midnight supper, also developed a searing toothache, and the travelers made haste to depart, not pausing to look at any of the monastery's artistic treasures and sacred sites. The first stage of the descent from the cliffs was nerve-wracking. "The car," Edith told Berenson, "had to be *let down by ropes* to a point about ¾ of a mile below the monastery, Cook steering down the vertical descent, and twenty men hanging on to a *funa* [rope] that, thank the Lord, *didn't break*." The image is an arresting one: twenty monks from the monastery lying flat on the terrace, one below the other, clinging to the stout rope for dear life; the car hanging out virtually in space, Cook in front gripping the wheel, Berry and Edith sitting frozen in the back. The Furies, as Edith Wharton put it, were not done with them yet. On the dash to Milan, where Berry was to take the night train to Paris and his own dentist, the Mercedes collided with a cart coming out of a side road, and

Edith's personal maid was flung out into a stream and nearly drowned.

All the glass was smashed in front, and when we finally got patched up again I had to sit till 11.30 P.M. holding my umbrella (inside the car) to keep the night wind off my maid's dripping head and Walter's tortured tooth! We reached the station 3 *minutes* before his train left, and I crawled back to the Cavour for two days' rest. *Et voila.*

Such was Edith Wharton's visit to La Verna. She never did get to Camaldoli.

Our exploration of La Verna in 1973 was a moving experience; but it has, in fact, yielded its place in our memory to a return visit two years later, in 1975, made in the company of Robert Penn Warren and Eleanor Clark. The Warrens were spending the autumn in a villa near Panzano, about thirty miles south of Florence. It belonged to John Palmer, then editor of the *Yale Review* and the dean of Silliman College at Yale. The situation sounded charming, but household problems were reported: no telephone, heat not working, a drive of several miles to get mail, and inadequate help. (The villa lay within the province of Firenze, but almost at the border of the province of Siena; the ancient rivalry still expressed itself in the glowering reluctance or even refusal of *operaii senese* to work for anyone living in Firenze.) Eleanor was also wittily acerbic about what she called the Anglo-American geriatric community, retired folk (as described), with little on their minds except telephone calls about the next lunch or dinner party and boring chatter with an interspersed and slightly phony Tuscan accent.

The Warrens drove up on a November afternoon and spent the rest of the day and the night in our roomy apartment in Villa San Francesco di Paola, atop a long slope on the south side of the Arno.* We had known each other since 1960, and well enough by 1967 for Red Warren to agree to become the godfather to our

* On our ten-month stay in Villa San Francesco, see Ch. 6.

infant daughter, Emma. On this occasion, Warren and I spent several hours in my immense high-ceilinged study (it had once been the studio of the renowned sculptor Adolf von Hildebrand), going over manuscript chapters (sent in advance) of his as yet unnamed novel-in-progress. It would be called *A Place to Come To*, and would be published in 1977. The novel comprised the first-person story of Jed Tewksbury, a country boy from Alabama who early on evinces a flair for classical and modern languages and literature, who gets himself admitted to the University of Chicago graduate school, and eventually becomes internationally famous as a professor of comparative literature and a scholarly expert on Dante and the *Divina Commedia*. The greater part of the narrative is given to Jed's emotional and erotic life, as they bear on the story's theme. The latter is put into words at a particularly poignant moment during the graduate student days, when Jed realizes with blank despair, "I had no place to go. Not in the world." He elaborates dismally: "Odysseus, even though guilty perhaps of dawdling on the way, had been, in his deep heart, lonely for his rocky isle, but . . . I had nothing, nothing in the world to be lonely for."

Warren and I sat close together at my big desk, turning the manuscript pages. He wanted (I judged) any kind of comment on the work; but he was especially interested in my response to his handling of the University of Chicago section (Jed's graduate years there, not to mention some of his extracurricular doings, coincided with mine), of Jed's wartime activities, and of the Dantean materials. Captain Tewksbury also finds himself behind German lines in central Italy, pushed there (he says in retrospect) by the "Blind Doomsters of Washington"; he is practicing his Italian with a band of partisans, deserters from the Italian army in the area around Siena who are bent on killing and dynamiting as many Germans as they can reach. Warren knew something of my Abruzzese and Tuscan escapades, and asked if his renderings were historically plausible. A little brushing-up of reference and detail proved necessary, and the relevant portion of the narrative (Ch. IV) was a good deal tightened in the rewriting. As to Dante, Warren hardly needed guidance from me: he had been reading

Dante assiduously from the 1940s onward, and drew on *The Inferno* for the epigraph to *All the King's Men* in 1946. If I could help at all, it was to summarize developments in academic Dante scholarship, and to say whether Jed Tewksbury's dissertation subject, "Dante and the Metaphysics of Death," was a likely one. (To tell the truth, it sounded too original and imaginative.)

Our editorial task concluded, Red Warren and I joined the others in the living room. Before the evening was far along, two events had been added to the folklore of the two families' relationship. By way of saying good-night to our three children—thirteen, ten, and eight at the time—Eleanor Clark unexpectedly launched into a song from her Connecticut childhood, "My Daddy Wouldn't Buy Me a Bow-wow"—we parents listening enthralled, and with the sense of a sudden and inexpressively endearing revelation. Later, to the children clustered on the bed of the youngest of them, Red Warren read aloud for half an hour from *Uncle Remus*—the parents this time hovering outside the bedroom door, spellbound, while that thick-accented Kentucky voice intoned tales and sayings of Brer Rabbit and his friends.

The next morning at 9:15 the four of us departed in a comfortable car conducted by our old friend and driver, Marcello Chirici, going up over the Consuma Pass and into the valley, stopping briefly at Poppi, then on via the town of Bibbiena up the twenty-six-kilometer road to La Verna.

La Verna is one of the genuine holy places of the earth. The desolate mountain with its rocky summit was given to Saint Francis of Assisi in 1213, four years after the founding of the Franciscan order, by the wealthy Count Orlando of the Casentino. Orlando had been much stirred by Francis's preaching and offered his mountain (for the salvation of his own soul, he said) as a place entirely removed from human life and suitable for solitary devotions and penance. Saint Francis went there in 1214 with a few companions; they built several little huts made of tree trunks. It was on his seventh visit, in 1224, that he received the stigmata.

On this occasion, Saint Francis found his customary hut insufficiently remote: he wanted (it seems) to extend the act of withdrawal to its uttermost; and after some searching he discovered a nearly unreachable place to which he gained access by a wooden plank over the cleft between two massive boulders. Here his companions left him. Saint Francis spent forty days in isolation, from mid-August to the latter part of September, and to this period a series of miracles have been ascribed: a visitation of angels; a falcon who awoke the saint in the dark just before matins; a sudden predawn light which bathed the countryside. It was within this light that the saint had a vision of Christ on the cross and heard the voice of Christ addressing him: "I have given thee the Stigmata that are the signs of My Passion, to the end that thou mayst be My standard-bearer." When the vision passed, Saint Francis's hands and feet were pierced by nails, and there was a wound in his side like that caused by the spear in the body of Christ.

> nel crudo sasso, intra Tevero ed Arno,
>   da Cristo prese l'ultimo sigillo,
>   che le sue membra due anni portarno.

So speaks Saint Thomas Aquinas in *Paradiso* XI, rehearsing for Dante the life of Saint Francis with a lyrical eloquence quite unusual for that doughty dialectician:

> On the crag between Tiber and Arno then, in tears
>   of love and joy, he took Christ's final seal,
>   the holy wounds of which he wore two years.

Two years: Saint Francis died in 1226.

As we moved through the churches, chapels, and walkways that make up the rich complex of La Verna (the monastery also contains an observatory, a museum, and a library—La Verna is in every respect a working monastery and a training ground of novitiates), we were to a degree following Saint Francis, from the less to the wholly remote. Almost immediately upon entering the monastery, we came to the *chiesina* of Santa Maria degli Angeli, the oldest portion of which was built by Saint Francis, aided by

The town of Poppi

Saint Francis of Assisi, below the monastery of La Verna

Count Orlando, in 1218. Here he often knelt in prayer with his brother monks, and here he said farewell to them at the end of the long vigil in 1224, before mounting the ass he was forced to ride since his wounded feet forbade walking. Enjoining the others to hold the mountain always in reverence, Saint Francis allowed himself for once to assume a monitory tone. The words are inscribed on the wall: "Let such as will not reverence this place be confounded and let God punish them."

In Santa Maria degli Angeli and in the larger church next to it—it is known as Chiesa Maggiore and was built in the mid-fourteenth century—there is an exceptionally beautiful array of terra-cottas by Andrea della Robbia. The *Assumption of Mary* over the altar in the Chiesina is superb; but the *Adoration* in the Chiesa Maggiore has an almost supernatural delicacy and grace, matched only by the *Adoration* in the church of San Francesco in Arezzo. In the same church, the Chiesa Maggiore, are a surprisingly large-scale *Ascension* and another of Andrea's masterpieces (some think it his supreme masterpiece), the *Annunciation* of 1480.

From the Chiesa Maggiore, we walked down the Corridor of the Stigmata—enclosed now, but for a long time open to the elements. Along this the monks for many hundreds of years have proceeded every morning to say matins in the Chapel of the Stigmata at the far end. A legend from about 1500 tells of one dark winter dawn when the snow was piled so high in the corridor that the *frati* could not struggle through it. When they returned later, footprints of birds and beasts showed that Saint Francis's brothers and sisters from the animal kingdom had made the procession for them.

Partway down the corridor (the inner wall of which is covered with crude but likable frescoes of the life of Saint Francis by a late-seventeenth-century Franciscan), there is a small grotto containing the slab of rock the saint used as a bed. We finally reached the Chapel of the Stigmata, built by, or at the behest of, Simone di Battifolle. Terra-cottas by Luca della Robbia, founder of the clan and the school, and by his nephew Andrea adorn the walls; and in the paving, a stone carries an inscription from the late-fourteenth-century indicating the exact spot where the miraculous visitation of 1224 took place.

There were other things to see, including the rock from which Saint Francis observed the figure of Christ on the cross, and the precipice, 230 feet above the valley, where attacking demons were periodically hurled to their doom. But by common consent we went back to the large terrace to gaze out at the whole sweep of the Casentino valley. We stood there, turning our heads and raising pointed fingers: at the tower of the Guidi castle in Poppi, motionless against the sky; at the long mountain range, running parallel to the valley, known as the Prato Magno (literally, the great meadow), and at its lower slopes covered with dark-green olive orchards, vineyards, and plowed fields.

Eleanor Clark had been a resident in Italy for many years (she was bilingual in English and Italian), but she confessed she had never seen anything quite like this. Drifting clouds were shredding and re-forming, creating an almost uncanny painterly background to the spectacle. Eleanor took hold of her husband's hand—he looming up, smiling, silent, watchful—and said that it seemed to her like the painting of a mystic vision, with thin gleaming lights shining forth. Eleanor was anything but given to remarks of this kind; but the genius of the place had affected her, too, Roman soul and all.

Postscript on the Guidis

After Campaldino, Florence initiated a more systematic effort to break the power of the Guidi counts, setting them against one another and taking every opportunity to seize their holdings. The campaign was delayed a little by another Simone di Battifolle, who in 1343 earned the city's gratitude by capturing the so-called Duke of Athens, temporary tyrant of Florence, locking him up in the Poppi castle, and forcing him to abdicate.* Tales of murder and other evil conduct continued to accumulate. For a period of

---

* On the Duke of Athens, see Ch. 4.

time in the fourteenth century, a certain Contessa Telda (seemingly the granddaughter of the notorious Guidonovello) is said to have summoned to her bed a series of young men from the town of Poppi and then to have had them sequestered and strangled, one by one, in the castle vaults. The enraged parents of the victims succeeded at last in having Telda imprisoned in her tower, and there made to starve to death.

The influence of the Guidis came to an end in the mid-fifteenth century with one Francesco, who—seeking revenge on Florence for its ruination of his father—allied himself with the Milanese and went about assaulting strongholds, burning vineyards, and murdering peasants. His atrocities were worthy of Bevisangue, but in 1440 a Florentine force besieged the Poppi castle and drove Francesco into exile in Bologna, where he spent his last obscure days writing poetry. Poppi and all the other Guidi castles came into possession of Florence, which now became the master of the Casentino.

Cosimo de' Medici, *il Vecchio*—patriarch of the family (and grandfather of Lorenzo)—had come into full power in Florence six years before, and would continue to hold power for another quarter of a century. The conquest of the Casentino was a further sign that, in 1440, the Renaissance city of Florence was coming into its own.

[3]

The Real City

of Arnolfo di Cambio

The Public Thing

One of the appeals of Florence is the sometimes passionate love
its citizens have had for it. Not that Florence is unique in this
regard: the fierce loyalty of most Italian *cittadini* for their cities—
for Naples, Bologna, Venice—is something for an American to
marvel at; they grumble, lament, and foresee disaster, but let no
outsider criticize. Italy is still a country of cities, much as, to its
damnation, was ancient Etruria. The spirit of urban independence
and rivalry runs strong; laws promulgated in Rome may go coolly
unacknowledged in Bologna; and intercity football matches are
recognizable modes of warfare. An incapacity, or unwillingness,
to "think along national lines" (as Franklin Delano Roosevelt used
to exhort his countrymen to do) is in daily evidence; it is a part
of the country's problem and a part of its charm.* But nowhere

---

* Political regionalism intensified to what some consider the danger point in 1992,
when the Lombardy League began to win respectable percentages in national elections
in Italy and as much as 33 percent of the vote in local elections (Mantua, for example).
The League, under the leadership of the vigorously demagogic Umberto Bossi, stands
among other things for the creation of an autonomous Italian state in the north,
entirely separated from the economically poor and Mafia-infested south. The League
may well be defeated in its major goal, but its program has ancient roots and appeals
to ancient prejudices.

View of Apparita

in Italy are urban pride and love so modified as in Florence by a meditative, sardonic, and disputatious temper.

In 1529, the Spanish troops of Charles V, marching north along the Arno valley to besiege Florence, came over the spur of a hill above Bagno a Ripoli and for the first time beheld the city. It seemed to them an apparition, and a village in the locale was so named: Apparita. As they gazed, spellbound, there came into view a horde of Florentines, fleeing their homes. A Spanish captain called out to the refugees: "If we had a city as beautiful as yours, we would defend it to the last man." "That," muttered one of them, hurrying by, "is why you don't have a city as beautiful as ours." In the mid-1860s, Florence was supposedly rejoicing and vaunting itself upon becoming the capital of the new kingdom of Italy (the blandly repressive rule of the last of the Lorraine dukes having come to an end a few years previously, and with it the long epoch that had begun in 1530). At that very moment of regained freedom and prestige, Florentines could be heard saying to each other: "How much better off we were when we were worse off!"

A heightened appreciation of the past, if not always so wryly expressed, is a persistent form of Florentine self-esteem. There is, to-day, a museum, and an attractively illustrated book drawn from it, called *Firenze com' era* (Florence as It Used to Be). Florentines as a rule tend to be knowledgeable about former times, or so it strikes the American visitor. Some years ago when we were being driven back to our Lungarno apartment, we asked the taxi driver the name of the domed church across the river; we had observed it many times but had never inquired into it. "It is San Frediano in Ce-stello," he told us promptly, and went on to give a little discourse about it: an eighteenth-century construction, *grandiosa*, with many decorated chapels and (he thought) a thirteenth-century statue of the Madonna in wood. By exaggerated comparison, we found our-selves wondering whether a New York taxi driver could give any sort of historical identification to Grant's Tomb. Recently, when I was cabbing into the center of town, I heard the voice on the car radio say something about Pistoia. "Pistoia?" I asked. "That's quite a distance." "No," the driver said, turning around. "It's a street here named Cino da Pistoia. He was a lawyer, or something, and a friend of Dante." So he was, and a good poet too; the street that bears his name is close to those named after other Dantean associates, Brunetto Latini and Dino Campagni. What information might a New Haven cab driver have to offer about a street named for Jonathan Edwards, or the residential college at Yale called Calhoun? One imagines him uttering an American version of the unspellable Florentine exclamation *"Beuh"* (which, accompanied by a shrug, means something like "How should I know?").

No citizenry has more enjoyed celebrating the achievements of its most talented members, from the moment (around 1285) when Cimabue's painting of the Madonna with the infant Jesus—so long and excitedly awaited by the populace—was carried in triumph through the streets to the sound of drums. When the foundation stone of Palazzo Strozzi was laid in August 1489 on Via Tornabuoni, a Florentine physician, Tribaldo de' Rossi, took his children to witness what the entire city regarded as a historic event. Tribaldo held his oldest son up in his arms, and gave him a coin and some flowers to throw down so that he would forever remember the occasion. (In another version, the father clapped his son so hard on the back that the boy fell forward on his face.) But no citizenry is more prone, at the same time, to dispute over its buildings and monuments. They have been at it for centuries. In the 1290s, there was considerable stir over the San Frediano gate in the new circuit of walls—some Florentines insisting it was too high, others arguing heatedly that it was exactly in scale with the other gates. When Michelangelo was completing his gigantic statue of David in 1504, there was a remarkable open-air argument among leading Florentine figures about the placing of it. And we can recall the agitation for a number of years in the 1950s about the rebuilding of Ponte Santa Trinità and the reinstallation of the statues of the four seasons.

Such instances of often rancorous public pride make one part of the context within which to examine the contributions, in architecture and city planning, of Arnolfo di Cambio; for it was during the period of his greatest activity in Florence, in the last two decades of the thirteenth century, that the Florentine concern for *la cosa pubblica*—the public thing—began to express itself.

The concern had been growing, inchoately, over a number of decades, and amid a number of contradictory processes; from the outset Florentine history at its liveliest has always been a matter of strenuously diverse impulses, pulls and pushes in radically opposite directions ("tensions" is hardly the word for it). Disruptive factionalism and unifying public spirit increased and intensified alongside one another. The urban conflict that had begun with the assassination of Buondelmonte de' Buondelmonti in 1215, and that had brought the peninsula-wide Guelph-Ghibelline controversy within the city walls, reached peaks of violence around the middle of the century. In 1248 the Ghibellines, gaining temporary ascendancy, battered down thirty-six Guelph tower houses, including the looming edifice—with a 250-foot tower— of the Tosinghi family in Mercato Vecchio, the first private building in Florence to be called a palazzo. Two years later the Guelphs came into power and replied in kind; whole streets were blanked out by the rubble from the destroyed Ghibelline homes. There followed a decade of precarious calm under the Guelph-dominated regime known as the *Primo Popolo*; but in 1260, the Florentine Guelphs met in battle with the exiled Ghibellines and their Sienese allies at Montaperti, above the river Arbia, near Siena, and suffered an utterly disastrous defeat. So total was the Ghibelline victory that the party leaders, meeting at Empoli, decided that now was the moment to do away with the city of Florence once and for all by razing it to the ground. Florence was spared by the intervention of Farinata degli Uberti, of the arrogant Florentine Uberti family, the chief warrior among the Ghibellines and, in Dante's view, a great-souled individual. Facing the assembly, Farinata declared himself to be a Florentine first and a Ghibelline second; with his own sword he would defend his native city. The Ghibellines thereupon took the more limited action (a Guelph document gives us the inventory) of completely destroying 103 palaces, 580 houses, and 85 towers—both inside and outside the walls—and badly damaging a good many others, including some shops, twenty-two mills, ten *tiratoii* (buildings where wool was stretched) along the river, and seven castles in the nearby countryside.

After the Guelphs regained control of the city in 1267, they rewarded Farinata's act of patriotic heroism by convicting the entire Uberti family of heresy and removing from the face of the earth the extensive Uberti holdings in what became Piazza della Signoria. It was also decreed that no building should ever again be erected on the accursed site; nor has there been. In *Inferno* X, Dante encounters Farinata among the heretics, and the Ghibelline chieftain, motionless but unbowed within his fiery tomb, asks the poet about the harsh reprisals taken against his family:

> "Why is that populace so savage
> in the edicts they pronounce against my strain?"

> And I to him: "The havoc and the carnage
> that dyed the Arbia red at Montaperti
> have caused these angry cries in our assemblage."

He sighed and shook his head. "I was not alone
in that affair," he said, "nor certainly
would I have joined the rest without good reason.

But I *was* alone at the time when every other
consented to the death of Florence; I
alone with open face defended her."

(John Ciardi's translation here misses a little of Dante's sympathetic irony—in speaking not of "angry cries in our assemblage" but, more literally, "orations," or devotional prayers, "within our temple." What Dante regarded as trumpery charges against the Uberti clan were probably made in the Baptistery of San Giovanni.) But for the surviving Uberti there may have been a certain satisfaction in the last chapter of this long history of internecine violence: the hostile elements that split the Guelph party asunder in 1300 finally set off a war of arson and, in 1304, according to Villani, burned down no less than 1,700 palaces, houses, towers, and other "dear places"—wiping out, in Villani's words, the very marrow and center of the city from Via Calimala to the Arno.

But during these same years, while the city was periodically tearing itself apart, it was also gradually gathering itself together. More precisely: it was coming into being for the first time *as* a city, through a series of parallel developments that led not only to stability and prosperity but to a new urban self-awareness, a sense of the primacy of the civic and the public over the private and the factional.

The Florentine merchants began to form themselves into guilds (or *Arti*), corporate associations, as early as 1206, when the Bankers Guild was founded. This was followed by the Wool Guild in 1212, the Silk Guild on Por Santa Maria in 1218, and on through the Calimala (importers of woven cloth), the Judges and Notaries, and the Dyers Guild in 1280. Eventually, there were seven "major" merchant guilds, and fourteen "minor" artisan guilds (butchers, bakers, blacksmiths, vintners, leather workers, shoemakers, and the like). There remains (for the nonexpert) no little confusion about the numbers, the exact professional purposes, and the distribution of political power among the guilds. But there is no question that the guilds were the source of stability and continuity in thirteenth-century Florence and later, forming a vital bureaucracy, as it were, that held the society together and kept the economy expanding while Guelphs and Ghibellines came and went. The surging Florentine economy was essentially based on international banking and on international trade in luxury items—leather goods, richly adorned vestments—worked over with an extraordinary meticulousness. The scrupulous preparation of an expensive piece of cloth was important for the economy, but it was equally a matter of civic pride. And it was a telling moment in the urban as well as the purely economic history of Florence when, in 1252, the first gold florin was minted, quickly to become the basic monetary measure of Europe. For it was engraved not, as had been customary, with the image of a Pope or an Emperor or some other individual leader, but with the symbols of the city: on one side, San Giovanni, the patron saint of Florence; on the other, the lily, the city's secular emblem. The Florentine coin was itself a public thing.

While the material and worldly interests of Florence were thus progressing in a manner at once shrewd and public-minded (what was good for the merchants' guilds, one can hear them saying with considerable sincerity, was good for the civic health of Florence), a new species of religious orders was settling in the Florentine neighborhood, with an almost immediate and a large and enduring effect upon the cityscape. These were the mendicant orders, mostly coming in from Umbria and Emilia to take up their assigned task of enriching the spiritual life of the city. In 1221, the Dominicans were given a little eleventh-century church on the site where, more than fifty years later, the church of Santa Maria Novella was built. Beginning in 1226, the Franciscans were located in an early version of the church of Santa Croce. By 1248 the Servites ("the servants of Mary," and the only native-born among the new orders) had found home in what became Santissima Annunziata. The Augustinians established themselves across the river in Santo Spirito at mid-century. Near them, in

Oltrarno, a little to the west, the Carmelites had their seat in the Basilica of the Carmine by 1268. Their places in the urban scheme, it may be remarked, were all of them *outside* the 1175 circuit of walls.

The mendicant orders differed from most other Florentine monastic centers in two important ways. Committed as they were to poverty, as well as to chastity and obedience, they were largely immune to the financial motivations of orders like the Umiliati and the Vallombrosans, who grew wealthy on the tolls collected, respectively, at Ponte alla Carraia and Ponte Santa Trinità. And they were anything but self-enclosed, as were the Benedictines in the Florentine Badia (Abbey)—originally founded, through an enormous gift of land and houses in the heart of town, by Countess Willa in 978; and, by 1250, a sort of walled and turreted city within the city, self-sufficient and self-regarding, with an astonishing complex of chapels, gardens, libraries, shops, apartments. Quite to the contrary, the Dominicans, the Franciscans, and the others faced outward, physically and psychologically, toward and into the city and the people of Florence.

They were "*urban* orders," Giovanni Fanelli has remarked with emphasis.* Their clearly defined role was to preach to the Florentine populace. The churches and convents which housed them were regarded by the Commune as public edifices, constructed "for the benefit of souls and the prestige of the city which oversaw the founding of them"; and when the building of Santa Croce seemed deplorably behind schedule in 1361, the Commune declared that the church "had been founded by the Commune of Florence, and if it is not completed, will seriously mar the city's image." One of the first needs of the new orders was a large public space in front of their churches where the *frati* could preach to the assembled crowds; and thus were created the great piazzas which, within the century, became and would remain one of the characteristic features of the city of Florence as a work of art. With Piazza della Signoria, they were the ones we linger in today:

* *Firenze: Architecture e città* (1973). On this extraordinary two-volume study and its special importance for the present work, see p. 335.

Santa Maria Novella, Santa Croce, Santissima Annunziata, Santo Spirito, the Carmine.

There were, of course, differences between the activities of the orders, and especially between Dominicans, with their traditional stress on theological education, and the Franciscans, with their spirit of compassion and generosity. But Fanelli has helpfully summarized the elements shared in common by the two leading orders and implicitly by the others:

Both pursued a popularization of religion, both were founded on prayer and charity, both were flanked by lay (and 'tertiary') confraternities to encourage the participation of the laity, both created spaces to affirm more vigorously their presence in the city . . . Several of the societies or companies associated with the Orders played a noteworthy role in the city. Members of the company sang hymns, put on religious dramas, and organized aid programs. The church itself was a place of daily social reunion, especially in the warm summer days.

What we would call soup kitchens were run by some of the orders; steaming *minestra* and chunks of bread were handed out each day at noon, outside Santa Croce, to lines of hungry citizens.

The first *political* expression of the rising urban sentiment in Florence was the *Primo Popolo*, established under Guelph control in 1250. The moment was timely. Florence had assumed the status of a Commune, a self-governing entity, early in the twelfth century; but it had not been recognized as such, by the Holy Roman Emperor, until 1183, and even after that was still formally regarded as under imperial rule, however remote the latter might be. Imperial authority, though, was almost fatally weakened by the death of Frederick the Great in 1250—a death which both encouraged and coincided with the popular uprising in Florence. It was genuinely "popular": a revolt in the name of the Florentine *popolo* against the power of the nobility; and the regime of the *Primo Popolo*, which the uprising served to institute, took as its mandate (in the modern phrasing) the subordination of the nobles in the political life of the city.

It did so, among other things, by waging a kind of architectural war against the "Society of the Towers." During the previous eight or nine decades, Florence had become a city—perhaps more accurately, a forest—of towers; some 150 of these structures jutted up in hostile proximity across the city, within the confines of the 1175 walls and in the nearby suburbs. Their average height was 225 feet. Their use, at this time, was defensive, and they were usually erected alongside the family houses whose fortification they provided during the incessant interfamily vendettas that kept Florence in an uproar before and after 1215—and in 1178, as one terrible example, left more than half of the city in ruins. Individual families banded together with other branches of the clan—like the Amidei and the Uberti—to form groups of self-protecting tower houses (the towers sometimes connected with little wooden bridges high above the street). From this there emerged the Society of the Towers; and Florence might imaginably have become not so much a city as an urban battleground of interlocking noble families. But other processes were steadily earning the strong support of the people; and the *Primo Popolo* took the first decisive step in affirming the primacy of public interest over private feud.

Its major act was to resurrect and then to enforce an ancient law which decreed that no private tower in the city could be higher than about ninety feet, considerably less than half the average height just noted. Representatives of the *popolo* set about reducing the towers, whether Guelph or Ghibelline, to the prescribed measurement—no easy feat, it can be added; the extreme toughness and thickness of the majority of the medieval towers along the river proved resistant even to German dynamite and shells in the summer of 1944.

The medieval Florentines had a healthy recognition of the power of symbols, not only in religious art but in the very physical manifestations of their city; and the *Primo Popolo*, having decreed the lowering of the family towers, proceeded, in 1255, to build itself a civic home, on Via Proconsolo, which incorporated one of those old structures. By this act, the government conspicuously transformed a private tower into a public one; and since the latter alone, in the entire city, retained its original size (about 190 feet), it rose commandingly to twice the height of the clan turrets sprinkled around and below it. (Indeed, this civic tower, in the first century of its life, thrust upward more assertively and clearly than it would do—than it does today—after the considerable enlargement of its host building in the mid-fourteenth century.) Urban fact and urban symbol went forward together. In 1267, the tower was given the ironically echoing name of Volgognona, after the Ghibelline family that had been imprisoned in it by the victorious Guelphs, who returned that year to permanent power in Florence. And the building it contained directly confronted the Badia, on the other side of the narrow Via Proconsolo—proudly affirming the new strength and importance of the Florentine civic element as against that most private and inward of religious centers.

The building in question is the one we know as the Bargello. Its first name was Palazzo del Capitano del Popolo—that is, of the elected representative, or captain, of the people; and it was the first specifically and designedly civic building to be constructed in Florence, the magistrates having hitherto met in rented private houses or churches or even the Bishop's palace. The destiny of the new palazzo, according to an inscription on its wall, was to provide a setting for men capable of "governing the city with a jocund heart" (*governare la citta con cuore giocondo*—one hesitates to translate the adjective). It was by intention a fortress-like building, militant-looking, even aggressive. But it did not, in fact, stand in a hostile relation to the Badia across from it. If its lofty tower announced dominion over the tower houses of the feuding nobility, it engaged rather in a kind of urban dialogue with the slim bell tower of the Badia—stoutly maintaining the rights and powers of the civic, as it were, but participating with the religious in the total urban enterprise. The dialogue is visible (if the solecism be permitted) from many vantage points in the city: the Bargello and the Badia constitute the most striking pair of adjacent and contrasting monuments in all of Florence. And as you gaze upward from the second-story balcony of the Cloister of Oranges in the abbey, the Bargello tower and the Badia spire seem actually to be bending toward each other, caught up in an unending conversation.*

The *Secondo Popolo*, which summoned Arnolfo di Cambio to Florence in 1284, had organized itself only a couple of years earlier. It was the creation of the upper echelons of the Florentine business community. The latter consisted of the seven major, or merchants', guilds, who now tied themselves more closely, for political purposes, with the five lesser, or craft, guilds. Executive power in the new city government was given to six Priors—later to be known also as *Signori*—drawn from all these guilds but, through astutely managed elections, usually taken from the merchants' assemblies. The Priors held office for two months and during this time were required to live and carry out their business in the same building—their official home after 1304 becoming the newly constructed Palazzo Vecchio, designed by Arnolfo di Cambio. The *Secondo Popolo* was solidly and programmatically middle-class. The great majority of the Florentine populace was excluded: not only the working classes (including the wool workers, who comprised nearly a third of the city's population) but, at the other end of the social spectrum, the "magnates," the nobility and the families of ancient wealth, like the Bardi and the Peruzzi. In the interest both of power and of civic good sense, the *Secondo Popolo* contained and intensified the war of attrition against the nobility begun by its predecessors. Magnates were declared ineligible for public office unless they inscribed in one or another of the guilds, which few of them ever got around to doing.

The nobles responded by flexing their social muscles, showing their contempt for the new urban, bourgeois atmosphere by public

---

* The present Badia campanile was rebuilt in 1330, after its tenth-century predecessor had been half destroyed during an anti-Benedictine uprising in 1307. It is topped by a very sharp steeple, above which there turns and twists a weather vane in the form of an angel: hence the old Florentine saying "to waver like the angel of the Badia." As to the 1255 palazzo, it was turned over to the head of the city's police force in 1574 and, under its new name of Bargello, became a place of torture and confinement. All the instruments of torture were publicly burned in 1782 by Grand duke Pietro Leopoldo of Lorraine, who also abolished the death penalty. In 1865, the Bargello was inaugurated by King Vittorio Emmanuele II as the National Museum. Its charming courtyard seems to have been created around 1340.

behavior of the most insolent and unruly sort. The *Secondo Popolo* bided its time and, then, in 1293 and under the indispensable leadership of the Prior Giano della Bella (himself an antinoble of noble family), passed a constitutional act called the Ordinances of Justice. The act came down as hard as possible on the nobility: not only were the nobles entirely excluded from the government, but severe penalties were exacted for any harassment by them of the citizenry; in serious cases, a nobleman could have his hand cut off, in extreme ones he could be executed.

The Ordinances did their work, but it took awhile. As late as 1300, younger and rasher members of the nobility were still displaying an aristocratic disregard for the common folk, and in one instance Dante Alighieri became involved. A youth of the Adimari family had been cited for lawless conduct, and Dante, one of the Priors at the moment, was asked to intercede. It was expected that, as a neighbor and dinner guest of the Adimari, Dante would see to a modest penalty for the young man. But as he made his way toward the Esecutore, the government representative, in the Adimari district (just off Via Calaiuolo), Dante began to think about things, and the more he thought the angrier he got. "This cavalier," Dante reflected (in the words of the humanist writer Franco Sachetti), "was a haughty young man, ungracious and proud, who when he went about the city, especially when on horseback, so spread himself over the street, which was not wide, that the toes of his boots rubbed against the passersby." The latter often had to back away and look for another street. After one exchange with the Esecutore, Dante ordered a heavier penalty for the loutish young Adimari than had originally been demanded. The family was furious; Adimari resentment was said to have been one of the reasons for Dante's exile in 1302—after which, in fact, one of the Adimari asked to be given the confiscated houses of the Alighieri. The feud continued into poetry, Dante observing caustically in the *Paradiso*, via Cacciaguida, that the whole race of the Adimari behaved like dragons before the weak, but in a cowardly and placating manner toward the strong.

On the more purely constitutional side, the Ordinances of Justice strengthened and clarified the role of the Priors and, importantly, added a seventh Prior, called *gonfaloniere*, or banner bearer; he was to serve as titular leader of his fellow magistrates. Another section of Giano's Ordinances increased the number of minor guilds by nine—making fourteen in all of these craftsmen's organizations; Florence's lower-middle class had thus the sense, at least, of enlarged participation in the governing of their city, though few of its members were ever in fact elected to the priory. Giano della Bella was a man of outstanding political wisdom, courage, and compassion, but these qualities served him ill; the other magnates regarded him, quite properly, as a traitor to his class (even Dante, in *Paradiso* XVI, suggested that Giano had rather let down the aristocratic side); others felt that, through his Ordinances, Giano had shown himself soft on miscreants. In 1295, he was accused of having led an uprising; he fled the city and went into exile in France, where he died. But the regime he was so instrumental in straightening and expanding would—with whatever lapses and challenges, and shifts in the actualities of urban power—endure for the unheard-of length of two centuries, until the demise of the republic.

The Works of Arnolfo

Arnolfo di Cambio must have been about forty when he came to Florence in 1284. Little is known about his early years, and indeed there is much yet to be done to flesh out the biography of this extraordinary artist. The scholarly inquiry will depend upon full recognition of Arnolfo's achievement—as the senior partner, so to speak, rather than (as in the usual history) the forerunner of Brunelleschi in the architectural creation of Florence. Such recognition began, very late, in 1830, when two huge statues of Arnolfo and Brunelleschi, placed side by side, were installed among the columns of the building facing the south wall of the Duomo. But even today allusions to Arnolfo di Cambio remain timid and vague, and in some quarters he is spoken of primarily as a sculptor (he was, of course, a very great sculptor). Only Giovanni Fanelli, to my knowledge, has thus far given Arnolfo something close to the enormous credit he deserves; and here, as so often, I am very much indebted to Fanelli.

Georgio Vasari, who wrote briefly but with a sort of confused respect about Arnolfo, saddled him with a German father named Jacopo, renamed Lapo by the Florentines whom he came down to serve (presumably bringing with him the rugged style of the German Gothic). And the Florentine Bargello seemed so clearly to anticipate the Palazzo Vecchio, as a father anticipates a son, that the Bargello was attributed to this Lapo, who is not certain even to have existed. In fact, Arnolfo seems to have been born of Tuscan heritage in the early 1240s, in the village of Colle di Val d'Elsa near Siena. He was probably in the sculpture workshop of Nicola Pisano in Pisa, and it is known that he performed as a junior collaborator with Nicola on the pulpit in the Duomo of Siena (around 1267). He did a monumental tomb for Cardinal de Braye in a church in Orvieto and, in the 1290s, a resplendent ciborium in the Roman church of Santa Cecilia. Vasari, in his representation of Arnolfo giving the Signoria his designs for the new walls, shows us (a traditional image, one supposes) a stocky, balding, thoughtful-eyed man with an air of unemphatic self-assurance.

Those designs led—after some forty years of labor—to a prodigious accomplishment: the second and final *communal* circuit of walls (the first being that of 1175).* It was prodigious by communal intention: a great wall to enclose and to shape a great city. The Florentines took considerable civic pride in the very statistics of the vast construct; some of the following data are taken from an inscription on the Porta al Pinti (since destroyed) on the northeast slant of the circuit. The length of the circuit was a bit less than five and a half miles. The walls were about seven feet thick, wide enough for two sentries to pass each other as they patrolled the pathways that ran along the top of the circuit; and these walls stood thirty-seven feet high. There were fifteen massive gates— one about every 1,900 feet—shouldering upward to as much as 115 feet; the citizens clustered about arguing pleasurably as they

* See outline-map of Arnolfo's circuit on p. 35.

watched the gates being built and, later, adorned with sculpture, frescoes, and family crests. Every 370 feet there was a tower, seventy-three in all, with an average height of seventy-five feet. The walls were the central element in a complex defensive and urban system. A road thirty-feet wide stretched along the walls within, all around the circuit, and another road of the same breadth extended immediately outside. Encircling both walls and roads was a sixty-six-foot ditch, beyond which were drinking wells and other conveniences for visiting travelers and their horses and mules.

Arnolfo's circuit was a masterpiece of defense—for its own time, anyhow. In 1526 the Medici Pope Clement VII, a refugee from Rome, had most of the gate towers lowered, as being too inviting a target for enemy artillery; and in 1544, Duke Cosimo I, fearing an attack upon the city by the Sienese, built a line of fortifications within the circuit on the south side, beginning on the Boboli hillslope, cutting across Via Romana and Via Serragli, and rejoining the old walls at Piazza Torquato Tasso.* But the 1284 walls were also an urban masterpiece. For one thing, they brought inside the city boundaries the religious centers of the mendicant orders, which for some time had been standing out in the fields at varying distances from the rim of the 1175 circuit. And within the grand new design, with its pronounced eastward tilt, the churches were more visibly aligned with one another— fixed points on the urban compass which, indeed, they helped to establish—Santissima Annunziata and Santo Spirito to the north and south, Santa Croce and Santa Maria Novella to the east and west. At the same time, Arnolfo's circuit, hospitably taking in the churches and the verdant areas surrounding them, created extensive natural spaces inside the otherwise thickly crowded city (spaces which would have a curious history). The 1175 walls, of course, had to be dismantled to make way for the larger enclosure; and upon their disappearance there sprang into view the *circonvallazione* mentioned in an earlier chapter, following the track of

---

* The fortifications were demolished in 1571, but you can see traces of them in the Boboli Gardens.

the former circuit from Ponte alla Carraia north, east, and south back to Ponte alle Grazie, and still clearly detectable on the average map of Florence. Arnolfo's workers recycled the materials of the 1175 walls, as we might put it, for use in building the city's new stone belt, and they exercised the age-old Florentine thrift as well by making use of materials from the rubble of destroyed Ghibelline and Guelph houses.

These formations—the grouping of the churches, the *circonvallazione*—found their places and their significance within the larger scheme, the circuit as a whole. In drawing up his designs, Arnolfo di Cambio reshaped the entire city along a new cross-axis articulated by the four gates at the geographical extremities: one line running from Porta San Gallo to the north (allow a little for the tilt in each case) to Porta Romana (originally called Porta San Pier Gattolini) to the south; the other from Porta alla Croce to the east to Porta al Prato to the west. But it was altogether characteristic of the Florentine spirit, in its urban creativity, that the new design contained rather than obliterated the older patterns and relationships. Preserve and indeed enhance the old while introducing the new: the Florentines would not have it any other way. So Giovanni Villani, for example, observed happily that the two axes were not only of almost exactly the same length but that they intersected in the Mercato Vecchio, which thus remained what it had always been from Roman days: the precise center of the city.

Similarly, the 1284 circuit, far from diminishing the urban role of the four bridges over the Arno, rather dramatized their importance and, strikingly, that of the river as well. The river now flowed straight through the walled city. And when the concrete *pescaie* were set up in the river west of Ponte alla Carraia and east of Ponte alle Grazie—as the solid river-section of the walls, the final element in the fortification—the bridges more clearly belonged to urban Florence. They were its only bridges, and, by architectural implication, the only ones it would have or need for the foreseeable future. In this as in other respects, there was a kind of aesthetic and urbanistic finality about the walled city of Arnolfo di Cambio. Florence would not push beyond, would have no impulse to push beyond, the Arnolfian boundaries for nearly six centuries. In a real sense, it has never exceeded them.

The city shaped and girdled by Arnolfo thought of itself as in direct descent from the ancient city of Rome. It was not only that Florence—as Villani reflected, visiting in Rome during the Jubilee year of 1300 and gazing at the ruins—was literally the "daughter and creation of Rome" and that upon its founding in 59 B.C. it was at first referred to as "little Rome." It was even more, and this was the point of Villani's meditation, that, as against the long-fallen and devastated classical city, Florence in 1300 was "on the rise" (*nel suo montare*) and "destined for great things." In its power and its beauty, Florence was to be the *new* Rome, at once the heir and the rival of its paternal city. The *Romanitas* of Florentine culture, as is well enough known, found expression in architecture and the interior designs of public and private buildings, and then in the classical themes and styles manipulated by painters, sculptors, and poets. In the course of time, *Romanitas* became a rallying cry at moments of crises: the tempestuous Rinaldo degli Albizzi, about to initiate a costly war with the Milanese in the 1420s, sought to galvanize his compatriots by saying, "I wish we were real men and could beat the Duke of Milan to the draw. It would be a greater glory than the Romans ever achieved." But on a deeper and more pervasive level, Florence's sense of the Roman legacy was at the root of its urban self-awareness and its civic pride. For what medieval (and, later, Renaissance) Florence inherited from Rome was, more than anything else, the Roman urban ideal.

It was said about ancient Rome, not long after it had passed into history, that it had "citified the earth"—meaning that it had planted cities all across the map. Intellectually speaking, it had gone a good deal further than that: it had urbanized the cosmos. The word *urbs* was the most compelling and complex word in the Roman philosophical vocabulary, along with words and phrases like *civis*, *civilis*, and *res publica*. In Cicero's *De Natura Deorum* (begun in 45 B.C.), one of the speakers contends that the gods themselves "are united together in a sort of civic society or fellowship, and rule the one world as a united commonwealth and city" (*unum mundum ut communem rem publicam atquae urbem aliquam regentis*). Enlarging on the idea, he goes on to say that the entire *mundus* ("world," or, better, "universe") is, "as it were, the common dwelling place of gods and men, or the city that belongs to both." If the world could be thus conceived as a city and a *res publica*, the human city was the object of the Roman heart's desire. Virgil begins the *Aeneid* by telling us that he will sing of a man who "suffered much in war until he could found a city."

So it is not surprising that historians like Villani devoted so much attention to legends and traditions about the *founding* of the city of Florence. But the Roman urban legacy, especially as formulated by Virgil, contained one striking and recurring component: the city sought for by the weary wandering Trojans in the *Aeneid*—the city that (prophetically) lay in store for them—was something *walled*. Praying to Apollo on an island stopover, Aeneas beseeches the god: "Grant us a walled city . . ." When the Trojans make for Crete, on the mistaken advice of Anchises, the ships are barely hauled up on shore before Aeneas is "eagerly build[ing] the walls of the longed-for city." And the wraith of Anchises, speaking to his son in the underworld, foresees for him "that great Rome," whose empire shall equal the world and who "shall surround her seven hills with walls, fortunate in a race of heroes." It was, symbolically and actually, by walling Florence that Arnolfo di Cambio created the city that was to equal and perhaps to surpass the city of Rome.

With the new communal circuit under way, Arnolfo set to work building or remodeling a number of the most important monuments the walls were to enclose—and to arrange. These buildings were conceived, under Arnolfo's supervision, not only as entities in themselves, each with its own quality and purpose, but in relation to one another and to public edifices (like the Baptistery and the Bargello) already existing. In 1285, Arnolfo turned his attention to the Badia and its central church of Santa Maria Assunta. Despite the confining surroundings of the Badia complex,

Arnolfo managed to enlarge the church's interior in the shape of a Latin cross; and he created a rugged new facade on Via Magazzini. He may also have begun the construction of the bell tower. Much of the interior of Santa Maria Assunta was destroyed by fire in the seventeenth century and entirely remodeled by one Matteo Segaloni; but in its own era and for several centuries the abbey church bore the stamp of Arnolfo, with an added strength and dignity that heightened its dialogue with the imposing Bargello across the way.

It seems to have been around 1290 that Arnolfo built a loggia for the grain and cereal market at Orsanmichele. The market had been set up by the Commune in 1240, on the site of a little eighth-century church named for San Michele (Saint Michael) and near a large vegetable garden, or *orto*—hence San Michele in Orto, and, eventually, Orsanmichele. Of late, it had been an open granary, a money-changing booth, a hangout for the poor of the city, a shrine for the Virgin. Arnolfo's loggia protected people from the rain and probably served to introduce system into the various goings on; but it had a short life span, being one of the chief victims of the great fire of 1304. Even so, it was, characteristically, the location of the loggia that reflected Arnolfo's urban intention. By situating it on the recently opened Via dei Calzaiuoli, Arnolfo meant to enhance the public role of that street as the connecting artery between Palazzo Vecchio and the Cathedral—neither of which, it must be added, was even designed, much less erected, in 1290. Nothing is more astonishing than Arnolfo's success in working, from 1284 onward, to fill out an urban scheme—by designing and relating the buildings within it—that existed only in his mind.

A much grander enterprise than the Orsanmichele loggia was the restructuring of the Franciscan church of Santa Croce, upon which Arnolfo began in 1295. The small original Santa Croce (vestiges of which were discovered under the debris caused by the flood of 1966) dated from the time of the arrival in Florence, in the 1220s, of the Frati Minori of the Franciscan order. The urban dialogue, in this case, was to engage the newly monumental Santa Croce near the eastern curve of the walls with the

Church of Santa Croce, façade before 1863

Santa Croce, interior with tombs

Dominican church of Santa Maria Novella (itself considerably enlarged starting in 1278) over on the western flank of the city. The Commune invested huge sums in Santa Croce, and wealthy private citizens contributed; the Franciscan monks handed over some money-making properties they had acquired from Ghibelline heretics. But it may well be imagined that the Franciscans, with their vow of poverty, their cult of simplicity, their active devotion to the poor and the wretched of Florence, were appalled by the sheer amplitude of their new religious home.

In size and bulk, Santa Croce was planned to exceed any church yet built in Florence, one of the first of several architectural affirmations (in the last decade of the thirteenth century) of the city's sense of its own expansiveness and its bulging population. Santa Croce is longitudinal in structure, about 385 feet in length, with three naves combining to a width of 125 feet and a transept 245 feet wide. Exteriorly, the church presided handsomely over the large piazza where sermons were declaimed, heretics were condemned, and food and charities distributed; and it dominated and centered the whole area (or *quartiere*) around it. The keynote of the interior is spaciousness: it is all an airy space, but a space measured and defined by columns whose upward thrust is controlled by the flat ceiling and the horizontal line of the cornices. One is conscious, in Santa Croce, of being surrounded by orderly space; one feels invited to walk around and to linger in it, as one might linger and look in a piazza or on a bridge. The Florentines felt this so keenly that beginning in the mid-fifteenth century they converted the right nave into a pantheon, a gallery of the tombs of illustrious Florentines, starting with the superb tomb of the chancellor Leonardo Bruni by Bernardo Rossellino. Among the funerary monuments that were later added, there are Vasari's huge tomb of Michelangelo—whose body had been snatched away at night, in Rome, and carried on horseback to Florence—and an uninspiring edifice for Machiavelli dating from the late-eighteenth century. But long before that, Giotto and then Taddeo Gaddi, Donatello, and others had, by their superlative frescoes and reliefs, made Santa Croce one of Florence's most gratifying places to wander in.

By the 1290s, Vasari writes, "no work of importance was under-taken by the Florentines without [Arnolfo's] advice." In 1300, the Commune exempted Arnolfo from any form of taxation, a vir-tually unprecedented gesture and due in particular to Arnolfo's leading role in the building of the city's new cathedral. It was evident, the Commune declared, that from the "visible and mag-nificent principle" of the cathedral, there was arising "the most beautiful and honorable temple in Tuscany."

The original Florentine cathedral had been built in the sixth century and named for an obscure Styrian martyr, Santa Reparata. Arnolfo's temple was to be called Santa Maria del Fiore, another religious-secular designation, which combined the Mother of Je-sus with the flower after which Florentia was thought to have taken its own name. Citizens, of course, continued for a long while, as citizens do, to speak of "Santa Reparata"; and after Brunelleschi added the enormous cupola in the 1420s, everyone has referred simply to the Duomo. Recent excavations, inciden-tally, have unearthed large portions of the original church, which lie open for inspection in cloistered spaces below ground level.

Santa Maria was to be the very expression, in its magnitude and splendor, of the newly walled city. If Santa Croce organized the southeastern section of the city, the cathedral would organize the city itself. Or perhaps more accurately, it would *represent* the city, both in its magnitude and in its design; and this Arnolfo understood. Fanelli puts it well:

For the first time, a building asserted itself as a material and conceptual dimension on the scale of the whole city, as capable of organizing into a unity all the dispersed elements of the preceding panorama. In the center of the city, the cathedral contained within itself an image of the city that contained it . . . like a little Florence with its own walls.

Its vast interior was designed as the city's greatest public and communal space, capable of containing some 30,000 persons at a single moment. William Dean Howells, in fact, moving through its immensities in the 1880s, found the Duomo "a temple to damp the spirit," one that gave an impression "of stony bareness, of drab vacuity . . . unless it is filled with people." But filled it always was in those earlier centuries, and not with guided hordes of multilingual tourists but with big clusters of citizenry coming together to talk and argue and discuss urban affairs. The interior was, accordingly, Florence's supreme piazza, a closed piazza within the open piazza that surrounded it. The piazzalike quality must have been the more apparent when people could circulate in and out, from one piazza to the other, through the four high doors on the north and south sides of the cathedral—before the doors on the north side were sealed off, a good time back, for reasons of security. The outside piazza, meanwhile, was enlarged and its shape and function were clarified, in part by Arnolfo di Cambio. Houses and towers were torn down and a salt market was removed; and Arnolfo more closely aligned the cathedral with the adjacent Baptistery by having the facing exteriors decorated with horizontal green and white stripes.

In 1294, the Florentine authorities, led by Giano della Bella, decided that the city needed a new and larger civic center, in addition to the Bargello, and chose Arnolfo di Cambio as the master architect.* The site selected was close to the river and next to the eleventh-century church of San Piero Schiaggato (itself largely dismembered and its remains taken into the huge administrative office building—the Uffizi—created by Vasari for Duke Cosimo I in the 1560s). The authorities were careful to forbid any use of the adjoining space, which had come into being when the hated Uberti holdings were demolished several decades earlier. That rubble-strewn surface in fact served as a quarry for Palazzo Vecchio. When the debris had all been cleared away, the emptied

---

* Almost everyone today agrees with Vasari that Arnolfo *was* the designer of Palazzo Vecchio, though there exists no document to prove the fact beyond doubt. It is not my purpose here or elsewhere to linger over the question of attribution. But if Palazzo Vecchio is not the work of Arnolfo, then we can only postulate, at exactly the same time in late-thirteenth-century Florence, another architect and town planner of similar genius and vision. There comes to mind the proposition of Stephen Dedalus, in Joyce's *Ulysses,* that the plays of Shakespeare were actually written by another man named Shakespeare. And, indeed, I have seen it argued that Arnolfo di Cambio the architect was not the contemporary sculptor of the same name.

The Cathedral of Florence, with Giotto's Campanile

The Cathedral, interior

space emerged as a piazza—Piazza della Signoria, to give it its present and probably permanent name—its irregular outline marking the successive locations of the old Uberti tower houses. Unlike the other Florentine piazzas, which were laid out to cover specific spaces for specific purposes, Piazza della Signoria, as it might be said, happened into being as an accident of the city's factional history.

The new palazzo was located in a direct linear relation, along a straight south-north axis, with the rising new cathedral. According to the original design, in fact, the palazzo's main entrance was to be on the *north* side, directly facing Santa Maria del Fiore, and the two monuments—the religious center and the civic center of Florence—were connected by a roadway that ran right up to the cathedral's south entrances and that has since been divided into Via dei Cerchi and Via Farina. Only later was that major instance of urban dialogue blurred a little when the connecting artery became Via dei Calzaiuoli, which more immediately links the two *piazzas* rather than the buildings themselves.

In order to keep the palazzo uncontaminated by a single inch of accursed Ubertian space, Arnolfo had to squeeze it into the corner of the permissible space. He brilliantly exploited the limitation in a construct that was systematically unsymmetrical; nonrectangular, with the main entrances over to the right, an uneven number of windows on either side of the facade, and a tower displaced sideways. If Arnolfo could not expand horizontally, he could build upward as far as money and materials permitted: Palazzo Vecchio is a 140-foot building topped by a 310-foot tower—the latter enclosing an older tower known as *la vacca*. The ringing of the tower bells was greeted by Florentines as the periodic mooing of the old "cow."

If Palazzo Vecchio—known at first simply as *the* palazzo (in Florentine speech as *il palagio*)—was an artistic triumph, it has also seemed to observers to possess an engaging human personality and at the same time to be a phenomenon not of art but of nature. Howells, who felt more at home there than in the cathedral, thought he detected a note of "kindliness" about it, but his lasting impression was of "a great, bold irregular mass, beautiful as some rugged natural object is beautiful." The narrator of the early Henry James story "The Madonna of the Future" recalls wandering by moonlight into Piazza della Signoria, where, opposite him, there rose "the Palazzo Vecchio like some huge civic fortress with the great bell-tower springing from its embattled verge as a mountain-pine from the edge of a cliff." Seated across from it in the piazza today and staring up at the great mass with its sky-challenging tower, I am myself always surprised by the palazzo's refusal (so it strikes me) to overwhelm; by its quality of being perfectly self-contained but not at all aloof; by the sense that it is communicating its presence with a personal intimacy of tone unlike that of any other monumental building in my knowledge.

Palazzo Vecchio was completed in unprecedentedly short order, and the Priors were able to move in before the end of the first decade of the new century. Arnolfo did not live to see the event: his death date is as uncertain as his birthdate, but he seems to have died around 1304. His task was complete: he had designed a city, the medieval city of Florence—an urban structure conceived as an artistic whole, an *insieme*.

Go up once more to Piazzale Michelangelo high above the south bank of the Arno, or further up to the convent of San Miniato, and look down upon the city in its wholeness—upon Arnolfo's still distinctly visible urban pattern: to the north, the cathedral (topped, of course, since 1426 by Brunelleschi's dome), and a dozen blocks due south of it, Palazzo Vecchio; in between, over to the west, the Badia and the Bargello, tower to tower; on the east, directly below the observer gazing downward, the extensive orderly bulk of Santa Croce, standing with massive assurance over against the elegant Santa Maria Novella to the far west; and all holding their appointed places, in consort together, within the lost but somehow palpable ellipse of Arnolfo's walls.

The Arnolfian shape of medieval Florence required one final internal restructuring—into *quartieri* (quarters). Tiny ancient Florence had also been divided into quarters, named for the Roman gates; but with the circuit of 1175, Florence was portioned out, as Venice still is, into *sestieri* (sixths). By 1349, with Arnolfo's circuit completed and his other buildings finished or nearly so, it became apparent that a new division was called for. The city was formally divided into the *quartieri* of San Giovanni (named for the Baptistery), Santa Croce, Santo Spirito in Oltrarno, and Santa Maria Novella. Florence has been a quartered city ever since.

It was a classic urbanistic instance of the one and the many: a political and cultural expression of the deepest meaning of the *insieme*. Each was named for a key monument, each had its own chief thoroughfare, and each its local pride. The spirit of competition grew apace; the *quartieri* became intense political, social, and vociferously athletic rivals of one another. One can still witness a fierce soccer battle between, say, San Giovanni and Santa Croce; I attended one not long ago, and, inured though I am to the violence of professional American football, I came away shaken by the exuberant brutality. The *quartieri*, moreover, and in perfect Florentine fashion, quickly subdivided into zestfully self-assertive neighborhoods. The unique vitality of Florence derived from such opposite flows of energies: the indrawing power of Arnolfo's rational urban scheme working in vigorous tension with the centrifugal pull of the four *quartieri*, each *quartiere* duplicating that inward-outward pattern, and imaging the Florentine's enjoyment of the disputatious and the quarrelsome. Within the created *insieme*, the city dialogue went on.

A Knowable City

The hallmark of the Florence of Arnolfo di Cambio was its reality; if one may use the word, its realness. By contrast, the modern Western city has been made to seem altogether otherwise:

> Unreal city,
> Under the brown fog of a winter dawn,
> A crowd flowed over London bridge, so many . . .

And later in *The Waste Land*:

The Real City of Arnolfo di Cambio

What is the city over the mountains
Cracks and reforms and bursts in the violet air
Falling towers
Jerusalem Athens Alexandria
Vienna London
Unreal

These are, of course, literary images, though they are not uncharacteristic of twentieth-century renderings of the urban scene. A sense of loss pervades the treatment of great cities in Henry James, Proust, Joyce, D. H. Lawrence, Virginia Woolf, Hart Crane. What has been lost is not really a sense of urban vitality. No one, except maybe T. S. Eliot, has denied the abundant, clamorous, sometimes explosive liveliness of the modern city; Hart Crane's most inimical description of New York, in *The Bridge*, is also the wildest and most agitated portion of the poem. It is rather the loss of a core of meaning, of a basic knowability, that these writers reflect.

Arnolfo's city was, and what remains of it is, supremely knowable. The relation of the parts to the whole could be grasped, could quite literally be *seen*, at a glance; and a perceptible meaning inhered in the confrontation of towers, of Franciscan and Dominican churches, of civic and religious monuments, of variously inhabited bridges. Compare that to early-twentieth-century New York City as observed by Henry James when he returned to his native town in 1904, and in the impressions he recorded of it in the New York chapters of *The American Scene*, written a year or so later. What struck James was a fantastic combination of immense vitality and almost total impenetrability: on the one hand, vast energy, a violence of noise, incessant change and movement; on the other, a perceptual chaos of which no sort of sense could be made. He stared at the thick crowds heaving along Wall Street, and the sight conveyed to him

confusion carried to chaos for any intelligence, any perception; a welter of objects and sounds in which relief, detachment, dignity, meaning, perished utterly and lost all right.

James ended by taking a bizarre satisfaction—his own word is "comfort"—in the incomprehensibility of New York. If it was simply too incoherent, too various, too far beyond any remembered scale of measurement, then he was released from the task of trying to take intellectual hold of it.

To be sure, one part of the modernist and postmodernist mystique has been a cult of the unknowable, an affection for the problematic; a distrust of rational and traditional meaning carried to a positive approbation of the unmeaningful (in slim distinction from the meaning*less*). The lack of graspable meaning in New York which James pondered—with an irony so vigorous and eloquent as virtually to overcome it—has proven to be a source of profound intellectual satisfaction to certain later writers and critics. But that is no country for old Florentines.

It should be acknowledged, on the historical as against the literary side, that efforts to alleviate the American urban chaos were already under way when Henry James made his 1904–05 tour of the country. What became known as "the City Beautiful movement" found its first focus in the World's Columbian Exhibition in Chicago in 1893. Visiting the exhibition, Henry Adams felt—it was one of the stranger lapses in his career—that he might be witnessing a reversal of the 700-year-long drift from unity to disunity. "Chicago was the first expression of American thought as unity," he wrote in his *Education*; "one must start there." A host of architects and planners—like Daniel H. Burnham and the firm of McKim, Mead and White—were at work, meanwhile, in cities across the land, attempting, in Burnham's much-repeated phrase, "to bring order out of chaos." "Make big plans," Burnham intoned, "aim high in hope and work . . . Let your watchword be order and your beacon beauty."

These men were inspired by Pierre-Charles L'Enfant's design for Washington D.C., by the great achievements of Frederick Law Olmstead, and, above all, by Renaissance Rome and Venice.* In their civic vision, cities were to be transformed by the introduction

* See *The American Renaissance: 1876–1917*, the catalogue for the exhibition that opened at the Brooklyn Museum in the fall of 1979; see especially the chapters by Richard Guy Wilson.

of squares, parks, monumental buildings, topographical rear-rangements, patriotic statuary, and moralistic inscriptions. There were a number of particular successes—the Boston Public Library, for instance, and the Henry Villard houses (later, for a time, the home of Random House) in New York—but the urban movement as such did not amount to much. Perhaps it is just as well. Daniel Burnham's plan for Chicago (as rendered by Jules Guerin) is a bit chilling: such implacable symmetry, such monumental sameness. The Florentine city of Arnolfo and, later, Brunelleschi—and it would have been a much better model than Rome, though not perhaps than Venice—*grew out* of the most spirited concerns, and the dialectic of concerns, of the Florentine people; it was an expression of the popular spirit. The advocates of the City Beautiful were seeking the impossible; they were trying to impose an outgrowth. The entire enterprise was unhappily belated, though it still goes on, here and there, in bits and pieces and sometimes to cheering individual effect.

A real city—that is, a knowable city—does good things for one's identity; in knowable surroundings, one arrives at a firmer grasp of the self. Again, in the literary depiction, New York has been thought to produce the opposite. As early as 1842, Emerson, after a visit to the metropolis, remarked in his journal, "In New York City, one seems to lose all substance." Fifty years later, in Howells's *A Hazard of New Fortunes*, when Isabel March is informed by her husband that the family may be moving down from Boston to Manhattan, she begins to jitter about a prospective loss of self. "New York terrifies me," she says piteously. "I don't like New York, I never did; it disheartens and distracts me; I can't find myself in it."

She cannot have meant this literally. In no city in the world is it harder to get lost than in Manhattan—thanks to the grid plan laid out in 1811, the rigorous scheme of north-south avenues and exactly spaced and numbered east-west streets; the same plan by which most other American cities were to be afflicted. This was New York's "primal topographical curse," in Henry James's magisterially biased view; "her old inconceivably bourgeois scheme of composition and distribution . . . [the] original sin of pettifogging consistency." Isabel March was alarmed, of course, not by the thought of physical but of psychological dislocation; she would not be able to find her *self*.

In Florence, quite the other way. After all the visits and years, I can still lose my immediate bearings there. I never set forth on a walk in the city without a map of Florence in my pocket; but even after inspecting it, standing at some intersection, I am likely to march off bravely in the wrong direction. The truth is, Florence is essentially unmappable; it isn't possible, on that flat surface and depending chiefly on straight lines, to provide a usable chart of the city, with its twistings and turnings and sly concealments. There is too much in Florence of what Henry James found New York least endowed with: "any happy accident or surprise, any fortunate nook or casual corner, any deviation, in fine, into the liberal or the charming." And except on a map so large-scale as to be *non-tascabile*, the little street you are looking for, though only two blocks from Palazzo Vecchio, is probably not even included.

But I am never really lost in Florence. It is not merely that I always know which *quartiere* I am in, and that in a moment or two, as I move along, I will come upon one or another monument that will at once orient me: the Badia, San Marco, San Lorenzo, the Carmine. It is rather that, partly because of such assurance, I have no panicky sense of a psychological loss of way. Florence, one feels, is a city that knows itself; and it encourages the resident, temporary or permanent, to do likewise.

In the early winter of 1504, a very distinguished group of Florentines, dialoguing together in public, paid remarkable if perhaps unwitting tribute to Arnolfo di Cambio. At issue was the proper placing of the gigantic statue of *David*, which Michelangelo had almost completed—carving it out of a block of Carrara marble that had itself been worked over clumsily by one Agostino di Duccio almost forty years before and, since then, left lying neglected in the courtyard of the cathedral. And the question came down to this: Should the colossus be associated with the cathedral

Palazzo Vecchio

Panorama of Florence, early nineteenth century

(Arnolfo's religious masterwork), or should it be associated rather with the other polar monument in the city, the Palazzo Vecchio (his supreme civic construction)?

There gathered in the courtyard, near the statue, on the chill morning of January 25, some two-dozen-odd personages summoned to consider "an appropriate and acceptable location" for *il gigante* (as it was called).* Among them were Leonardo da Vinci, Sandro Botticelli, Andrea della Robbia, Giuliano da Sangallo, the architect known as il Cronaca, Perugino, Fillipino Lippi, Piero di Cosimo, and two heralds representing the Signoria, the Florentine governing body. It was an exemplary debate: the Florentine community at its characteristic best. There was little, if any, shouting (though there was a certain amount of anxious stammering—a genuinely grave matter was at stake). The tone was courteous, thoughtful, concerned; almost every disputant began by speaking admiringly of his predecessor's remarks, and then, in many instances, went on to voice a different, even the opposite, opinion.

Michelangelo's statue had originally been intended to be placed high up on an east-end buttress of Santa Maria del Fiori, as one of a series of twelve monumental prophet-figures which had been in the planning stage since the time of Arnolfo. By 1504, this idea had been abandoned: probably because of the near impossibility of hoisting a seventeen-foot stone statue to so lofty a position, from where, in addition, its magnificent features would not have been easily perceptible to people staring up at it from the piazza far below.† In fact, only a few of the disputants favored locating *David* even in the vicinity of the cathedral; but one of these was the sixty-year-old Botticelli, perhaps the most religious-minded of the group, a vocal *piagnone*, or mourner, for the monk Giralomo Savonarola, by whom he had been converted and who had been hanged and burned in Piazza della Signoria six years before.

---

* The verbatim (*de verbum ad verbum*) text of the argument is contained in *Michelangelo's David: A Search for Identity*, by Charles Seymour, Jr. (2nd ed., revised, 1973), as an appendix to this superbly informative monograph.

† The only prophet-figure actually to be set up on the cathedral—where it stood forth in lonely dignity until the seventeenth century—was the *Joshua* of Donatello, in 1410, and this was made of the much lighter terra-cotta.

Botticelli proposed placing the statue on the steps of the cathedral. "I judge it would go well there," he said briefly, "for it is the best place of all."

To Botticelli there responded Giuliano da Sangallo, one of the finest architects in that great age of architecture (Palazzo Strozzi, among many other things, resulted from his design). "My judgment too," he began politely, "was much inclined in favor of the corner of the Duomo." Then, after an imaginable pause, he continued: "But consider that this is a public thing." *E cosa pubblica:* the phrase had lost none of its vibrancy in two and a half centuries. Consider, too, he urged,

the weakness of the marble, which is delicate and fragile. Then, if it is placed outside and exposed to the weather, I think that it will not endure. For this reason as much as any, I thought that it would be better underneath the central arch of the *Loggia* of the Signoria: either underneath the center of the vault, so that you can go in and walk around it, or else behind it as a sort of tabernacle. Remember that if it is put outside, it will soon weather badly.

The Loggia of the Signoria favored by Giuliano—and as beautiful and influential an architectural creation as one can readily think of—had been built in the 1370s, at right angles to Arnolfo's palazzo. It had three arches facing the square and another at the east end facing the palazzo. Here, on the enclosed platform above the short flight of steps, official ceremonies took place; and this fact gave some of the speakers pause. "I agree that it should be in the Loggia," Leonardo da Vinci remarked; but (here he evinced a certain wariness toward his younger rival) he did not want it to stand conspicuously and obtrusively under the central vault; rather, he preferred to have it placed "on the parapet where they hang the tapestries on the side of the wall, and with decency and decorum, and so displayed that it does not spoil the ceremonies of the officials."

A fife player named Giovanni Cellini, the father of Benvenuto, gave somewhat jumbled reasons for thinking that the statue should not be in the Loggia at all. He seemed to be saying that, even though covered in the Loggia, it would still be exposed to the weather; and he worried whether the giant might not be too big for the central vault.* Also, said Cellini, if you put it in the Loggia, "it would be necessary to go round it there, and, besides, some wretch might damage it with a stave."

One reads those words with a sigh, for wretches with staves, or the equivalent thereof, have left their traces in recent years on the Loggia statuary. It was the Medici Dukes Cosimo I and Ferdinand I who loaded the hitherto empty platform with statues in the sixteenth century: Benvenuto's world-famous bronze *Perseus* holding up the head of Medusa; by Giambologna, with his predilection for the outsized, the looming, swirling *Rape of the Sabines*, and *Hercules Fighting the Centaur*; at the rear, six stone figures of Roman matrons. Not long ago a Florentine student, exuberant on *vino* after passing his bar exams, swung himself vigorously on one of the big stone feet of the *Sabine* group and broke it off. I remember the almost audible groan of the Florentine population when the news was reported; and the somber faces of the crowd in the Piazza della Signoria, as they gazed silently at the damage. The foot has been repaired, but further if less serious harm has been done to some of the other pieces. So now the entire Loggia is chained off; no admittance. It is no longer possible, owing to these wretches, to "go round" anything there. And works like those of Cellini and Giambologna, which were built precisely to be walked around for a full viewing, can only be looked on in front, while you stand on the steps craning your head irritably forward.

Those who favored placing Michelangelo's young giant in the area of Palazzo Vecchio, on that January morning, outnumbered those who voted for the cathedral area by six to one. It was not only that the David was in every respect a secular figure—it had been commissioned and designed, even when intended for the buttress of Santa Maria, as representing Florentine civic freedom and civic grandeur. But by 1504, as well, the civic concern, the

* Professor Seymour, *op. cit.*, made an experimental photomontage showing the *David* under the central arch of the Loggia, where it fits to physical and symbolic perfection.

cosa pubblica, far outweighed in strength the pulses of religious piety. There was a difference of opinion, however, among those who felt that the statue should be related to the city's official doings.

A couple of them wanted to establish it in the courtyard inside the palazzo—"a place worthy of it," said the fife player Cellini, winding up his discourse. Others, and there were more of them, felt the statue would be better situated outside the palazzo in public view, and proposed placing it in the *ringhiera* (literally, railings), ordered by the Commune in 1323 as a little section of the piazza where Florentines could in a more orderly manner fulfill their need to *arringare,* harangue, one another. Francesco Filareti, First Herald of the Signoria, advanced the notion in what appears to be a carefully composed speech, and one that reflects the Florentine habit of connecting the proper condition of the city's public elements with the well-being of the city itself. Filareti proposed removing Donatello's statue of Judith and the slain Holofernes from in front of the palazzo and replacing it with Michelangelo's *David;* and this on grounds of both seemliness (or sexism, to use the later term) and superstition—the Donatello group had been moved to the palazzo at about the time (1494) that Pisa had broken away from Florentine control.

Judith is an emblem of death, and it is not fitting for the Republic— especially when our emblems are the cross and the lily—and I say it is not fitting that the woman should kill a man. And even more important, it was erected under an evil star, for from that day to this things have gone from bad to worse; for then we lost Pisa . . . My preference [is] for where Judith is now.

A few of the speakers remarked that Michelangelo's own views should be decisive—"I believe that the master sculptor would know best," Fillipino Lippi said—but the herald Filareti probably expressed the official position. For the Signoria, after (one supposes) studying the transcript of the debate, gave word that the *David* should be set in the *ringhiera.* It was lifted onto a cart by ropes and pulleys, a tremendous feat, and in a highly symbolic ceremonial act it was transported from the courtyard of the cathedral to the Palazzo Vecchio.

It remained there through all seasons and epochs until 1873. Then, in another highly symbolic act, Michelangelo's *David* was taken away—again by the use of ropes, pulleys, and carts—and placed in the Accademia on Via Ricasoli. (A copy of the statue was then set up on the original spot.) The understandable reason for the displacement was the fear of damage from continuous exposure to the weather, and perhaps from vandals with staves. The *David* is an unparalleled work of art that overwhelms the moment one enters the gallery and sees it looming up at the far end. But it is now no more than an item, however big, in a museum. It no longer participates in the life and the history of the city, no longer embodies the city's battle for political freedom.

[4]

Medici Country

Florence Becomes a Work of Art

Via Lamarmora—it was named for an Italian artillery general and
minister of war (died 1878)—is a residential street in the northern
part of Florence's historic center. It begins at a point near Porta
San Gallo, the northernmost gate in Arnolfo's circuit of walls;
from there it descends to San Marco square, where, changing its
name to Via Ricasoli, it continues on into the Piazza del Duomo.
During the winter and spring of 1963, Nancy Lewis and I, with
our infant son, occupied a penthouse seven stories above this
slender, ingratiating avenue, and we endlessly studied the surrounding urban landscape—a section of the city hitherto not very
well known to us. Below us stretched the lovely Semplici Gardens
(the name refers to medicinal plants), which proved to be an
inviting place for all of us, especially the one-year-old; and only
a step beyond, as it seemed, the Duomo itself, surprisingly intimate in the gathering dusk, awe-inspiring when the moon rose
behind it. Explorations on foot helped us, after a bit, to identify
the notable places nearest to us: the church and convent of San
Marco; over to the left of the Duomo, Piazza Santissima Annunziata, with the church of the same name and the Ospedale degli
Innocenti (Hospital for Foundlings), with its infinitely elegant
loggia; away to the right, the big, rough-faced church of San

Lorenzo, containing its Old and New Sacristies; and, in between, the compact mass of Palazzo Medici. It slowly came home to us—after frequent consultations with our guidebook, the 1950 edition of the Touring Club Italiano guide to Florence—that, as inhabitants of Via Lamarmora, we were residing in Medici country.

More specifically, we were in that area of Florence that had been organized and monumentalized by Giovanni de' Medici and, after Giovanni's death in 1429, by his son Cosimo, the two of them drawing successively on the virtually unrivaled architectural genius of Filippo Brunelleschi and on the lesser, softer genius of Michelozzo.

It took longer to discover that the Medicis were only the first, though by all means the most important and far-grasping, of the half-dozen wealthy and powerful families that, over the fifteenth century, divided Florence into a series of family dominions—the others being the Rucellai, Pazzi, Strozzi, Pitti, and, until their ouster in 1434, the Albizzi. (Another matter that had to be learned was that this last name is properly pronounced with the stress on the first syllable—AL-bizzi—rather than on the second, which had sounded more natural; and that it could be spelled indifferently with one or two z's.) This development, in its several manifestations, brought about the first significant change in the configuration of Florence since the late-thirteenth-century days of Arnolfo di Cambio.

During the century and a quarter following Arnolfo's death, the most striking additions to the cityscape served essentially to amplify the Arnolfian urban design and to enhance the structures he had initiated. To take one overpowering example, Giotto's sublime bell tower, begun by the aging artist in 1334, is the supreme artistic achievement of the fourteenth century; it lifts itself skyward in a manner at once resolute and reverential, and at nearly three hundred feet it was the temporary winner in what has been called the Florentine battle for space. But the Campanile was conceived and executed as an adjunct to the cathedral of Arnolfo—work upon which had just started up again after a lapse of nearly three decades, and now under the supervision of Giotto as *capomaestro*.

In 1337, the year of Giotto's death, three Florentine architects —Francesco Talenti, Neri di Fioravante, and Benci di Cione— undertook the reconstruction of the granary-cum-tabernacle of Orsanmichele, expanding on Arnolfo's design for the earlier Orsanmichele, which had been destroyed in the holocaust of 1304. There was thus gradually realized (with interruptions, the work took twenty years) Arnolfo's vision of a religious-urban construct to abut the passage between the city's religious center, his cathedral, and its civic center, his Palazzo Vecchio; and to stand in a short west-east line with the other religious and civic pair, the Badia and the Bargello. With Orsanmichele, it might even be said, the Arnolfian scheme was at last complete; for Orsanmichele concluded and closed the urban rectangle otherwise comprising the cathedral, Badia-Bargello, and Palazzo Vecchio—the defining urban statement of medieval Florence.

As early as 1323, the Commune, seeking to make the role of the Priory more visible and dramatic, saw to the construction of a *ringhiera* in front of Palazzo Vecchio: a flight of stone tiers where the Priors could sit facing the assembled *popolo*, take counsel, announce judgments, and harangue (*arringare*) the citizens. It was later decided to erect a second, covered *ringhiera* in which deliberations could go on even in inclement weather, and this became the grandest of Florence's loggias (there will be another word on this shortly), at right angles to Palazzo Vecchio and in expressive communion with it. But long before that, in the decade of the 1340s, Florence had suffered a calamitous interval, brief in duration but of almost incalculable consequence.

We can go back to the late 1330s and take stock of the condition of the city of Florence. Most of the following facts and statistics come from Giovanni Villani, who was the first of Florence's historical statisticians. The population of the city was upward, perhaps well upward, of one hundred thousand. Of these, some thirty thousand worked on various levels of the wool industry, in about two hundred "laboratories." Ten thousand children were in school learning to read and write, and we may pause over this.

The remarkable and sustained high rate of literacy among Florentines and the peninsula-wide supremacy of the *lingua Toscana* (though most effective, according to one adage, when pronounced by the *bocca Romana*) have been very considerable factors in Florentine history; and credit is said to be due the Emperor Charlemagne, who perhaps established a school system in Florence around 800 A.D. There were about eighty banks, or places of exchange, in 1330s Florence, and six hundred notaries (take heed of that extraordinary figure), sixty doctors and surgeons, several dozen bakeries, and assortments of dyers, carpenters, vintners, goldsmiths, jewelers, and the like. A great deal of the commercial and workshop activity—especially that of the bankers, dyers, and silk workers—concentrated in and around the Mercato Nuovo (what we know, in its reduced modern form, as the Straw Market), and this became another of the chief gathering places for the lively conversations and transactions of the citizenry.

The religious life was similarly flourishing. "The churches in Florence and the *borghi*," writes Villani, "including the abbeys and the churches of the religious orders, amounted to 110." To avoid the distracting, if not deafening, sound of several score of church bells ringing at once, a schedule was worked out whereby each church in any given sector had its own turn. More than ever, the religious scene permeated the urban one. Energetic preaching and the singing of lauds went on as always in the open spaces—most of them, by now, recognizable piazzas—outside Santa Croce and the others. But there were also multiple religious celebrations, processions, publicly held rituals. New occasions for these were regularly being contrived: in addition to the fifty-two Sundays in the year, there were more than forty religious holidays—the chief one being June 24, the day of the city's patron saint, San Giovanni—in fourteenth-century Florence. It may be remarked that, while the number of such holidays has been curtailed in most Italian cities, they remain in force in the outlying districts. What traveler in the Italian countryside has not arrived at some remote village, with one day to spend there, only to discover that everything is closed up tight in honor of Saint Qualcheduno?

City life was a daylight affair. The sixteen gates clanged shut at sundown, and the serving women hurried to the nearest well—there was one communal well in each of the city's fifty-seven parishes, still another site to forgather and chatter and pass the news—to draw the evening's supply of water. In their homes, the Florentines sat long over meals. It has been estimated that they consumed, in varieties of pasta, more than 2,000 bushels of wheat a day, and quaffed down 70,000 quarts of wine. They were—and have remained—devoted eaters of meat, slaughtering for their dinner tables 100,000 sheep, goats, and swine a year, as well as about 4,000 cattle. During the day, the urban scene was bustling, colorful, and congested. The Florentines were perhaps the first and the most lively of the street people and standers-in-doorways; their insatiable curiosity about what might be going on in the street outside, their eager desire to participate, has been a constant and an ever-beguiling phenomenon. Shopfronts pushed out into the narrow curving streets, and wares were displayed on wooden benches, making progress more difficult for passengers on horseback and for donkeys loaded with merchandise. There were preachers everywhere, and beggars abounded; heralds made their way about the city giving voice to the latest communal decrees. Nor was this frenetic activity limited to particular portions of Florence: each of the *quartieri* was a total mix of magnates, merchants, *frati*, artisans, and *popolo minuto*, the poorest segment of the population; of church, palazzo, workshop, inn, market, flower stall. The visitor to Florence today can find something of this same mix in Piazza Santo Spirito in Oltrarno.

Violence, physical violence out in the open, was abating, and blood-spilling factionalism had virtually disappeared in the decades since the Blacks and the Whites had striven so aggressively with one another. Acts of atrocity now tended to be individual matters, like those of the magnate Carlo Adimari (the example, in fact, is taken from a somewhat later epoch), who, before being rounded up, raped and decapitated a country maiden, seized and repeatedly violated another adolescent girl from the same village, and then, going entirely berserk, murdered two men, one of them an abbot, and burned down the houses of three other citizens.

The Florentine zest for the disputatious increasingly took the less bruising form of simple quarreling, passionate disagreement, public debate—and endless litigation. Florentines, as the fourteenth century moved forward, seemed never happier than when engaged in a lawsuit; it was not unheard of for a man to denounce his own brother in court as a magnate, thus making the latter ineligible for public office. The man of law was the most sought after of citizens, and it is hardly surprising that the city needed ten times as many notaries as it did doctors and surgeons.

But this, too, was a sign of irrepressible vitality. Florence in the late 1330s seemed, indeed, to be more than ever "on the rise," to borrow the phrase Villani applied to the city in 1300. The great things Villani saw destined for Florence were already by way of being accomplished: not only in the great public monuments, in the new proliferation of paintings by artists liberated through the work of Giotto from the stiff Byzantine style, and in letters (Boccaccio would shortly make his return to Florence)—but in the city's enormous financial and mercantile power and, above all, in its exemplary political arrangements.

Then came a time of terrible tribulation. The city had survived the frightful inundation of 1333 and the heavy losses of life and property computed by Villani; the three wrecked bridges were on the verge of being rebuilt—Ponte Vecchio, with its three handsome arcades, resulted (Vasari says) from a brilliant design by Taddeo Gaddi. But the disaster of 1342 was man-made, even self-imposed, and it is one of the most mysterious episodes in Florentine history. What happened, briefly, was that the Florentines called in a certain Count Walter of Brienne, known for some obscure reason as the Duke of Athens, to take charge of the city's armed forces; whereupon Count Walter immediately made himself the despotic ruler of the entire city. It was not uncommon for Italian cities to call in a "strong man" to protect the vested interests, and elsewhere on the peninsula (Dante had lamented the fact three decades earlier) this had led to a number of tyrannies. But Florence had always been more cautious: when, for example, they had invited the assistance of the Duke of Calabria, the son of the King of Naples, to come to their aid in 1325, they circumscribed his authority and limited his term of control to ten years—and managed to get rid of him a good deal sooner than that. But the Florentines seem for once to have lost their political nerve in the summer of 1342; after being installed as the town's commanding general, the *soi-disant* Duke of Athens solicited and acceded to a request by the citizenry that he be given absolute power over Florence for the rest of his life. The Priory was abolished, and the Duke, behind squads of armed guards, exercised sole authority in Palazzo Vecchio—adding to the latter's fortress-like character by shutting off the *ringhiera* and barricading the heavy entrance doors. After a year of the Duke's ruthless conduct, the Florentines—that is, the guild members working together—chased him out; he fled to the Guidi castle in Poppi, whence he was removed and dispensed with.

The best explanation for this untypical interlude, apparently, is that the Florentine bankers had turned to the Duke of Athens in a moment of panic. The boyish and headstrong Edward III of England—*il piccolo re d'Inghilterra,* in Villani's patronizing phrase —had underwritten an invasion of France, a few years before, by a loan of more than a million gold florins from the Bardi and Peruzzi banks in Florence. When Edward's attempt to make himself King of France came to grief, he took the easy way out and casually repudiated his debts. The Bardi and Peruzzi promptly failed, and other businesses and banks went down in catastrophic succession. Workshops closed their shutters; unemployment soared; the *popolo minuto* faced starvation. There was reason to fear a savage popular uprising; and it was to prevent this or beat it back (so the plausible argument runs) that the Duke of Athens was summoned. In a familiar and melancholy political pattern, the savior soon threatened to become the destroyer, as the Florentines responsible realized just before it was too late.

But the dismissal of the Duke of Athens, while belatedly reaffirming the congenital Florentine loathing of tyranny, did little to ease the economic situation. Matters, indeed, grew worse. The city's finances were still in alarming disarray when, in 1346, the countryside around Florence suffered the worst crop failure within people's memory. Now there was genuine starvation, and rioting in the streets by frenzied and desperate workers. What might have developed can be guessed at from the actual and temporarily successful revolt of the wool workers in 1378. But on this earlier occasion, the most colossal disaster in European annals intervened to put an end to all other considerations. In the spring of 1348, Florence was visited by the Great Death.

We now know that it was a form of bubonic plague, and that though its geographical origins were much more remote, it was brought to Europe on trading vessels from the Crimea, carrying infected rats and parasitic fleas. It is now commonly referred to as the Black Death. For the Florentines, as for people elsewhere, it was more simply Death itself, death on so great a scale as to be beyond human calculation. Boccaccio remarks that the number of deaths reported on any given day or night (four thousand on average) was "so enormous" that it was almost impossible to believe. Before the pestilence had run its five-month course, he concludes, "it is reliably thought that over a hundred thousand human lives were extinguished within the walls of the city of Florence." And he adds: "Yet before this lethal catastrophe fell upon the city, it is doubtful whether anyone would have guessed it contained so many inhabitants."*

It has since been reckoned that the death toll in Florence was closer to sixty thousand, or about three-fifths of the city's population, but Boccaccio's first-hand account of the plague in Florence, the introduction to *The Decameron*, remains not only the most vivid but the most suggestive that we have. He indicates the sudden Florentine discovery of a preposterous shortage of doctors (only threescore, we recall), and observes that the host of amateur medicos who thrust themselves forward did incomparably more harm than good. He is exceedingly shrewd about the varying responses to the horror: those who withdrew into an isolated and carefully abstemious life; those who turned to extravagant self-indulgence—so many priests and lawyers having been wiped out that there were too few left to enforce "the laws of God and man." The customary period of public mourning was

* Translation by G. H. McWilliam, in his Penguin edition (1972) of *The Decameron*.

perforce abandoned; men, women, and children died too swiftly and in numbers too great for burial rites to be performed. When all the graves in the consecrated grounds were exhausted, trenches were dug in the churchyards, and here "new arrivals were placed in their hundreds, stowed tier upon tier like ship's cargo, each layer of corpses being covered over with a thin layer of soil till the trench was filled to the top." The very scale of the calamity, Boccaccio writes, produced before long an attitude of sheer indifference:

no more respect was accorded to the dead than would nowadays be shown towards goats . . . More often than not bereavement was the signal for laughter and witticisms and general jollification—the art of which the women, having for the most part suppressed their feminine concern for the salvation of the souls of the dead, had learned to perfection.

The Decameron, begun in 1349 or thereabouts, is on one level a literary enactment of this conversion of horror into comedy.

Before moving on from fact to fiction, Boccaccio offers a sorrowing epitaph for the devastated city:

Ah, how great a number of splendid palaces, fine houses, and noble dwellings, once filled with retainers, with lords and ladies, were bereft of all who had lived there, down to the tiniest child! How numerous were the famous families, the vast estates, the notable fortunes, that were seen to be left without a rightful successor!

He thereupon brings to the scene the seven young ladies and the three young gentlemen who, after meeting in the church of Santa Maria Novella and making their plans, proceed to a roomy and beautifully appointed villa a few miles outside Florence, near Settignano, for ten days of storytelling and gracious living.

Boccaccio stresses the loss to Florence of "famous families" and "vast estates," and as we shall see in a moment, he was not altogether wrong to do so. Meanwhile, his analysis of Florentine reactions to the Great Death provides a clue to the plague's aftermath. Nothing is more astonishing than the cultural resilience displayed by the Florentines in the years following, and even while the pestilence was making briefer and less horrendous return visits. The experience may have had a somewhat diminishing and diversionary effect upon painting, which for a period became rather stiff and formalized—as against the supple naturalness and humanity of Giotto's frescoes—and applied itself to topics like the Last Judgment and the Triumph of Death. But Florentine art showed no real or profound imaginative involvement with death, of the sort evident in other countries. In fact, the daily encounter with death, the daily witnessing of hundreds and thousands of bloated corpses seems instead to have heightened the Florentine consciousness of the sheer value of life. *The Decameron*, one of the very liveliest of the world's literary masterpieces, is itself a product of the dreadful adventure.

In urban matters, Florence recovered its stride almost at once. A specially appointed Committee of Eight guided the city through the worst days, maintaining at least an adequate order within the walls and doing what it could to dispose of the bodies. The plague had barely subsided before a number of rich families donated 350,000 florins to Orsanmichele, as the city's chief shrine for the sickly and anxiety-ridden; and Andrea Orcagna, in 1349, set to work constructing a glittering tabernacle to enclose Bernardo Daddi's painting of the Madonna alle Grazie, thought or hoped to be as efficient in producing miracles as the previous one destroyed in 1304. (There is a curious disagreement about Orcagna's tabernacle: Fanelli is not alone in thinking it artistically overrated and incoherent; others, including the present writer, find it breathtaking.) Work resumed once more on Santa Maria del Fiore and went ahead with such vigor that by 1380 the Arnolfian cathedral, now much expanded, was virtually complete.

By 1376 the Commune was ready to proceed with the century's greatest new civic monument in Florence, the loggia in the Piazza della Signoria, funds for which had been voted only a few years after the deadly visitation. It was probably designed by Andrea Orcagna, and executed by Benci di Cione and Simone di Francesco Talenti: framing a vast interior space, with three immense arcades

Loggia dei Lanzi, with statuary

facing the piazza and another, on the left flank, opening toward the Priors' palace. It received the name Loggia dei Lanzi after Duke Cosimo I installed a company of Swiss lancers there; originally it was known merely as the Loggia della Signoria. In republican Florence, the loggia, as its first title indicated, was the place where the Signori assembled and conferred, and where citizens could sit at their ease and watch the goings on in the piazza. So made use of, the loggia became what Leon Battista Alberti (the comment was quoted earlier, with reference to the little piazza on the Ponte Vecchio) would say every loggia should be: the chief adornment of the piazza, which is in turn the chief adornment of the city.

The building of the Loggia della Signoria took place during the years in Florence dominated by the Revolt of the Ciompi. This strange word seems to mean wool workers, or perhaps wool carders; it referred, anyhow, to the sizable number of persons engaged in the wool industry, who were excluded from guild membership, lived on starvation wages and in squalid circumstances, and had no say whatever about their condition. More broadly, it referred to the whole of the *popolo minuto*, the little people, the impoverished and disenfranchised of the city. In 1378, when the uprising began, the city was still controlled by the *popolo grasso*, that minority of citizens who belonged to the seven major and the fourteen minor guilds; in fact, the seven Priors and the *gonfaloniere* were still chosen from the major guilds of merchants and bankers. For the working class, things had not improved since the somber days of the 1340s and the Black Death; a fifty-year-old workman in 1378 could have a sickening memory of that dark period of famine and failure. And for the first time, ghettolike sections had come into being in Florence, around Santa Croce and even more in Borgo San Frediano, near the Carraia bridge, where thousands of wool workers were crowded together in ramshackle housing.

So, in the summer of 1378 (Florentine disturbances customarily occurred in the hot season), the Ciompi revolted. They came storming into Piazza della Signoria, took over Palazzo Vecchio and sent the Priors flying for their lives, exultantly rang the tower bells, and, amid continuing commotion, pressed their demands until they were granted three new guilds of their own and, equally important, representation by three new Priors. The minor guilds, their number thus increased to seventeen, contained 13,000 members; if they had hung together, they could have overwhelmed the merchants and bankers at the polls. But the older artisan groups feared and detested their new wool-working associates (one thinks of recent American social history, and the tensions between working-class whites and the emergent black and Hispanic population). There were fresh divisions and alliances; power shredded away; and early in 1382, the major guilds dispatched a band of thugs into the slum districts of Oltrarno and beat the *ciompi* into submission. Legislation of a nakedly improper kind was hurried through, revoking the new guild charters. The merchant-bankers were in full command of the city.

Like every truly significant change in the structure of a society, this one—the coming into being of an oligarchy in Florence—

had been long in the making. It was one of several developments whose origin can be traced back to the year of the Great Death. Another novel feature of Florence at this time was a slave population, amounting perhaps to five thousand: non-Christians imported from Dalmatia and elsewhere, mostly to work as domestics, presumably to replace the countless servants who had died in the plague. ("I know not whether your own experience is similar to mine," Pampinea says to the other young ladies with whom she is organizing the villa party in *The Decameron*, "but my house was once full of servants, and now that there is no one left apart from my maid and myself, I am filled with foreboding and feel as if every hair on my head is standing on end.") The Signoria legalized slavery in 1364, and in chillingly dispassionate language: "Whoever purchases them may receive, possess, use and exploit them as his slaves, and may do his will with them."* With the drastic reduction in the citizenry, there was also a new distribution of power and money, and new invitations to greed. Out of the turmoil, a relative handful of merchant and banking families moved steadily to the forefront; and it was this process that came to a head in 1382, when the Florentine oligarchy almost openly declared itself as such.

The process was inevitable and, all things considered, not entirely unfortunate. It is true that the Great Death killed off a larger percentage of the poor than of the rich, mainly because of the packed and vulnerable living conditions of the poor. But as it has been remarked, Florence had not been divided geographically along class lines; every section had its wealthy, its well-to-do, its modest, and its impoverished, and the ranks of the upper bourgeoisie had likewise been woefully invaded by the pestilence. Boccaccio had been quite right to sigh over the many "famous families, the vast estates, the notable fortunes" that had vanished utterly from the face of the city. With the disappearance of the *many* powerful families, there arose the opportunity for the *few* to take charge, which was precisely what they did. The social

---

* On slavery in Florence, see p. 156 and footnote.

spectrum of Florence in the late 1370s showed a few families at the top and the many families of the working class at the bottom, huddled close together in the new ghettos.

Even so, Florence prospered after 1382—materially, politically, intellectually, artistically. Flexing its revived military muscle, the city gradually established its sovereignty in southern and western Tuscany. Arezzo was won in 1384 and Montepulciano in 1390; Pisa in 1406 and, by purchase, the port of Livorno in 1421. It was in part the heady sense of Florentine hegemony within its particular world that released a flood of eloquent urban self-congratulation. In his *Laudatio Florentiae Urbis* (*Praise of the City of Florence*) in 1402, Leonardo Bruni—chancellor, or permanent secretary, of Florence, and the first distinguished writer of classical, as against medieval, Latin prose—compared Florence surrounded by its territories to the moon surrounded by stars, each in its fixed place: "which is beautiful to see." Florence, in Bruni's elaborating figure, was the center of a perfect aesthetic order: the principal and dominating circle within a series of concentric circles. The city was encircled by walls, and they in turn by "beautiful *borghi*." The *borghi* (suburbs) were surrounded by the outlying villas, "and the villas similarly by the other territories and castles."

Further testimony to the supremacy of Florence was offered a year later by Coluccio Salutati, a successor to Bruni as chancellor, a singularly adroit diplomat and administrator, and a writer of such rhetorical skill that one of his state papers was said (by Gian Galeazzo Sforza of Milan) to have the political value of a thousand horsemen. Salutati addressed himself to the matchless blessings of the immediate urban scene:

What city, not merely in Italy, but in all the world, is more securely placed within its circle of walls, more proud in its palazzi, more bedecked with churches, more beautiful in its architecture, more imposing in its gates, happier in its wide streets, greater in its people, more glorious in its citizenry, more inexhaustible in wealth, more fertile in its fields?

More telling than the generalized extravagance of Salutati is the acute survey of the city's specifically urban composition by the humanist historian Goro Dati in his *History of Florence from 1380 to 1405* (written in 1423). Dati's commentary is the best evidence possible that the early-fifteenth-century Florentine fully appreciated the "real city"—the coherent, knowable, and superbly designed city—in which he lived. I will quote selectively, especially since the text has been considerably emended by recent scholarship.

The city is well walled-around, with strong towers on the walls, and with ten open gates all of great height . . . The streets inside are straight and wide; and the internal circuit runs seven miles . . . One street departs from one gate and goes directly to another gate across a diameter two miles in length. Another street likewise goes from one gate to another and forms a cross (with the first street) in the middle of the city, or nearly, that is, in Mercato Vecchio. There are still other streets leading from gate to gate, and across the middle of the city and over the river Arno. On the river at mid-city are many mills of marvelous beauty . . . And then there are four bridges in the city all of stone (*concia*) and gracefully composed. Among them is one on which there are beautiful shops everywhere, all made of stone, so that you would not think you were on a bridge were there not a piazza in the middle, from where you can see the river above and below them. Then, at the end of the city, on the *tramontana* side, are many other mills which between them grind as much grain as the city needs, which at the present is 100 *moggia* [bushels] or thereabouts. Almost in the middle of the city in a great square stands the palace which is the habitation and residence of the Lord Priors, all in stone and wonderfully strong and beautiful . . . In the square off the Palazzo there is a great and magnificent loggia of stone all the way to the ground, with four arcades of notable beauty . . .

The wall circuit with its gates and towers; the pattern of streets and the cross-axes meeting at the center of the city, Mercato Vecchio; the river, the mills, the bridges, and especially Ponte Vecchio with its shops and its little piazza; Piazza Signoria, Palazzo Vecchio, the Loggia della Signoria—all mentioned, all perceived in relation *to* and measurable distances *from* each other. We listen, in Dati's discourse, to the first explicit identification of

Arnolfo di Cambio, 1844 bust   Filippo Brunelleschi, 1447 bust

the actual and palpable city of Florence as itself a *work of human art*. We listen as well to what is in effect the final tribute to the Arnolfian city and its design; for as of 1423 a new, or at least a critically revised, urban *insieme* was soon to appear.

Brunelleschi's Vision

The *gonfaloniere* of Florence in May–June 1378 was one Salvestro de' Medici. He was a fairly prosperous merchant and a member of the oligarchy; but like several other decent-minded oligarchs, Salvestro seems to have become outraged by the wretched state of the *popolo minuto* and the wickedly repressive treatment to which they were subjected. Adopting the traditional and inestimable role of traitor to his class, Salvestro, in the last days of June, let it be known that in his view the moment for a large-scale uprising was at hand. He left office shortly before the wool workers charged into the piazza; but the name of Medici was thenceforward a popular one, even a rallying cry, among the lower orders of the city.

The Florentine Medicis apparently began drifting into the city, around 1200, from the Mugello, a handsome mountainous district not far to the north. The name Medici, if it means anything (which is unlikely: the family name Pazzi would literally mean "crazies," which some of them may have been but which *it* doesn't), means "doctors." I have seen it speculated that some early members of the clan may have had something to do with medicine or pharmacy, and that the five round balls on the family crest, which no one has otherwise been able to explain, may have been so many white pills. More probably, the Medicis were originally peasant farmers, of the sort Dante was to speak of so resentfully: "smelly peasants from the countryside," who degraded the makeup of the citizenry.

In Florence, at any event, these country folk gave their energies to business affairs. They were obviously good at it: soon after the *Secondo Popolo* was formed in the 1280s, members of the family were inscribed in the major guilds, and in the 1290s a certain Ardingo de' Medici was elected Prior and then *gonfaloniere*. Perhaps their peasant beginnings continued to color their outlook as their fortunes grew through the fourteenth century: there are attractive and, it seems, insoluble psychological mysteries about the earlier Medici; one would like to know just what impelled Salvestro not only to sympathize with the little people but to take the daring step of giving the signal for their revolt. But if, because of that, the Medicis captured the enthusiasm of the commoners, they also and for the same reason aroused the suspicion and distrust of the traditional oldsters among the ruling group. It is with Salvestro's nephew, known as Giovanni di Bicci, that the chronicle of the Medicis as the first family in Florence usually begins; and Giovanni was long regarded as a newcomer, an upstart, not really a dependable member of the club.

He was a reserved man, Giovanni, not at all given to display or the conspicuous pursuit of power. He did not seek or much enjoy public office. "Let the palace come to you," he aphoristically advised his children, and the palace did so; willy-nilly, Giovanni was elected time and again to the Signoria and once was made *gonfaloniere*. His interests were primarily financial; he was the first Medici to concentrate on banking rather than merchandise, and though he began in relatively modest circumstances and was for a period reduced almost to poverty by the intrigues of jealous rivals, he ended in command of perhaps the greatest fortune in the city. He provided dowries for the daughters of impecunious friends; he gave generously to the poor, and made a point of keeping on good terms with the common people. Another bit of advice he passed on was: "Never hold an opinion contrary to the will of the people, even if this same people should prefer something that is perfectly useless." A cautious and honorable man, sufficiently devious (some would have said knavish) to survive and even flourish on the hectic Florentine stage, with blunt features and shrewd, kindly eyes that betrayed a faint, curious expression of anxiety, Giovanni de' Medici lived out his life in a quietly adroit evasion of drama.

In 1386, he was married to eighteen-year-old Piccarda Bueri, Verona-born but of Florentine origin, and known as Nannina (the name would be handed down to females in the line for six hundred years). She was a skilled administrator of the household, and showed a knowing interest as well in her husband's banking ventures. "I commend Nannina to your care," Giovanni told his two sons upon his deathbed. "You must see to it that my death does not deprive her of the honor and respect she has always deserved." The sons followed this request faithfully during their mother's few remaining years.

Of those two sons, we hear little of the younger one, Lorenzo. He was content to subordinate his activities to those of his brother Cosimo, both in the expanding banking business and in art patronage. Lorenzo died at the age of forty-five, to Cosimo's intense grief. Among his sixteenth-century descendants were a famous assassin and Cosimo I, the first Duke of Florence and later the first Grand Duke of Tuscany.

Cosimo de' Medici was forty years old when his father died in 1429. It soon became evident that the new head of the family was prepared to take political advantage of the Medici popularity with the masses to a far greater degree than his father; and no one was more aware of this than Rinaldo, the intemperate leader of the Albizzi clan which had been the ruling element in Florence since the destruction of the Ciompi guilds in 1382. Following a disastrous effort to bring the city of Lucca under Florentine control, Rinaldo degli Albizzi, feeling the need to reestablish his authority, decided to get rid of his most dangerous rival.

In September 1433, he summoned into being a special committee, allegedly to discuss governmental reform (it was an ancient, infrequently used, and unconstitutional instrument), and oversaw election to it by the simple device of sealing off the entrances to Piazza della Signoria and allowing only those favorable to the cause to slide through and vote. The committee, or *balia*, had Cosimo brought in from his country home in the Mugello, placed him under arrest, and shut him up in a little cell high up in the Palazzo Vecchio tower. Despite Rinaldo's prodding, however, the committee, thrown off balance by the pro-Medici tumult throughout the city, refused to condemn Cosimo to death.

Cosimo took it for granted that an effort would next be made to assassinate him in secret, most probably by poisoning, and for several days refused to eat or drink anything served him—until his jailer assured him that he himself, if necessary, would taste the food in advance. "I have no wish," Cosimo was to remember the jailer saying, "to dirty my hands with the blood of anyone, and most especially of yours, who have never done me harm. So be of good cheer, eat your food, and keep yourself alive for your friends and for the country." Varied sums of Medici money were passed around; the committee voted to send Cosimo into exile; and Cosimo, along with his brother Lorenzo and several supporters, was led to the Tuscan border and made his way to Venice. Here all were received as royalty and heroes. A year later the Florentines elected a priorate of Medici persuasion, and in October 1434 Cosimo and his followers rode back into a wildly cheering city. Rinaldo degli Albizzi, who was of course promptly exiled in turn, sent Cosimo a message: "Watch out; we are not asleep." "I can believe it," Cosimo replied dryly. "I have made it impossible for you to sleep."

Cosimo—the Elder, or il Vecchio, as he came to be known—has long seemed to me the most interesting and impressive of the Medicis. He lacked the dash and glitter of his grandson Lorenzo il Magnifico, not to mention Lorenzo's genuine literary flair and his capacity to seize and exemplify the cultural moment; and certain claims to preeminence might be put forward for those two of the Medici descendants who became popes as Leo X and Clement VII. But in addition to several appealing personal qualities in Cosimo, both as a man and as a paterfamilias, no one contributed as much to the well-being of his native city as he did. No one so effectively brought the urban personality into focus and, as it were, saw to its training and education. Renaissance Florence was, in truth, begotten by and under the auspices of Cosimo de' Medici, and the authorities were wise, upon Cosimo's death in 1464, to have inscribed on his simple tombstone in the church of San Lorenzo the phrase that most aptly became him: *pater patriae*, the father of his country.

Contemporary and near-contemporary, as well as later, testimony is surprisingly unanimous in its assessment of Cosimo. Machiavelli, in his history of Florence, summed Cosimo up as a man who expended his life for the good of his city; and another Italian historian (Marcello Vannucci), citing that judgment four and a half centuries later, remarks upon the "many civil works, churches, monuments, streets" that Florence owed to Cosimo, who paid for no few of them out of his own private means. Those means were, of course, enormous, and by the 1440s the public resources (Cosimo was adept at mingling the two revenues) were close to immeasurable. Branches of the Medici bank could be observed in action in Rome, Venice, Pisa, and Milan, and outside of Italy throughout the European world: in Lyons, Paris, Brussels, Antwerp, Basel, Cologne, London, Barcelona, Lübeck, and elsewhere. Philippe de Commines, that astutely skeptical French onlooker, pronounced it the greatest commercial house that had ever existed; which makes it the less surprising that during Cosimo's rule in Florence (the figures come in fact from grandson Lorenzo, who discovered them in an old account book), the sum

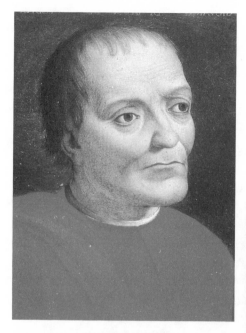

Giovanni di Bicci

Cosimo the Elder

Lorenzo de' Medici

of 663,755 florins was spent on "buildings, charities and taxes."* By any financial reckoning of the era, so vast a number of florins were staggering; the florin—*fiorino*, named for its place of coinage—being now the accepted coin of every European realm.

With the money, needless to say, came the power. "He it is who decides peace and war and controls the laws . . . He is king in everything but name." So spoke one of the most clear-sighted and cultivated of Cosimo's Tuscan contemporaries, Enea Silvio Piccolomini, the humanist, poet, and statesman who became Pope Pius II in 1459. Cosimo remained a private citizen by title, in what continued to be called a republic; but no private citizen since the days of Rome, in the words of the learned Florentine historian Francesco Guicciardini, had ever enjoyed such a standing. What had happened in political reality was that the oligarchy, which had pretty well taken over from the republic decades earlier, now gave way to one-man rule. What must be added in invoking that last formula about Cosimo il Vecchio is that this authority of his was rooted in the support and affection of the working masses and that it exercised itself *against* the assertive power of the oligarchs, the *magnati*, the big fellows (in a modern transphrasing) who controlled the great guilds.

Cosimo himself, with the passage of time, grew more doubtful about the durability of Medici power than about the permanence of the urban monuments he had helped bring into being. He confided to his friend and memoirist Vespasiano da Bisticci, bookseller and scholarly librarian: "I know the humors of my city. Before fifty years have passed we shall be expelled, but my buildings will remain." The political prophecy had a short-range accuracy: within three decades of Cosimo's death, the Medicis (in the form of another Piero) were expelled. But after forty-some years of Medici going and coming, a namesake of il Vecchio had supreme power conferred on him as Duke Cosimo I; and the Medici dukes were thereafter the lords of Tuscany for almost

---

* The period covered in the account book actually runs from 1434 to 1471, and thus includes the five years of the regime of Cosimo's son Piero the Gouty and the first two years in power of Lorenzo himself. See *The Rise and Fall of the House of Medici*, by Christopher Hibbert (1974), p. 74.

exactly two hundred years until, with the death without heir of Gian Gastone in 1737, the Tuscan grand duchy became the property of the house of Lorraine.

But Cosimo's architectural prophecy could not have been sounder. "My buildings": the urban buildings completed or begun during the rule of Cosimo de' Medici—the Duomo, the churches of San Lorenzo and Santo Spirito, the church and piazza of Santissima Annunziata with the Ospedale degli Innocenti, the church and convent of San Marco, Palazzo Medici—enacted the grand design of Renaissance Florence, a design which carried forward from the medieval city of Arnolfo di Cambio and transformed it. Two architects in particular, as we noted earlier, drew up the individual designs and, as circumstances permitted, saw to the execution of their plans: Filippo Brunelleschi (1377–1446), perhaps the greatest of Florence's city architects, and the somewhat younger Michelozzo Michelozzi (1396–1472), a less venturesome spirit, but an artist of immense ability and Cosimo's personal favorite.

Brunelleschi was a hot-tempered, fiercely argumentative figure, driven by genius and by an urban vision which no one else in his Florentine time ever quite grasped or entirely shared. He was the stuff that artistic-historical myths are made of; his personality lent itself to illuminating encounters and telling anecdotes, all representative of his huge *idea* of the city as an architectural entity and of its relation to authority and tradition. The matter of Santo Spirito—mention was made of this in Chapter 1—is a major case in point. Around 1428, Brunelleschi was asked by the Commune to prepare a model for a new church on the site of an old Gothic church and an Augustinian convent dating back to the mid-thirteenth century (and also of a school so lively in its discussions of metaphysics and physics that Boccaccio, out of admiration, bequeathed his library to it). The site is on the southern side of the Arno, not far below the Ponte Santa Trinità. Brunelleschi conceived the plan of having the facade on the north end of the church face out into a piazza which would itself extend some meters farther to the river.

It was a stupendous proposal. As Fanelli has written, Brunelleschi always took as fundamental the relation between building and city; and so, as an example, Santo Spirito was imagined not so much as one more addition to an urban context that would continue to grow and unfold in time but rather as an element that would serve to reorganize in a permanent way the *quartiere* of Santo Spirito named for it and fit that *quartiere* into the urban context, which was in turn perceived as an architectural whole. Church-and-piazza fronting the river, moreover, would have brought the Arno more intimately into the urban life; and, as a contemporary remarked, visitors coming into town along the river from Pisa would have been able to look across the piazza at the facade of a great church.

But a number of houses and shops—so it was argued, though this has been disputed since—would have had to be demolished to make way for the new piazza, and the owners concerned, powerful men, refused to countenance the plan. The present church has a facade facing *south*—and, as must be admitted, into the most inviting of piazzas, with trees at one end and a small elegant fountain in the middle; rectangular in shape and containing on one side the *signorile* Palazzo Guadagni, possibly by Baccio d'Agnolo. Piazza Santo Spirito of a morning is enlivened by a local open market (look in particular for peppers and olive oil); and no area on the south bank is more attractive to lounge in at any time of day. But a special opportunity was lost when Brunelleschi's scheme was defeated. The opposition demonstrated the still considerable clout of the magnates and, no less, the fact that Brunelleschi's urban idea was simply not understood.

Brunelleschi was, of course, anything but easy to deal with. He tended to make difficult matters worse by his impatience and pugnacity with the slower-witted authorities. During the hearings about a new dome for the cathedral in 1419, Brunelleschi grew so obstreperous and noisy (the issue was the possibility of vaulting the center by a giant dome without buttresses) that he was carried out of the church bodily by attendants and dropped on his back in the square. But these were qualities in a man who was artistically alive and urgent in every fiber, and who responded on the instant to any challenge or suggestion. It is told of him that, loitering one day near the Baptistery with his friend Donatello and chatting about ancient sculpture, he heard Donatello speak of a beautiful antique marble vase he had recently come upon in the town of Cortona. Excited by the news, Brunelleschi then and there set forth on foot for Cortona (a distance of some 120 kilometers, or 75 miles), still in his working clothes and wooden shoes, and returned a few days later with a drawing of the vase to show the unbelieving Donatello.

He also liked to stroll about the old market with Donatello, so Vasari reports, listening to the voices and absorbing the language of "the people." And this may be the main clue to the man. The artist who was an ardent student of geometry (Vasari tells us) and who envisaged architectural forms in pure geometrical shapes—witness the interplaying semicircles and rectangles of the Old Sacristy in San Lorenzo and the Pazzi Chapel next to Santa Croce—had at the same time, in the same temperamental mix, a tremendous consciousness of the *human* world in which he lived and for which he worked. Of this remarkable melange, the new dome for the cathedral of Santa Maria del Fiore is the superlative expression.

The building and the setting-in-place of the Duomo by Brunelleschi was, as has been frequently declared, an unparalleled feat of engineering as well as a fabulous architectural accomplishment. Brunelleschi was alert to the challenge. "There is no doubt that great undertakings are always difficult," Vasari has him saying to the cathedral wardens and the syndics of the wool-workers guild, "but this one even more so than you are fully aware. Not even the ancients raised a vault so enormous as this one will be." Some time later, he drew up a statement that was read aloud by a tribunal: "The difficulties of this erection being well considered, magnificent signors and wardens, I find it cannot be in a perfect circle because the huge span could not bear the weight of the lantern . . . The thickness of the base of the vault must be seven feet, and it will diminish like a pyramid towards the top where it must be two feet thick. A second vault must be built as a protective roof for the first. The parts of this shell, lighter than the dome, must meet the inner vault at the top"—and so on, in detail.* The cupola was effectively completed in late 1436, and it was consecrated in an elaborate ceremony (Vespasiano da Bisticci describes it) wherein the Pope, the cardinals, innumerable bishops and subdeacons—"the whole court of Rome duly arraigned"— proceeded along a bridge from Santa Maria Novella to the cathedral, passing between blue-and-white draperies, with benches on either side.

Work on the lantern was begun about 1435, under the supervision of Michelozzo, and completed twenty-odd years later. The bronze ball and cross at the top of the dome were fashioned by Verrocchio and put there in May 1471: "The canons and others went up and sang the *Te Deum*" in the lantern on that day, as we learn from the diary of the apothecary Luca Landucci.

Filippo Brunelleschi was unquestionably the architect of the cupola, but in the first stages he was forced to accept the collaboration of Lorenzo Ghiberti, his old rival from the days, in the early 1400s, when the two youthful artists had competed to decorate the bronze doors of the Baptistery. Ghiberti won that event, and by 1420 he had become one of the most highly regarded sculptors in the city—and a figure far more congenial than Brunelleschi to the powers that were.† Brunelleschi was so filled with rage and despair at the proposed sharing of authority that

---

* Those interested in the technical aspects of this achievement might begin by reading Vasari's life of Brunelleschi, in which the architect is quoted holding forth in lengthy specifics about the task.

† The theme of the Baptistery competition was the Biblical story of the sacrifice of Isaac. Brunelleschi and Ghiberti both produced superb panels: Brunelleschi characteristically freezing the final dramatic moment as though for eternity; Ghiberti no less suggestively showing the event as it developed in episodes over a period of time. Modern opinion tends, if anything, to agree with the judges who voted for Ghiberti.

Ghiberti's first doors were finished in 1424; the second doors, known as the "Gates of Paradise" because Michelangelo so labeled them, took twenty-seven years more to complete. Brunelleschi's panel, incidentally, may be found in the Museo dell'Opera del Duomo; and there also, sorrowfully, are all of Ghiberti's Baptistery panels. The panels we see today, as we walk around the Baptistery, are late-twentieth-century copies.

he was half inclined to destroy his models and tear up his designs, and was only kept from doing so, if Vasari is to be believed, by the soothing encouragement and comfort of Donatello and Luca della Robbia. Before long, and by a variety of stratagems, Brunelleschi managed to get rid of his would-be partner and was himself alone in charge.

Leon Battista Alberti, coming to Florence in 1434, was overwhelmed by the spectacle of the cupola, and would write about it in a book dedicated to Brunelleschi:

A structure so great, rising above the skies, large enough to shelter all the people of Tuscany in its shadow, built without the help of any centering or of much woodwork, of a craftsmanship [which] perhaps not even the ancients knew or understood.

If not, in fact, large enough to cast its shadow over the whole of Tuscany, it was certainly large and striking enough to dominate the whole of the city of Florence in the mid-fifteenth century, and ever since. But this raises a key issue about the Florentine cityscape.

The Duomo as constituted does not relate primarily to any other single Florentine monument. Arnolfo di Cambio's original cathedral, for example, related directly and distinctly to Palazzo Vecchio, its civil counterpart; and at the same time, it served to organize the city by providing its representative architectural and urban structure. But the Duomo of Brunelleschi related rather to the entire city; and in doing that, it *created* an entire city; it made the city into a single harmonious totality. Everything now related to it: Palazzo Vecchio and Santa Maria Novella and Santa Croce and the city wall and the gates. Florence in that mid-century had become, as though by urban-architectural magic, a single unified entity. Giovanni Fanelli is emphatic and eloquent on this miraculous happening; but it is also what any visitor today instantly intuits the moment that eyes are laid upon the Florentine skyline. The Duomo is what pulls everything together; it is the reason why the Florentine *insieme* is indeed an *insieme*.

At the same time, there is an age-old question about the Duo-

mo's sheer visibility, from anywhere near close up. Hippolyte
Taine, the French historian and philosopher, raised the question
in his book about Italy in 1877. He was filled with admiration for
the pride and patriotism which had given rise to Arnolfo's cathedral, but with a demurral:

Let us, accordingly, look at the celebrated Duomo—but the difficulty is
to see it. It lies upon flat ground, and, in order that the eye embrace its
mass it would be necessary to level three hundred buildings. Herein
appears the defect of the great medieval structure . . . The spectator
catches sight of a fragment, some section of a wall or the facade; but
the whole escapes him.*

Mary McCarthy, in *The Stones of Florence*, has voiced a harsher
verdict. "The Duomo, outside," she says, "still astonishes by its
bulk, which is altogether out of proportion with the narrow streets
that lead up to it." Indeed, she writes, the Duomo is something
you simply stumble upon in your wanderings through the town,
and are always startled by.

It is true that if you approach the Duomo from a few blocks
away—coming up Via dei Calzaiuoli, perhaps, or along Via de'
Cerretani—your view of the cathedral is blocked, and the experience of coming suddenly upon its multiform magnificence is
invariably startling and stirring. But apart from an obvious failure
to understand the architectural *role* of Brunelleschi's dome, about
Ms. McCarthy's final contention one could almost say that the
opposite is true. You get at least a glimpse of the Duomo from
everywhere: you see it as you cross Ponte Vecchio heading up-
town; from the cloister at San Lorenzo you can see the top of the
Duomo plus the lantern, and if you go up one flight you can see
the whole thing—and this is only two blocks away. We could see
the Duomo every morning from our kitchen window overlooking
Piazza Santa Croce. From a greater distance, the Duomo is the
never-failing landmark; from Fiesole and Bellosguardo, you locate
other buildings, their spires or towers, by reference to the cupola;

* Translated by J. Durand, in the fourth edition of *Italy* (New York, 1875).

Brunelleschi's Duomo

and coming into Florence by train—say, the night train from Paris—you begin to peer intently through the window, the moment you have left Prato behind, for your first view of Florence —that is, your first sighting of the Duomo. It commands even as it composes the Florentine panorama. As an example of urban view-making, it may be added, the Duomo is a striking illustration of Brunelleschi's mastery of the art of perspective, an art which he helped introduce into the fifteenth-century Florentine aesthetic and which he taught (for one) to young Masaccio.

Taine, overcoming his disapproval of the church's limited visibility, gave vent to a brilliantly worded description of the whole edifice:

The chancel and transepts bubble out into rotundities and projections, in petty domes behind the church in order to accompany the grand dome which ascends above the choir and which, the work of Brunelleschi, newer and yet more antique than that of St. Peter, lifts in the air to an astonishing height its elongated form, its octagonal sides, and its pointed lantern.

Then, as though carried beyond himself by his sense of the historical wonder represented in the walls and columns and engravings of the church, in its "assemblage of all forms," Taine concluded: "The entire past, shattered, amalgamated and transformed, seems to have been melted over anew in the human furnace in order to flow out in fresh forms in the hands of the new genius of Giotto, Arnolfo, Brunelleschi and Dante."

Brunelleschi's work on the Duomo began during the lifetime of Giovanni di Bicci de' Medici, and was completed during the early years of Cosimo's rule. It was Giovanni as well who was instrumental in the commissioning of Brunelleschi to remodel the church of San Lorenzo, heading a group of well-to-do parishioners who offered to support the Communal financing of the enterprise. There had been a church on this site—just outside the Roman wall, to the northwest (and now a step away to the west from Via Cavour)—since the late fourth century, and named for the youthful victim of a savage religious persecution. It had been enlarged in 1260, and, until the building of Santa Reparata later in the same century, it had served as the Bishop's seat.*

For about a decade, from 1419 or so to 1429, Brunelleschi devoted himself to what became known as the Old Sacristy (the New Sacristy, so-called, being the one designed or anyhow sculpted by Michelangelo in 1520 and later). The modestly sized Sacristy is decidedly one of Brunelleschi's masterpieces, a rhythmical play of geometrical shapes as though conceived by the mathematics of music, and carrying the eye upward into the rounded, multisegmented dome. It was perhaps the first clear expression of a new architectural style—it would be recognized as the "Renaissance style"—and it struck the clustering onlooking Florentines as just that. Antonio Manetti, Brunelleschi's disciple, assistant, and reverential biographer (he executed the Sacristy dome after the master's death), recalled the scene: "The sacristy went forward before anything else and arrived at that state which aroused the marvel, for its new and beautiful style, of everyone in the city and of the strangers who chanced to see it. The many people constantly assembling there caused great annoyance to those working."†

Giovanni, as we know, died in 1429, and his wife Piccarda Bueri in 1433. The two of them are buried in a sarcophagus (by Buggiani, 1434) under the marble table in the middle of the room. Another family resting place nearby in the Sacristy is the porphyry-and-bronze sarcophagus of Piero the Gouty and Giovanni de' Medici, the two sons of Cosimo il Vecchio, beautifully designed in 1472 by Verrochio, who was commissioned by Lorenzo il Magnifico and his brother Giuliano to honor their father and uncle.

For the rest, the decoration of the Old Sacristy was entrusted to Donatello, who, between 1435 and 1443, did some of his finest

---

* In early January 1993, the Florence newspaper *La Nazione* announced the forthcoming celebration of San Lorenzo's 1,600th birthday. There would be suitable services and gatherings; and listing these, *La Nazione* rehearsed the story of the church, from its founding outside the city walls, and mused over the phenomenon of "sixteen centuries of history."

† Translated by Catherine Emgass, in Antonio di Tuccio Manetti, *The Life of Brunelleschi*, ed. Howard Saalman (1970).

work there. In the cupola are four scenes from the life of Saint John the Evangelist in polychromed stucco roundels; in the lunettes are the Four Evangelists. Most engaging of all are the two bronze doors on either side of the altar: above them, painted reliefs of San Lorenzo and San Stefano (on the left), and of San Cosmas and San Damiano (on the right); and covering the doors, a number of panels, two groups of five on each door, displaying pairs of conversationalists and disputers—martyrs on the left door, apostles and church fathers on the one opposite. Eve Barsook describes it vividly: "Here Donatello explores all the dramatic possibilities of discoursing figures: greeting, listening, arguing, agreeing, or running past one another." If the Old Sacristy itself, in its ideal harmony and luminous coherence, represents the new spirit of architecture, the doors of Donatello represent the Florentine cultural ideal of life: the principle and the art of *dialogue*; that same spirit of dialectics that produced the Camaldoli disputations memorialized by Cristoforo Landini (referred to in Chapter 2, earlier), and the published dialogues of Leon Battista Alberti and others.*

Among those Donatello was himself disputing with, in his bronze door panels, was his old friend Brunelleschi, in a matter of considerable historical consequence. A dispute of some sort there almost certainly was. In Antonio Manetti's account, Brunelleschi was critical of the doors, on the grounds that their pictorial figurines and the structures that contained them broke the rhythm of his architectural scheme. Manetti even advances the mind-twisting opinion that Donatello "knew little of pictorial composition."† The fact is, of course, that Donatello's doors *do* break the architectural upward flow. This was exactly Donatello's in-

---

* I drew upon Donatello's doors in a graduation talk I gave at the American School in June 1978, saying, among other things, that "dialogue is of the essence of the Florentine spirit" and "this is a city which discussed and disputed and fought its way into a splendor of being"; that "dialogue is the one indispensable element in the educational experience" and, beyond that, "a pretty good principle for the conduct of one's life."

† As Manetti's anecdote expands, Brunelleschi appears as a wise, even-tempered, quietly amused individual, and Donatello as edgy and resentful—an exact reversal of the two personalities, according to every other source.

tention, his artistically companionable intention, as we might say, and a sign of his (at the time) avant-garde notion of pictorial composition. A similar purpose and effect are visible within the main body of the church of San Lorenzo itself.

The church in its own aesthetic terms is a masterwork nearly beyond praise. It is at once the first and, as many have thought, the ultimate Renaissance church in Florence or even in Italy. Luciano Berti has written (1967) that "the whole conveys an unforgettable impression of the revolutionary novelty of this church, the first of the Renaissance"; and he goes on, in words worth attending to, to say that the final effect "is that of a conception carried forward from the mysticism of the preceding age to a level of high rationality and humanistic intellectualism." In that carrying forward, Berti insists, "the religious theme is still respected," but it is transferred to, or transposed into, the elevated aesthetic rationality.

Visitors to San Lorenzo can experience this effect, and find their own phrasing for it—taking note of the stately flow of graceful Corinthian columns, joined above by rounded arches and flanking the broad central nave, everything in movement toward the transept and the high altar: the two side naves and the chapels along them; arches seeming to echo or mirror arches; the line drawn down the middle of the central nave to declare the exact equality of the two halves of the building.

Within that structure, as separately observable elements, are two pulpits carved, in part, by Donatello. They are situated close to the end of the central nave. In the pulpit panels on your left, as you face the altar, are the *Crucifixion of Christ*, the *Descent from the Cross*, and the *Entombment*; on the right, *Christ in Limbo*, the *Resurrection*, and the *Ascension*. As you walk around these depicted scenes and study them, what begins to strike you is that the figures in them are constantly breaking the rectangular form: in the *Crucifixion*, Roman soldiers are pushing out of the frame to the right; in the *Entombment*, an unidentified character has actually stepped wholly outside the frame and stands there, looking away; in the *Resurrection*, it is Christ himself who has broken not only out of the tomb but out of the panel, his head pressing against the border above. Once again, Donatello is engaging in an artistic argument with the Renaissance canons of ideal form —as represented by Brunelleschi's architectural composition. The statement seems also, on Donatello's part, an expression of an intensely personal set of feelings, of a sort unprecedented in Florentine or perhaps European art.*

The pulpits more or less enclose the marble roundel at the foot of the main altar, which marks the spot where Cosimo il Vecchio was buried in 1464 (he died on August 1 of that year), after a ceremony in the basilica. The transcription tells us that "Cosimus Medicea" rests there, and that by public decree (*Decreto Publico* —the Signoria had issued such pronouncement some years before, ordering that it be inscribed on his tomb) he had been declared *pater patriae*. The inscription informs us that Cosimo lived for seventy-five years, three months, and twenty days. With the entombment of Cosimo il Vecchio, San Lorenzo became more firmly than ever the family church of the Medicis. Three generations of Medicis are buried in the main church and the Old Sacristy; the fourth generation, that of Lorenzo the Magnificent and his ill-fated brother Giuliano, would eventually be interred in the New Sacristy.

Perhaps the most appealing contribution of Brunelleschi to the look and shape of urban Florence was the singularly beautiful Ospedale degli Innocenti, which he designed and constructed (with the help of his assistant Francesco della Luna) between 1419 and 1425. The Ospedale, superb in itself, also in effect created what many have thought to be the handsomest square in Florence, that of Santissima Annunziata; and it added a significant

---

* John Pope-Hennessy, in a book on Italian Renaissance sculpture (1958), argues that not even with the later etchings of Rembrandt "do we feel ourselves trespassers among private beliefs and personal emotions, as we do in San Lorenzo." The most striking such moment, we may say, is the image of Christ rising from the grave: "with something still of torpor and the great sleep in his movement," as Luciano Berti has said. The two pulpits were the last works by Donatello, and the great sleep was almost upon him. They are dated June 15, 1466; the eighty-year-old Donatello died six months later.

Brunelleschi presents his design for San Lorenzo

San Lorenzo, exterior

San Lorenzo: the Old Sacristy   Donatello's Doors, the Old Sacristy

San Lorenzo, interior

new dimension—something humane and social—to the cultural makeup of the city.

The Ospedale was not a hospital, properly speaking, but rather a shelter or home, a place of refuge for abandoned infants. It was established in 1419 by the Arte della Sete, the silk guild; and in 1421, the Arte petitioned the Commune for official recognition as the sole patron of the place. It spoke of the new building and of its purpose. The guild, it said,

has begun to construct a most beautiful edifice in the city of Florence and in the parish of S. Michele Visdomini . . . [It] is a hospital called S. Maria degli Innocenti in which shall be received those who, against natural law, have been deserted by their fathers or their mothers, that is, infants who in the vernacular are called *gitatelli* [literally, castaways; foundlings].

Giovanni de' Medici did his part to help the guild fund the building of the Ospedale.

The care of these "Innocenti"—the name was intended to recall, pointedly, the Massacre of the Innocents by Herod, the biblical story that Ghirlandaio illustrated in a painting contained in the Ospedale's Pinoteca (Giotto inaugurated what would be the recurring motif of the massacre in his awesome dramatic panel in the Scrovegni chapel in Padua)—was a sometimes heartbreaking affair. The hospital record books, as Iris Origo has written, were kept "with meticulous care by the treasurers, with a very Tuscan mixture of shrewd realism, careful cheeseparing and rough kindliness." One entry, of December 5, 1451, reports that two female twins had been brought in during the night.

We caused them to be baptized and gave them the names of Sandra Innocenti and Nicolosa Innocenti. They came from the house of Agostino Capponi, born of Polonia his slave; they were brought by Monna Dorotea, the midwife . . . wrapped in two linen rags, without being swaddled. They were half dead; if they had been two dogs they would have been better cared for.

Some days after that, it was recorded that "Sandra died on January 30th in the hospital. God gave her his blessing."*

It was for this uniquely charitable enterprise that Brunelleschi built the Ospedale, along with the church (of Santa Maria degli Innocenti) and the cloisters for men and for women on the inside. On the outside, facing the piazza, is the loggia, with its nine supremely lovely arcades (two were added in later centuries), the shapely columns holding their place with geometric precision atop a long flight of steps. Above, in rounded "windows" —Brunelleschi planned them to remain empty—are the exquisite medallions of swaddled babies, the *gitatelli*, against the blue background, done by Andrea della Robbia in 1487 and possibly his finest single work of art.

Brunelleschi's portico for the Innocenti, in the mysteriously energizing and proleptic way of art, created a piazza that was not literally and technically completed for two hundred years. There is really no doubting the historical achievement. The Piazza Santissima Annunziata, says one expert commentator flatly, was "designed by Brunelleschi and [is] surrounded on three sides by porticos. It is the most beautiful square in Florence." The observation, which accurately elides a long process, takes in the Innocenti portico; the colonnade directly across from it, the one

---

* These two infants, as was indicated, were the children of a slave girl. Iris Origo, in "The Domestic Enemy" (*Speculum* XXX, 1955), says that of 7,500 children registered over a ninety-year period at the Innocenti and the adjoining hospital of San Gallo, nearly 1,100, or 14 percent, were the children of slaves, and that the figures may well have been larger.

As to the phenomenon of slavery itself, Marchesa Origo discovered that of 357 persons sold as slaves in Florence between 1366 and 1397, 274 were Tartars, 30 Greeks, 13 Russians, 8 Turks, 4 Circassians, 5 Bosnians, 1 Cretan, and the rest "Arabs" or "Saracens." Perhaps more tellingly, of that same number no less than 329 were female, and of these, 34 under the age of twelve and 85 between twelve and eighteen.

The fathers of the abandoned slave children might be the heads of the household, as was the case with little Sandra and Nicolosa. In another Ospedale entry, it was mentioned casually that the father was a priest named Ser Andrea: "He has taken the child from her mother and sent her to the hospital, and has made the slave [i.e., the mother] give suck to the child of a fellow-townsman." Marchesa Origo also suggests that, though the treatment of slave women could in certain situations be appalling, their legal and domestic status was not entirely wretched. They were regarded as members of the household and, indeed, of the family, in the same way as the servants were treated.

Piazza Santissima Annunziata

built around 1520 by Antonio da Sangallo and Baccio D'Agnolo for the Confraternity of the Servants of Mary; and a third portico, created in the early 1600s at the head of the piazza in front of the church (which we will return to) of Santissima Annunziata.

The later Florentine artists, in the sixteenth and seventeenth centuries, were—quite consciously, there seems no doubt—working out the implications of Brunelleschi's loggia and its placement, adding elements by artful relation to the first portico. In the course of time, there appeared the big rearing equestrian statue of Ferdinand II by Giambologna, the sculptor's final work, finished in 1608 by his disciple Pietro Tacca; and the two charming and entertaining fountains by Tacca in 1620. Such artistic entities—with the imposing Palazzo Grifone, built by Ammannati in about 1560 for a secretary of Duke Cosimo I, and filling out the urban space on the *south* side—were designed to take their place within what was recognized as a preexisting scheme of Brunelleschi. So was slowly born the Piazza Santissima Annunziata.

There is a different kind of point to be made. As Fanelli puts it, the theme of the Ospedale was that of a *"luogo di vita,"* a place of life for the innocent castaways; and that theme "rises here, as a consequence of Brunelleschi's architecture, to a dignity through which it becomes itself an essential element in the urban image, on a par with the civil and religious architecture." The point once more can be made visually and geographically: a home for the foundlings, with the piazza it served to create, took its position on one of the main axes of the city—in a direct line from the Duomo and connected to the great religious edifice by the straight-running Via dei Servi; and at only a certain remove, along the same axis, in a line from Palazzo Vecchio, the civic center.

The Dominion of Cosimo

Some years after his return from exile and his entrance into financial power and political authority in Florence, Cosimo il Vecchio began to think about a new Florentine home for his family. In 1416, Cosimo, then twenty-seven, had married Contessina de' Bardi, of a noble Florentine family dating back a century or so (it is the Bardi chapel in Santa Croce that contains Giotto's paintings of the life and death of Saint Francis of Assisi). The Bardis too were bankers, and had joined the Peruzzis in the ill-fated loan to King Edward of England. The Bardi family home was a palazzo in Oltrarno, near the river and on the street that now bears their name. Contessina is reputed to have been a good-natured woman, fat and cheerful, skilled, like Piccarda Bueri, in running the household, cautious with money, and full of sound advice for her husband as he set off on his travels. She bore Cosimo a son, Piero, during the first year of their marriage; a second son, Giovanni, followed in 1421. There was also a bastard son named Carlo, born to Cosimo during a long stay in Rome by a slave girl, Maddalena, with whom he consorted; Contessina took this child's presence in good part, like most Florentine wives in the same situation, and Carlo was brought up and educated with the two legitimate sons (he later became the rector of a church in Prato). This was the family for whom Cosimo sought a new domicile.

For about a dozen years, Cosimo and family had lived in Palazzo Bardi; then, after the death of his father, Giovanni, Cosimo moved into the paternal home near the Piazza del Duomo. He wanted not only a home of his own making but one sizable enough for the conduct of his business and state affairs, which he intended to move from Palazzo Vecchio. Cosimo wanted the palazzo to be within sight of San Lorenzo, and he invited Brunelleschi—just then overseeing the completion of San Lorenzo—to be its designer and builder. According to Vasari, Brunelleschi was never happier than when he was at work on the design for the Medici home; but when Cosimo saw the plans and the wooden model Brunelleschi had constructed, he rejected them, pronouncing them too sumptuous and likely to arouse criticism among his rivals. It was the envy Cosimo feared, Vasari believed, rather than the expense. Brunelleschi, on hearing this news, flew into one of his violent rages and destroyed the model. It seems apparent, though, that the design itself was spared, and was followed in some part by the architect to whom Cosimo then turned, Michelozzo.

Michelozzo di Bartolommeo Michelozzi (he is usually referred to by his first name) was born in 1396. As a youth, he studied sculpture and worked with Ghiberti (on Orsanmichele) and Donatello (inside the Baptistery). In the 1420s, he designed the Palazzo Communale for the town of Montepulciano in southern Tuscany; like many another in the region, it displayed the healthy influence of Palazzo Vecchio in Florence. Michelozzo became an intimate friend of the Medici family and accompanied Cosimo into exile in Venice in 1434. In retrospect, he was inevitably compared with Brunelleschi. The spirited chronicler Benedetto Bardi called Brunelleschi "the king of the world," and spoke of Michelozzo, by contrast, as "the architect and sculptor for everyone"; Brunelleschi's intellectual intransigence was deftly set against Michelozzo's "mercantile flexibility." Antonio Manetti, jealous at every turn for his master's status, was careful not to mention Michelozzo; but Vasari spoke of him as the most orderly and accommodating architect of his time. A modern biography of Michelozzo (by Miranda Ferrara and Francesco Quinto, 1984) suggestively sums up the relation between the artist and Cosimo: "a reciprocal influence," it is said, "a technical assimilation on the part of

Cosimo, an assimilation of Cosimo's prudence on the part of Michelozzo." The working relation began with Palazzo Medici.

It was built at the start of Via Larga (now Via Cavour), which really was a "broad street," wide enough for joustings and chariot races and ending with open fields between the palazzo site and the city wall. It was a massive affair, the new palazzo, but not excessively so: a mix of the bulky and the delicate, as it was of medieval heft and sobriety with classical shapeliness and charm. The rough stonework of the ground floor gave way (in the process called "rustication") to the increasingly smoother surfaces of the upper two stories; and the whole was crowned by a splendid cornice. It was, altogether, striking and dignified, with no evident desire to overwhelm; though it did not escape angry claims—far from baseless—that its aim was the enhancement of the Medicis rather than that of the city. But it was in its age a genuine family affair, with stalls, workrooms, shops, and servants' quarters clustered on the north side; a good deal less grandiose than it would become after the Riccardis took over in the 1700s, did away with all appendages, and—with a view to outdoing the other palazzi which had come into view along Via Larga over the centuries— added seven windows to the original ten.

Upstairs, Michelozzo built the family chapel, which was consecrated in 1444 and which shelters on its walls Benozzo Gozzoli's enchanting *Journey of the Magi*. In another room is Fra Filippo Lippi's *Madonna and Child* (from about 1442), no doubt painted in the studio arranged by Cosimo in the palazzo for that most renegade of artists and perhaps the most poignant rendition of its theme ever made. Cosimo did not move into Palazzo Medici to settle until 1459. With him came his wife, Contessina; their older son, Piero, with his wife, Lucrezia Tornabuoni, and their five children—Lorenzo (later, the Magnificent), Giuliano, Maria, Lucrezia, and Bianca, known as Nannina; the second son, Giovanni, his wife, Ginevra degli Albizzi, and their son, Cosimino. To his grandfather's great sorrow, the boy Cosimino died before his sixth birthday, and two years later Giovanni died of a heart attack. It was at this time, after the losses, that the aging Cosimo was heard to mutter that the palazzo was too big for so small a family. In

Palazzo Medici, and jousting on Via Larga

San Marco: the Cloister

fact, Cosimo always enjoyed life out at the villas more than he ever did in the city. He particularly cherished the villa at Careggi, a few kilometers to the northwest of Florence (beyond Rifredi), where he held his richly stored and ever-growing library. He bought a villa nearby Careggi for his young friend, the writer and humanist Marsilio Ficino. We find Cosimo, in 1562, writing to Ficino: "Yesterday I arrived at Careggi . . . Let me see you, Marsilio, as soon as possible, and do not forget to bring with you the books of our favorite Plato—which, I presume, according to your promise, you have now translated into Latin."

Palazzo Medici is a historic marker: the first town house in the postmedieval period, and the first that was not essentially a fortress. It was also a determining feature in a newly emerging urban entity—the Medici family segment of the city of Florence. To the church of San Lorenzo and the Medici palace, which formed the southern portion of the dominion, there were added before long the church and convent of San Marco, lying farther up Via Larga, and, over to the east a bit, the church of Santissima Annunziata. All these were the creations of Michelozzo Michelozzi.

San Marco was begun in 1436. There had been two previous convents of San Marco, going back to early medieval days; by the 1430s, the second of them was falling into ruin. The Dominicans were now given permission by Pope Eugene IV to take over the site, and the following year Cosimo il Vecchio assumed the immense financial burden of building an entirely new complex. The costs were enormous, but Cosimo kept pouring money in, maintaining that the expense was an atonement for his sins (chiefly, the sin of usury). At one moment, the *frati* actually protested against Cosimo donating such huge amounts, but he kept it up.

The result is generally regarded as Michelozzo's masterwork and Cosimo de' Medici's finest contribution to Florence. The church's facade, from about 1480, forms a neoclassically cold exterior for an airy and pleasing interior, with its single broad nave and chapels. Michelozzo is also responsible for the nicely composed sacristy and apse; and on the left-hand tomb slabs, one above the other, are the names of Lorenzo de' Medici's humanist associates, Angelo Poliziano and Pico della Mirandola. The *convent* is an atmospherically rich harmony of diverse parts: the cloister of San Antonio, the larger cloister of San Domenico, the small and the large refectory, the chapter house, all on the ground floor; and, on the floor above, the dormitory, with its forty-odd cells, and the astonishing, gracious library (which Cosimo turned into the first *public* library in Europe).

The convent is a collaboration, hard to match elsewhere in Florentine annals, between architect and painter, Michelozzo and Fra Angelico, the latter supplying assorted frescoes of the life of Christ for cloister and chapter house and, with the help of assistants, for the cells upstairs. Baptized Guido da Fiesole when he was born in 1387, the artist took the name Giovanni when he became a monk in Fiesole, and was given his better-known name in part because of (in the words of Christopher Hibbert) his modesty, simplicity, and holiness. Fra Angelico did not come down to Florence until 1436, when he was nearly fifty. Cosimo persuaded him to take up painting again, with special attention to the convent of San Marco (where Cosimo retained a double cell for periods of retreat and meditation). One unforgettable consequence is the *Annunciation*, which greets you coming around the bend onto the last short flight of stairs to the dormitory, and is one of the gentle glories of the world.*

The space outside the church and convent was slow to become a proper piazza, and can hardly be labeled a Renaissance creation. A certain liveliness ensued when the Medici Duke of Urbino (in 1515) built some stables on the east side, to which Cosimo I added a riding academy. The University of Florence found an early home on the same site. Grand Duke Pietro Leopoldo, of Lorraine, had a small and unexpectedly charming palazzo built in 1780 for his mistress, the Roman ballerina Livia Raimondi (Casa Livia, on the west side of the square), perhaps recalling that Bianca Cappello,

---

* The Museo dell'Angelico was opened in the convent in 1869. It houses on its four walls a number of Fra Angelico's most beautiful and heartfelt paintings, brought in from around the city: among them, the tabernacle painted for the linen drapers' guild (the *linaiuoli*), with a frame by Ghiberti; and the Deposition from Santa Trinità.

Duke Ferdinand's mistress and wife-to-be, lived on the southern side of the piazza when she was still married. Today, the piazza is a pleasant meeting ground for students, including foreign students, and writers and professors of various denominations.

Santissima Annunziata, a short way along Via Battisti eastward from San Marco, is the mother church of the Servite Order—known as *Servi di Maria*, Servants of Mary (hence the name of the street heading like an arrow from the Duomo to the piazza, Via dei Servi)—founded in 1234 by a group of wealthy and pious young Florentines. Michelozzo designed and built the church itself, on the site of a mid-thirteenth-century oratory; the tabernacle; a most impressive tribune, or choir gallery (later modified by Alberti); and the Chiostro dei Voti, the Cloister of the Votive Offerings, which is what you come into when you pass through the portico from the piazza outside. The cloister offers for view frescoes by Pontormo, Andrea del Sarto, and, among others, a lovely rural rendering of 1460 by Alesso Baldovinetti.

The church of Santissima Annunziata was the final ingredient in Cosimo's domain-within-a-city; but the Medici connection is, in fact, somewhat stronger with Piero the Gouty than with his father. It was the thirty-two-year-old Piero who took Santissima Annunziata as his own special churchly interest, and who commissioned Michelozzo to build the tabernacle just mentioned. It appears in the interior, immediately on the left, and holds the painting of the Annunciation whose history goes back to 1250 or so, when it was allegedly completed by an attending angel. The surviving fresco was painted in 1350, and its place is one of the most celebrated devotional shrines in Italy.

Whatever the intention, Piero's tabernacle expresses an "outward" and worldly sense of things; it is a not unattractive or ill-conceived statement about his Medici self (Francesca Petrucci makes the point in a 1992 booklet)—and compares with the cell at San Marco, where Fra Angelico's fresco of the Epiphany (painted with the help of Benozzo Gozzoli) and his *Pieta* encouraged the prayers and thoughts of father Cosimo. Piero the Gouty, in this regard, bespoke the Florentine future.

The Day of the Palazzi

Benedetto Dei, the much-traveled agent of the Medicis, and especially of his friend Lorenzo il Magnifico, observed in his *Cronaca* of Florentine life and history (completed some time before his death in 1492) that thirty palazzi—palaces, private homes of magnitude and splendor—had been built in the city between 1450 and 1470. The motif of the rambling chronicle was *Firenze bella* (or Fiorentia, or Florentia, or however he chose to spell it), and a major dimension of that *bellezza*—along with the fabulous amounts of money, the famous families, the guilds, the warriors—was the great number and variety of its buildings, among them, especially, the recently arising palaces.

The year concentrated on was 1472, at which moment, by Dei's count, there were in the city:

106 churches, open day and night, "with marvelous choirs and chapter houses and refectories and infirmaries and sacristies and libraries and bells and towers" and so on;

50 *piazze* "within the city," each with a church, a palace, shops. Dei named most of them, including the Signoria, San Giovanni (the Baptistery), Santo Spirito, Santa Croce, Santa Maria Novella, San Marco, the Innocenti, the Mercato Vecchio;

a great many shops: 270 belonging to the wool guild, 83 to the silk guild, 98 for artistic woodworking, 54 for stone and marble work, numerous shops for silver and gold items and jewelry; not to mention butcher shops and the like;

33 major banks.

But it was in its buildings, Dei implies, that Florence should take most pride. During the time of Cosimo de' Medici, he wrote, there came into being some thirty-three "very great buildings of great fame and very great costliness." He mentioned, among others, the cupola of the cathedral; the churches of Santo Spirito, San Lorenzo, and San Marco; and then the palaces—of the Medici, the Pitti, the Rucellai, the Tornabuoni, the Pazzi, and many others. *Fiorentia bella*, he here suggests, reached its truest expression in these lordly edifices.

He was partly right. The fifteenth century was the pivotal age of palace building in Florence, the long period in which what we now look upon as the palatial landmarks were undertaken and in some cases brought to completion. Palazzo Medici, one way or another, was the crucial factor, the certifying or challenging instance; and after it, one can name, in particular, Palazzo Pitti, Palazzo Rucellai, and Palazzo Strozzi (not listed by Dei, since it got under way too late—1489—for him to recognize it). These, with some others, may be said to have set the final stamp on the city of Cosimo; but they also began the process of fundamentally transforming it.

Palazzo Pitti is probably the best example of the process at work. It was commissioned by Luca Pitti, an ambitious and (if we credit Machiavelli) vainglorious, even a rather stupid, man, who was also among the city's richest citizens. (Dei, cataloguing the *"maggiori ricchi di Firenze"* in 1472, lists Lorenzo de' Medici and kin, Giovanni Rucellai and a brother, and then Luca Pitti and relatives; Pazzis, Capponis, Tornabuonis, Soderinis, and the like follow after.) Luca, who was in fact a fairly good friend of Cosimo, was exceedingly jealous of Piero de' Medici, and yearned for something larger and showier and costlier than the recently completed Palazzo Medici. The structure that was finally built was attributed by Vasari to Brunelleschi, and it seems likely that it was based closely on a grand design by Brunelleschi—quite possibly the one he originally drew up for Cosimo's palace. The actual building, however, was not even begun until after Brunelleschi's death, and then by Luca Fancelli (1430–1495).

Palazzo Pitti was a decidedly striking construct when it first came into sight; but it was far from the colossus it would become. It was a solid three-story building, with seven evenly spaced windows on each of the upper two stories. Exact Brunelleschian equality—of the size and shape of stories and of windows—is the controlling principle; and this, with the reddish-gold-colored stone and the long-running balustrades, helps account for the slight dazedness that can affect the observer today after staring

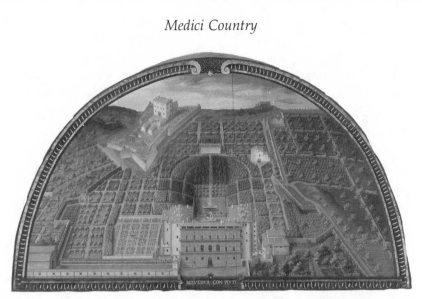

Palazzo Pitti, with the Boboli Gardens

at it for some minutes. Sheer size, of course, contributes to that effect; but Palazzo Pitti did not assume its enormous dimensions until the seventeenth and eighteenth centuries, during which time it virtually tripled in the length of the facade (on the ground floor and the one above it) and in the number of windows (these seem literally countless; there are, in fact, twenty-three); and two huge wings were added to the north and south. Palazzo Pitti as it became is simply too big for comprehension or enjoyment; and to see it—either as a work inspired by Brunelleschi or as a sign of the cultural temper in c. 1480—one must think it back to its original proportions. Today, of course, after having served as the Tuscan ducal abode for three centuries and briefly (in the 1860s) as the Italian royal palace, it houses one of the great art galleries of Italy and of the world.*

---

* The Pitti in our times has been not undeservedly the source of ironic wit and satire. In Cole Porter's *Kiss Me, Kate*, the male lead sings longingly of the women he must give up on the eve of his marriage and, among them, wonders about the one called Alice—

> Where are you, Alice?
> Still there in your pretty itty bitty Pitti Palace?

(The line should be said or sung slowly, with a stress on each of the echoing adjectives.) And in *The Custom of the Country*, Edith Wharton's most unrestrainedly satirical novel, the young billionaire Elmer Moffatt, remarried to Undine Spragg, presents his

Even with its original and relatively compact size and its seven bays, Palazzo Pitti made an extraordinary impression upon fifteenth-century Florentines; even Machiavelli admired it. This was due not only to the strength and beauty of the edifice but also to the grandiose piazza which was laid out before it, and to make room for which Luca Pitti had destroyed a great many houses adorning the start of Via Romana. No other private home in Florence, hitherto, had had its own exclusionary piazza in front of it.

While his building was going up, Luca Pitti is said to have boasted that it would have a courtyard large enough to enclose the entire Palazzo Strozzi (he also averred that the windows were to be the size of the big portals at Palazzo Medici). The story is probably apocryphal—the dates don't seem to work out—but the legend testifies to the reputation of the Strozzi palace even before it was begun. The making of Palazzo Strozzi was without question the architectural event of the epoch for downtown Florence, and it is worth a moment's rehearsing.

Filippo Strozzi, the family representative, sought by means of a magnificent new structure to restore the family's standing, after half a century of singularly and uncharacteristically savage treatment by Cosimo the Elder and his successors. Filippo's banking father, Palla Strozzi, had at one time been the richest man in Florence (some said, in the world); but he was of a modest and retiring disposition, interested in the encouragement of literary learning and the founding of libraries. Cosimo, on his return from exile in October 1434, took strongly against Palla (imaginably, as a rival version of what he, Cosimo, aspired to be), and sent him into exile with all the other male members of the clan. Cosimo kept him there until Palla's death in 1462. The family fortune, however, increased during the long term of exile, through adroit maneuvers; and Filippo, from outside, began buying up property in central Florence, toward the creation of a family home there.

---

bride with a town house on Fifth Avenue in New York, "which is an exact copy of the Pitti Palace in Florence."

The "Catena": panorama of Florence, c. 1470

Work began on the palazzo after Filippo's return in something like triumph; and popular excitement was so aroused that a large crowd gathered to watch the laying of the foundation stone. The date was August 1489, and the Medici friend Tribaldo de' Rossi, as was remarked earlier, took pains to impress the historic moment on his young son's memory. The building process dislocated the city's center; there was dust everywhere, workmen crawling and climbing about, pedestrian and carriage traffic slowed almost to a halt. But Palazzo Strozzi, when at last Filippo's offspring moved into it in 1503 (Filippo himself had died in 1491), fulfilled all expectations.

In the genealogy of great Florentine palaces, Palazzo Strozzi descends from Palazzo Medici rather than, for example, from Palazzo Rucellai. That finely wrought latter-named work on Via della Vigna Nuova was designed by Leon Battista Alberti and completed in the 1450s for Giovanni Rucellai.* Alberti stipulated in his 1450 treatise on architecture that palaces should not be fortresslike; they should instead be "easy of access, beautifully adorned, and rather delicate and polite than proud and stately." Delicate, beautifully adorned, and even polite are fitting words

---

* Giovanni Rucellai, ever on the lookout for the good connection, himself married Palla Strozzi's daughter, and later managed to arrange the marriage of his son Bernardo to Cosimo de' Medici's granddaughter Nannina. He was also financially responsible for Alberti's facade for Santa Maria Novella.

for Palazzo Rucellai, the contemplation of which (as you step back into the little open space across from it) is a continuing pleasure for the Florentine resident; but they hardly apply to the Strozzi creation. Here a medieval heritage is evident in the heavy masonry; but there is a fresh and striking clarity of surface design. The powerful stone blocks, as Eve Barsook says, each have "a clear biting profile, and not a stone projects further than its neighbor." The windows, nine to a side, have a certain distinction; and within is a cortile of agreeable mass and grandeur.

Palazzo Strozzi is not infrequently named the most beautiful of the Renaissance palaces in Florence. Some people, using varying criteria, will prefer Palazzo Medici or the Rucellai or even the Pitti; but whatever the differences, what these architectural statements have in common—along with the palazzi of the Gondi, Pazzi, Tornabuoni, and others—is a pride of family self-aggrandizement. Each one affirms the role and power of the family to which it belongs; not one of them affirms much of anything about the city and community in which it has its location.

A disregard for the urban context is sometimes aggressively apparent. Fanelli underscores the fact that Palazzo Pitti and its piazza broke up the age-old corridor, a feature of Oltrarno, that led from the river to Via Romana to Porta Romana (Benedetto Dei, singing the praises of the *quartiere* of Santo Spirito as richly illustrative of Florence's *bellezza*, leads off his list of twenty-seven marvelous streets with the one that runs "from Ponte Vecchio all the way to Porta Romana"). The new palaces really took no part in the urban design of the city, as the great buildings traditionally had done. Palazzo Medici, still of an older period, could perhaps be plotted in relation to San Lorenzo and San Marco. But Palazzo Pitti, Palazzo Strozzi, Palazzo Rucellai: these, whatever their diverse and outreaching attractions, occupied each a space wholly to itself. The day of the palazzi ushered out the age of communal architectural expression; or, in the formula of J. S. Ackerman (*The Architecture of Michelangelo*, 1961): "Contrary to what is commonly believed, the architecture of the early Renaissance signaled the end rather than the beginning of an urbanistic system."

[5]

The Making and Unmaking
of Modern Florence

The Interval: 1500–1850

Cosimo de' Medici died in 1464; his son Piero the Gouty (his promising career as city leader cut short by several ailments), five years later; and Lorenzo il Magnifico, at age forty-three, in 1492. There followed four and a half decades of intermittent and sometimes drastic changes in Florentine political power. A republic of sorts appeared in 1494, after Lorenzo's son Piero had been thrown out because of his pusillanimous behavior with the invading French king. Then came the short and morally agitated tenure of the Dominican friar Girolamo Savonarola, who was finally hanged and burned in Piazza Signoria by order of the Borgia Pope Alexander VI. The republic, restrengthened, continued until 1512, at which time the Medicis returned to authority, in part through the maneuvering of Lorenzo's second son, Giovanni, who had been made Cardinal at the age of sixteen and would soon become Pope as the energetic Leo X. The republic was reborn briefly and one last time in 1527, only to collapse during the long siege of Florence by the imperial troops in 1529–30. In 1530, the nineteen-year-old Alessandro de' Medici was installed as Duke of Florence; he was quite possibly the illegitimate son of Pope Clement VII, the former

Giulio de' Medici, who saw to the installation.* Alessandro gave a vacillating performance as Duke of the city-state until, in 1537, he was assassinated—stabbed to death while waiting, naked in a darkened room, for a spurious appointment with a virtuous married woman—by his kinsman and companion Lorenzaccio, who, in an age-old and continuing impulse, was seeking celebrity status by murdering an authority figure.

Alessandro had no heirs. The European powers concerned, among them most notably Emperor Charles V, then selected as Duke of Florence a Medici from another line, a descendant of Lorenzo, the younger brother of Cosimo il Vecchio, and gave him the title Cosimo I. He was later (in 1569) made Grand Duke of Tuscany; and the Medicis thereafter held absolute rule over the Tuscan realm for nearly two hundred years.

In the story of Florence's shaping and its significant adornment, the era of Cosimo is the last chapter of consequence until the 1860s, and it repays some attention. Cosimo, personally, was a silent, watchful man, adept at hunting, though not otherwise much given to the pleasures of life; handsome and graceful, in a cavalierish manner; attached and apparently faithful to his highly competent wife, Eleonora of Toledo; undemonstrative toward his eight children, though he mourned at length and in solitude the death by malaria, at seventeen, of his daughter Maria. He was resolute in external affairs, prosecuting the war against Siena with exceptional ruthlessness over many years, until Siena succumbed to annexation in 1557 (leaving a residue of intense anti-Florentine spirit which has far from vanished in the present day and even infects foreign-born residents in the two provinces). Meanwhile, Cosimo as Duke earned the strong support of the poorer and the impoverished classes in the city, evincing a genuine and practical, if not unprecedented, concern for their well-being, and taking an active part in the fraternity of San Marino, which organized and distributed anonymous assistance to the unfortunate. To be sure, it was also Cosimo who ordered the construction of a ghetto near

---

* Alessandro has also been said to be the bastard offspring of the Lorenzo (died 1519) who became Duke of Urbino.

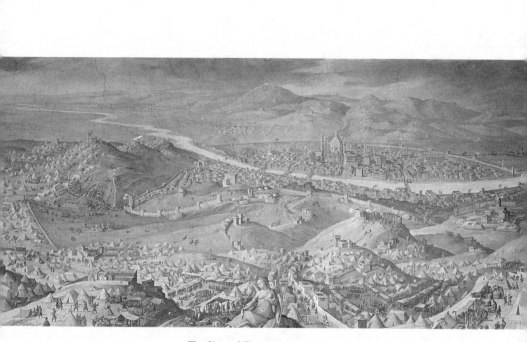

The Siege of Florence, 1529–30

Duke Cosimo I

Eleonora of Toledo

Mercato Vecchio, where all Florentine Jews were henceforth required to live; it was designed by Buontalenti, and was officially opened in July 1571. In part, Cosimo was following recent anti-Jewish papal policy (the horrific edict of persecution, the papal bull *Cum Nimis Absurdum*, had been issued in May 1555); but he was also seeking to protect the Jewish population from attacks by citizens inflamed by that policy, or so it has been argued; and later generations even felt that the ghetto life had been "a powerful preservative of communal solidarity and of traditional culture."*

As to the look of the city, it was under Cosimo I, according to the historian Eric Cochrane, that Florence "was becoming a work of art."† Florence, in fact, as we have suggested, began to become a work of art around 1300, and it was a full-fledged work of art by 1450, with the contributions (Duomo, Loggia degli Innocenti, San Lorenzo, Santo Spirito) of Filippo Brunelleschi. But it is not to be doubted that Duke Cosimo inherited the sense of his city as an *opera d'arte*, and saw to a series of major additions to it.

Among these was the superbly graceful Ponte Santa Trinità, designed by Ammannati around 1570. The Uffizi, neighboring the Palazzo Vecchio and built to contain the city's public offices (hence the name), was begun under Vasari's supervision and on his design in 1559. The Mercato Nuovo, the new market, was started in 1547 on a site dating back to the 1200s; it became a powerful, noble-spirited display, intended at the time for the merchandizing of gold and silk; the merchandizing of straw came in much later (it is now frequently called the Straw Market), and the porcelain boar (Italians tend to call the place Porcellino, or piglet) was a 1640 copy by Tacca of a Hellenistic statue in the Uffizi (and modeled also on a live wild boar that Tacca kept in a cage).

During the same years, Vasari constructed his corridor from Palazzo Pitti, the new ducal home, across and above Ponte Vecchio and into the Uffizi, via which the Duke could proceed unscathed to his administrative offices in Palazzo Vecchio. Likewise for the new Medici palazzo, purchased from the last and sorriest

* Cecil Roth, *The History of the Jews of Italy* (1946), 389.
† *Florence in the Forgotten Centuries: 1527–1800*. This outstanding work of historical narrative was published in 1973.

of the Pitti, Ammannati in the 1550s built the cortile, towers of dun-colored curving blocks gazing east toward the hillside, generally looked upon as one of the masterpieces of the century's architecture; while a variety of artists collaborated to decorate the new gardens, called Boboli in a mispronunciation of the name (Bogoli or Bogolini) of the family whose lands Cosimo bought up for garden purposes. Piazza della Signoria and Ponte alla Carraia were skillfully repaved; and Cosimo, like his remote kin Lorenzo il Magnifico, did much to further the building or enlargement of city palaces.

Cosimo must be given a good deal of the credit for the cultural atmosphere in Florence in the decades around the mid-century, the extraordinary hospitality to new artistic energies. He liked to consort with artists, and to talk with them about their creative methods; and when, for example, Benvenuto Cellini came to town on a family visit in the early 1550s, Cosimo quickly commissioned him to do a statue of Perseus. It was placed in the Loggia of Piazza Signoria, and soon became one of three statues—with the adjacent *Judith and Holofernes* by Donatello and the *David* of Michelangelo (the latter placed there, we recall, in 1504)—that for many a year symbolized the Florentine love of freedom; Cellini, well reimbursed, stayed on in the city, to fraternize, quarrel, and create. Agnolo Bronzino, kindest and most mannerly of individuals, could be called the court painter, if anyone was; he did the most widely admired portrait of Duke Cosimo (and then did an identical copy); and for the chapel walls of Eleanora of Toledo's apartment in Palazzo Vecchio, he composed a series of striking scenes, mostly from the Old Testament (the Crossing of the Red Sea and others). For a chapel in Santa Croce, Bronzino did a Pietà, for San Lorenzo, a painting of the church's patron saint, and to the cupola in the little church of San Felicità, at the head of Via Maggio, Bronzino added his portrait of Saint Mark to the portraits of the other three Evangelists by his master Pontormo. (The cupola is visible if you can find the custodian and arrange for enough light.) Pontormo, that great innovative and almost pathologically reclusive painter (Bronzino used to force him to eat a decent meal of chicken and veal every Sunday), was doing his unexampled, posthumous portrait of Cosimo il Vecchio (now in the Uffizi), his frescoes for Santissima Annunziata and elsewhere, and his disorientingly dramatic scenes from the Passion for the Certosa.

Throughout the epoch, Giorgio Vasari (1511–74), not a Florentine by birth but originally from Arezzo, was busy everywhere. He was responsible for the series of attractive Austrian settings in the cortile of Palazzo Vecchio, designed for the forthcoming arrival of Joan (Giovanna) of Austria before her marriage to Cosimo's son Francesco. With a team of assistants, he undertook to cover the vast ceiling of the upstairs Salone dei Cinquecento (it had been built for Savonarola's city government, and its ceiling was now raised about twenty feet) with "real" and allegorical scenes depicting past triumphs and recent glories of Florence; the picture of Arnolfo di Cambio presenting his plans for the wall-circuit to the city's Priors, as one instance, is at the end of the central axis. Vasari was a great historian in paint; but even before these enterprises, he managed to complete what Eric Cochrane with reason calls "the first great masterpiece in art history—and . . . one of the great masterpieces of history in general." This was his *Lives of the Most Eminent Painters, Sculptors and Architects*, published in 1550. With this work, in the words of Michelangelo, who is the book's hero, Vasari became known as "the man who revives the dead and prolongs the living."

Vasari laid out the pavement for the New Sacristy in the church of San Lorenzo. But the stupendous achievement of the Sacristy itself—the meditative seated figures representing the Medici Dukes Giuliano of Nemours and Lorenzo of Urbino, with the four allegorical nude beings reclining beneath them—is, of course, the work of Michelangelo, who left it partly unfinished when he quit Florence for good in 1534, three years before the accession of Cosimo I. The Sacristy was commissioned by Giulio de' Medici, before he moved up from Cardinal to Pope (as Clement VII); and it was Cardinal Giulio as well who persuaded Michelangelo to take on the design for the vestibule, and what became its great staircase, in the Laurentian Library attached to the church: one of the most stirring experiences for the viewer today (who should look at it from many different angles) that Florence has to offer.

The Uffizi, piazza and porticos

The Mercato Vecchio

These undertakings, whatever their dates of origin, were completed under Cosimo I, and made part of the tremendous new urban exhibition.

"Cast your eye about you," said Scipione Ammirato, the learned Medici court historiographer, as the century waned. "You will see nothing but marvels and wonders—loggias, granaries, two public palaces, four bridges, and so many towers . . . that no one can count them."* The Florentine capacity for knowing self-appreciation had happily not dwindled, though, as against the emphasis on shapeliness in the fifteenth-century eulogies (like that of Goro Dati, quoted from earlier), Ammirato seems rather to take pride in size and numbers. (Americans will recognize the tendency, as when this or that locale declares itself to be the fastest-growing city in the region.) And even as Ammirato spoke, plans were under way for a gigantic mausoleum within the San Lorenzo area. It was planned by Cosimo I as a dynastic resting place for himself and his ducal followers. Work did not actually begin till after 1600, but it went forward until the end of the Medici regime; large teams of stoneworkers handled the main tasks, while captured Turkish slaves labored to cut the stone into the right-sized pieces. What resulted was a cavernous affair, some thirty yards wide and sixty feet high, and in the course of time there were placed within it the sarcofaghi of Cosimo I, II, and III, Ferdinando I and II, and Francesco I.

It aroused gasps of amazement when it was first opened for inspection, and was regarded as one of the wonders of the world. Doubt and wonder, in fact, are what seize you today as you walk through it, shaking your head at the always intriguing excesses of baroque art: especially when, as here, money was never for a moment in question. But like the New Sacristy—the point is obvious, but needs to be repeated—it was also an expression exclusively of the power and prestige of the Medici family. Arnolfo presented his grandiose plans to the elected representatives of the Commune of Florence; the majestic tombs of the Medici dukes had nothing to do with the city as such, much less with

* See Cochrane, *op. cit.*, 106ff.

[*178*]

its living community. This is a chief reason why the peak of Medici self-aggrandizement—say, about 1600—is also the date when the decline both of the Medicis and of their state began to become apparent.

Historians of Florence and Tuscany vie with one another in pinpointing the moment of greatest decline in the story of the city between 1600 and 1850. Some find the era of Cosimo II a nullity, though in this book's perspective there is an occasional flicker of vitality: as in the dignified and well-formed granary loggia on Via Leoni (just below Palazzo Vecchio), and, in Piazza Santa Croce, the Palazzo dell' Antella, jutting out fashionably over its row of struts, its facade covered with frescoes painted by a supervised and synchronized team in twelve days in the 1660s. Other chroniclers would pick, as the dreariest epoch, the colorless reign of Cosimo III, which seemed to go on forever—he died in 1723 at over eighty years, after half a century in Palazzo Pitti. The period was marked by, more than anything, the Grand Duke's suspiciously sex-minded intolerance, as indicated by his threat to whip any young girls who sang May Day songs in the streets, and his proposal to remove all nude paintings from the Uffizi gallery. Yet in those same years, two striking additions to the Florentine profile came into existence: Palazzo Corsini, on what is now Lungarno Corsini, and, facing it at an angle, on the other side of the Arno, the church of San Frediano in Cestello. Their urban neighborliness is not entirely accidental: the same architect, the gifted Antonio Ferri (died 1716), who helped design the large-framed palazzo—with its cortile, its lateral wings, its double loggia, and its rooftop terraces dotted with statues and vases—also designed the cupola of San Frediano, looming up over the river for every visitor and stroller to admire, as the nearby church of Santo Spirito, three hundred years before, was intended to do.

So urban art did not expire in Florence in this long epoch. But it was hemmed in, shackled in good part to the interests of the absolute ruler of an absolute state. Venice, it has been argued, offers a telling counterexample. The great sixteenth-century Venetian painters—Titian, Tintoretto, Veronese, Bellini—were not the last of the line; Tiepolo, two centuries later, was painting until 1760, Canaletto until 1768, and the Guardi brothers until almost 1800. These individuals flourished within what was in certain real respects a continuing republic. The political system brought into play in thirteenth-century Venice, Hugh Honour remarks in well-chosen words, "removed the demagogue from the political scene" and "placed the government in the hands of a large body of men whose commercial prosperity and mutual jealousy prevented any one family from acquiring supreme influence or power." So effective was this system, Honour concludes, "it survived unchanged for half a millenium."

The decade of the 1730s has been selected by at least one learned observer as the worst moment in the sorry downward process, as "the lowest point of political disintegration, economic depression and intellectual disillusionment in eighteenth century Italy."* The air of dilapidation that afflicted Italy generally prevailed not least in Florence, where Gian Gastone was bringing the Medici rule to its close. Gian Gastone had shown signs of leadership as well as an authentic interest in philosophical thought as a young man; but disappointment and indolence led him to gross over-indulgence. He fell to drunken, publicly obscene behavior and to vomiting at the dinner table, and spent the last eight years of his life in bed. After his death in 1737, the succession passed to the house of Lorraine, with Grand Duke Francesco Stefano.

Pietro Leopoldo of Lorraine, who held sway from 1765 to 1790, added a little to the city's appearance. He opened the Cascine parks to the public and saw to the completion of the twin-sectioned facade of the church of San Firenze, down the slope from Palazzo Vecchio, on Via del Proconsolo.† As was mentioned, he also had constructed for his mistress, a ballerina from Rome named Livia Raimondi (a mediocre dancer, says one historian, but "a splendid girl"), a classically handsome little palazzo on the west side of Piazza San Marco, on the site of what had been the extensive

---

* Franco Venturi, quoted by Cochrane, *op. cit.*, 342.
† On this building and the Piazza San Firenze that encloses it—surprising, neglected sources of Florentine enjoyment—see Ch. 8.

Medici gardens (these latter founded by Cosimo the Elder in the empty space between his palazzo and the city wall).

This same Grand Duke also devoted some time and energy to promoting the literary and scientific life in Florence. But after his departure, the saga of the Lorraines began to resemble that of the Medici at the turn of an earlier century, with one Grand Duke, Ferdinando III, fleeing for safety in 1848, coming back in 1849, and running away permanently in 1859. The following year, 1860, the citizens of Tuscany voted to join the newly established Kingdom of Italy, under King Vittorio Emmanuele.

One very striking development in the history of the Florentine image (so to call it) began to become evident in the late-eighteenth century. A first sign of it was a notable increase in the number of tourists. There had been foreign visitors to Florence, of course, since earliest times, but it was in the 1770s and 1780s that they began to appear in abundance: often young English gentlemen making the grand tour at the behest and expense of their wealthy and well-born parents. New hotels and inns sprang up, older ones were enlarged; new attractions were added to menus—for example, something called *gelato*, based on a Neapolitan recipe and first provided in 1790 at an ice-cream house a little distance above the Duomo (this is the ancestry of such contemporary *gelaterie* as Vivoli's). Guidebooks proliferated. These too were anything but a novelty: the earliest document that falls within the genre, *Memoriale di molte statue e pitture della città di Firenze*, came out in 1510; a text closer to the modern mode was the appropriately titled *Bellezze della città di Firenze*, by Francesco Bocchi, in 1591, updated and expanded in 1677 by Giovanni Cinelli. A century later, guidebooks were being put out in several languages, with pages of practical information about lodgings, places to eat, itineraries, and prices.

Obviously, the shrinking of Florence as a political power and as a center of new creative energy coincided with a deepening attraction to the beauty of its cityscape and its art treasures; and contributed, in the paradoxical ways of culture, to the gathering awareness of the city's extraordinary historical *past*. If the English led the way in the tourist inflow—as they did among foreign settlers and residents in Florence, the English colony by 1800 being by far the biggest and most visible of its kind—they were also groundbreakers in their literary attentiveness to the phenomenon of Florence. This is the most significant aspect of the matter. It has been well argued that the seminal text in the begetting of an "idea of Florence"—that is, of a cultural concept or imaging of Florence as developed by foreign observers—was the *Life of Lorenzo de' Medici, Called the Magnificent*, published in London in 1795 by William Roscoe, a Liverpool attorney and a dedicated liberal activist, a forceful opponent of the slave trade, and a passionate adherent of the French Revolution. Roscoe's biography of Lorenzo was followed, in 1805, by his four-volume *Leo X, the Son of Lorenzo*. Both texts exalted the period of the Florentine Renaissance in general and, without reserve, the role within it of the Medici family.* As we shall later be noticing, William Dean Howells, writing in the late decades of the nineteenth century, could not have disagreed more with this verdict.

In a certain sense and on a certain level of cultural alertness, then, Florence in a part of itself was ready for the huge adventure of the 1860s when it served, over a five-year span, as the capital of Italy's young kingdom.

Poggi and the City Shape: The 1860s

It was on March 15, 1860, that the Minister of Justice Enrico Poggi (brother of the architect) announced from a window in Palazzo Vecchio to the crowd assembled in the piazza the results of the vote on Tuscany joining the Kingdom of Italy: more than 336,000 in favor, about 15,000 opposed (77% to 23%). King Vittorio Emmanuele made his first appearance in Florence a month later, and five months after that he returned to open an extensive and heavily attended national exposition—of industry and craftsmanship—at the Porta al Prato. It was a *nationalizing* experience for the

---

* Eugene Garan, in an article contained in *L'idea di Firenze*, 1989. On the conference that gave rise to the volume just named, this writer's part in it, and the general implications of an *idea di Firenze*, see Ch. 7.

local citizenry, as for the country at large: "It was Italy that came to Florence and Tuscany," writes the historian Marcello Vannucci. In the wake of that event, Massimo d'Azeglio, the influential Piedmontese writer and man of political affairs, was suggesting that Florence, with all its artistic and literary glory, might well become the national capital. For the moment, with Rome in an indefinite state and Venice in the hands of the Austrians, Turin was serving as the administrative base of the monarchy.

Four years passed before a parliamentary convention in September 1864 more or less agreed—the terms were not altogether clear—that if the French troops withdrew from Rome, the Italian government would guarantee sovereignty to the papal estates in that region, and would then move the capital from Turin to Florence. It would, that is, abandon the idea of making Rome the capital. Knowing observers interpreted this strategy as a step *toward* shifting down to Rome; but meanwhile, in November of the same year, parliament voted 270 to 70 in support of the proposition that "the capital of the kingdom will be transferred to Florence within six months."

The municipal authorities in Florence, catapulted into action, immediately set up a commission to study the urban needs for the city's new role. On November 20, it appointed Giuseppe Poggi head of the office entrusted with the work of enlarging the city. Poggi was told to have a plan ready by early February 1865; he presented his plans by that date and they were approved on February 18. It was barely in time: on the third of the month, Vittorio Emmanuele had left Turin with his entourage at eight in the morning, had proceeded south on the new railroad train that carried the royal group through Piacenza and Bologna—with frequent stops for appearances and greetings—and arrived in Florence at eleven-thirty in the evening. The king slept that night in Palazzo Pitti.

It must be admitted that Poggi was confronted with a staggering challenge, and he was not fully prepared for it. The forty-two-year-old Florentine had earned a solid reputation as an architect of eclectic tastes and talents—his Villa Favard on Lungarno Vespucci, which is always worth citing and looking at, is a happy, engaging mix of the Renaissance and the neoclassical; but he had little experience at architectural city planning. (Nor had anyone else in Florence, for that matter, since the days of Brunelleschi.) To a degree, the moment was propitious. Proposals to "improve" the city's interior had been bruited since 1860, and some action taken in that direction. The very narrow stretch of Via Tornabuoni from Palazzo Antinori to Palazzo Strozzi was being widened; west-running Via Oriuolo was broadened to give its strollers a better view of the Duomo; and the streets between the Duomo and Piazza Santa Maria Novella were given similar treatment for a similar good purpose. What seemed at the time a magnificent addition to the city's splendor was a new facade for the church of Santa Croce, set in place in 1863 by Nicola Matas and based on a design going back at least to the seventeenth century. It is in the familiar polychrome style; but in Fanelli's somber words, there thus "disappeared one of those great mute walls that hang over the major piazzas of Florence and that correspond in depth, as no fabricated design ever could, to the Florentine spirit." (Still visible "mute walls," of course, are those of San Lorenzo and Santo Spirito.) The center of the original facade was a gilded bronze statue of San Ludovico by Donatello; it was removed to the nearby museum, where it is currently on show.

As to the conditions of the city in the winter of 1865: it held a population of 150,000 (the numbers had increased notably in the previous fifty years), and with every expectation that another 20,000 would very quickly be pouring in—members of the vast new monarchical administration, dignitaries from England and the Continent, interested persons from the rest of Italy. Lodgings must be found or created for this horde, and spacious offices for the ministries. The Minister of War, in fact, took over a building on Via Cavour; the Director of Taxes settled in the convent at Santa Croce, the Minister of the Interior at Palazzo Medici, and the head of the Public Works in the convent at Santa Maria Novella.

But beyond that, there was an official feeling abroad, evident in public statements, that a good deal must be done to transform

Florence into something that *looked like* the capital of a great kingdom. Part of the process might be the introduction of order and clarity into the network of little streets that angled and twisted across the city's center. Adding to the large-scale confusion were the new means of transportation: horse-drawn omnibuses, departing from Piazza della Signoria and making their way to the various city gates (two million omnibus tickets were sold in 1866); and horse cabs to escort one or two passengers (500 of such in 1866).

Elegant grandiosity: this, it was said in the local newspaper, must be the principle of the newly shaped Florence. In some of Poggi's envisionings (the designs have survived), grandiosity tended to smother elegance: as in the vast new piazza to be presided over by Porta alla Croce, which was to have faced south over a huge triangulated space dotted with fountains and statuary to a monumental porticoed building backing onto the river. Broad new city arteries were also suggested, avenues fit for a capital city, like the one proposed from Piazza Santa Croce west through Via Condotto, Via Porta Rossa, and Via Parione to Ponte alla Carraia, cutting a broad swath and pushing aside shops and palazzi as it went. Cab drivers in our time might have welcomed these new routes: getting from Santa Croce to the Carraia bridge by taxi in this day and age means endless turns and pauses, and edging past always startled and disbelieving pedestrians; but the interior highway would have done wrenching damage to that portion of the city-as-a-work-of-art.

The chief focus of both the authorities and Giuseppe Poggi, in any event, was the overall image of Florence, and the city's immediate imperative to expand and magnify its visible body. In Poggi's own words (written in 1882), the need was "to enlarge and beautify a city which must serve as the seat of a new government, a city which, even if rich in monuments, was wretchedly ill-proportioned." The best way to achieve such a regal new look, it was generally agreed, was a grand encircling boulevard. And what would be the path of that boulevard if not the one followed by the wall-circuit begun in 1284 by Arnolfo di Cambio? As early as the end of November 1864, the municipality sent Poggi a formal letter declaring that "for some time the need has been felt to enlarge the circuit of the city," and that under the new circumstances the need had become "imperative and urgent." The letter continued: "It is believed that the desired enlargement requires the *demolition of the actual walls and the formation of a grand public passageway following the path of the walls*" (italics added).*

Poggi was allowed the final say in the matter, as it seems, and he did not hesitate. The destruction of the walls on the right bank began before the summer of 1865 was over, with tons of explosives being used (the old stone materials went into the making of the new *viale*); and the deadly work was completed within four years. What eventually took the place of Arnolfo's circuit, and deploying contemporary names, was a boulevard of a dozen kilometers in length, beginning on its eastern flank at the bridge of San Niccolò. It proceeds north, slanting westward and following the ancient path, circling around Piazza Beccaria, then performing a large oval around Piazzale Donatello, and reaching its northern vertex at the rectangular Piazza della Libertà. It then swoops down, south and west, making an enormous loop around Fortezza da Basso, rejoining itself at Porta al Prato, and so down to Piazza Vittorio Veneto and the river at the Ponte alla Vittoria.

Poggi's intention had been to preserve all the actual gates, the big stone edifices that punctuated the circuit—to monumentalize the medieval design and its history, so to say, by making the gates the successive centers of piazza-islands; but he found it necessary to get rid of Porta al Pinti half way up the eastern curve and the two smaller gates of Giustizia and Guelfa near the river, since they got in the way of his onward-driving boulevard. The gates that remained stood, then as they do now, in a kind of isolated splendor, in an uncertain historical-artistic relation to their modern surroundings. They are not without charm. Ottone Rossi has remarked winningly about one of them, Porta alla Croce in Piazza Beccaria, that the old stone portal stands in the middle of the piazza like an elderly gentleman, with his head covered in old-fashioned style, still capable of giving us lessons; at once stiffly

* See *Firenze Scomparsa*, by Edoardo Dati, 2nd ed., 1977, 34.

erect and at ease, he tells his stories of old-time battles in defense of Florence.* And, indeed, looking at the Porta, it does seem, with its slightly curving and slightly rakish roof (the "hat" in Rossi's image), as if a brownstone being stood there, engaging us in talk.

Poggi's initial scheme had a certain bravura of imagination: the city outlined anew, and dramatically, by a great boulevard twenty-nine meters wide and lined by trees, with pavements on each side three meters wide and elevated by three meters; the whole punctuated by large handsome piazzas enshrining the ancient gates and embellished with greenery and fountains. But of that plan, only Piazza Beccaria and what is now Piazza della Libertà came to fruition. The second of these provided special problems. The area had been called Piazza San Gallo originally, by association with a nearby convent and the gate of that name. During the Risorgimento, it became Piazza Cavour; in later years, continuing to reflect Italian history, it was rechristened Piazza Ciano (after Mussolini's son-in-law and foreign affairs representative), and in 1945, it swiftly took the name it now holds, Piazza della Libertà. When the wall was torn down, the old gate stood facing a massive Arco di Trionfo, raised by the first of the Lorraine grand dukes in 1745. Poggi set a pool and a fountain in the space between gate and arch, surrounded that scene with trees, and built a rectangle of big porticoed buildings (the influence of Brunelleschi's Innocenti hospital is apparent) to enclose the entire piazza.

In an age of horse-drawn carriages, Piazza Cavour could have been properly awesome, even though the various elements—gate, arch, pool, plantings, porticos—fail to come together in a harmonious formation (De Chirico is said to have been struck by the disjointed, surrealistic nature of the display). But automobile traffic has long since submerged it. There are seven streets and three boulevards now leading into and out of the square, endless streams of automobiles and buses and trucks spin along from all directions and in all directions.

* *Via Toscanella*, 1930.

Portion of the old wall, today

The fact is, the destruction of the walls (Fanelli has emphasized it) meant the destruction of what had been a crucial urban definition: the distinction between *inside* the city and outside it. "So great a task it was to found the Roman people," Virgil declaimed. But founding the Roman people, Virgil makes clear from the outset, meant founding a *city*; and this, in turn (as remarked earlier), meant building a *walled* city. Florence had been a walled city for five hundred and sixty years; with its walls removed, it was no longer a distinct and integral urban reality. What had been the city now blurred with or faded into the outskirts, the suburbs, the rapidly filling periphery. The great *viale* itself was supposed to supply a distinctive contour for the city; but with the remorseless trend of modern history, in the guise of the automobile traffic that thunders and jostles along its surface, that contour has virtually disappeared.

This was on the north side of the river. The south side was a different proposition. Here Poggi could disregard the Arnolfian circuit; and indeed he left much of it intact, as it went up the slope to Fort Belvedere and from Porta Romana west along Viale Petrarca and Viale Ariosto. Exploiting the wooded hillside that ranged upward from the Arno, Poggi brought into being a magnificent boulevard, Viale dei Colli—of the hills—that ascends in long, sweeping curves, and calling itself Viale Michelangelo, to the summit and to Piazzale Michelangelo; then down, still generously snakelike, and now Viale Galileo, to Piazzale Galileo, and finally, as Viale Machiavelli, to Porta Romana. The boulevard of the hills is Poggi's undoubted masterpiece; and its triumphant crown is the piazzale, from which one can look down and across at the Florentine panorama as from no other vantage point. Poggi planned to place a statue of Michelangelo at the center of the great square named for him, but publicity forces in the town hall insisted instead on yet another copy of the statue of David. Meanwhile, Poggi designed a loggia to be pressed against the hillside leading to San Salvatore al Monte; about this, which is now a pleasant cafe, there has been critical disagreement (both as to artistry and location). Poggi also arranged for a series of ramps descending from the piazza to the spot that would carry his name, Piazza Poggi; an easy and enjoyable walk back down to the river.

In the later decades of the century, Poggi suffered a barrage of criticism for his works of destruction and enlargement; and he was further embittered by a harsh inquiry into the cost of the boulevards. He himself seems never to have openly acknowledged any regret or afterthought concerning the demolition of the walls. But as old age overtook him (he died in 1901), he let it be known that he wanted no tomb among the famous Florentines in Santa Croce, nor did he want to be buried with his kin in the spacious cemetery of Porta Santa, outside Porta Romana. He ordered his ashes placed in the communal graveyard of the Trespiano cemetery in the hills north of the city.

Destruction at the Center: The 1880s

After the incorporation of the papal states into the Italian kingdom in September 1870, the nation's capital was transferred from Florence to Rome. King Vittorio Emmanuele left Florence for the last time, en route to Rome (and reportedly with much relief), in late June 1871. The urban refurbishings already under way went forward apace; among them, of particular note, the stretches along the Arno on either side: Lungarno della Zeccha Vecchia, Lungarno Serristori, and Lungarno Torrigiani. The new facade for the cathedral—designed by Emilio de Fabri and completed by Luigi del Moro—was inaugurated in May 1887 with extravagant festivity, including a staged tournament with a costume ball in Palazzo Vecchio, much of the display being illuminated by the first electric lights in the city (Henry James, a temporary resident in Florence, wrote home enthusiastically about the procession of Florentine nobles decked out in the medieval costumes of their ancestors). About the facade itself, opinion was and remains vigorously divided; but it has impressed its aspect upon one's vision for so long that critical judgment falls silent.

The preoccupying urban issue in the postcapital years was that of the city's center: the literal center, the precise midpoint space that sheltered the age-old market, the Mercato Vecchio, which stood on the identical spot where the Forum, the center of the Roman city, had stood two thousand years before, with its temples and its Capitol and its area for public meetings and conversing. The Mercato had been the scene of food marketing since at least the early-twelfth century, taking the name Vecchio when a new market opened up nearer the river. Eve Borsook evokes the market spectacle in medieval days:

During Carnival there were hens and capons and for Lent there were mountains of onions, garlic, shallot tarts and spicy herbs fried in batter. The favorite meat then, as now, was veal . . .

Everyone came to the Mercato Vecchio: merchants, housewives, farmers, beggars, pickpockets. Women and girls of good family were carried about in litters. Vegetable sellers and venders of junk of all kinds threaded their way through the loggias and stalls crying 'Bruccia Pistoia' (Pistoia's burning) for red watermelons, 'Eccolo il vero medico' (Here's the real doctor) for baked pears. Other criers were hired to call out lost property or help wanted (wet nurses, for example). Above the crowd, communal heralds on horseback announced death sentences, exiles, war news and bankruptcies.

The Mercato Vecchio over the years gathered along itself town houses of families on the rise: Ubaldini, Caponsacchi, Medici, Davanzati, Adimari, and many others. Several of the oldest churches in Florence stood nearby. A stone column with a statue by Donatello, suitably an allegorical image of Abundance, was set up in the piazza in 1431. In 1567 Vasari, commissioned by Cosimo I, built the sturdy and graceful Loggia del Pesce for the use of the city's fishmongers.

In the same era, however, the Mercato Vecchio began to undergo a grimmer admixture of history. Cosimo (to repeat) arranged to have a portion of the zone, covering the area from the upper part of the present Piazza della Repubblica to Via de' Pecori, as the newly framed ghetto for the city's Jewish population.* The latter was moved by ducal order, households and all, up across the river from Via Ramigliani where it had resided for perhaps two hundred years (the street in fact was formerly known as Via Giudici, a name meaning Jews—from *Giudico*, and not from *giudice*, judge). Jewish agents had run loan-bank operations, with the encouragement and support of the city authorities, since some time in the fourteenth century, and had prospered in particular during the rule of Cosimo il Vecchio and his grandson Lorenzo. Their banks were set up in Via de' Neri, Piazza Santa Trinità, and other central points, but they themselves were forbidden to live within the city proper. Now, with the ghetto, they had their own territory, but it was decidedly and somberly a place of confinement, a kind of penitentiary, shut in by big walls, with three small and carefully spaced entrances (one from the Mercato Vecchio).

Periods of limited tolerance alternated with stretches of vicious harassment; conditions within the ghetto grew more and more miserable. But beginning around the middle of the eighteenth century, Florentine Jews won certain real measures of civil rights.

---

* The ghetto occupied something like a rectangle, going north from the Piazza along Via Roma, back along Via de' Pecori, and south down Via Brunelleschi to the Piazza.

The word *ghetto*, incidentally, is itself Italian in origin, and seems to derive from the name of the little Venetian island occupied exclusively by Jews.

The ghetto was self-governing, and in 1782 it was in effect given control of its own property. Florentine community leaders also, as one small sign of strength, pressured a city theater into setting aside a number of boxes throughout the season, and to prohibit any malicious reference to Jewry on stage. By 1800, the municipal statute on racial segregation had been abolished, and Jews could live anywhere they wanted to.

As the Jews moved out of the ghetto, the worst elements of Florentine society unhappily moved in: thieves, cutthroats, pimps, prostitutes. The human ordure, as one enraged observer called it, spilled over into the Mercato Vecchio itself. The whole area fell into decay; as though by anticipatory symbolism, the column displaying Donatello's statue of *Abundance* collapsed (in 1721) and the statue was smashed. (It was replaced by another statue of *Abundance*, by G. B. Foggini; what we see today is a copy of Foggini's work.*) In 1835, the old city center, now a scene of squalor, gave rise to a disastrous cholera epidemic. In 1881, an impassioned Florentine journalist, Giulio Piccini, who wrote under the name of Jarro, gave voice in *La Nazione* to a popular cry: *"Date aria, date luce! Il che vuol dire: date salute, moralità!"* "Give air to this place! Give light! In other words, give it health, give it morality!"

The ghetto was evacuated in 1885. But the process of cleaning up only seemed to gain momentum, and over the next decade wholesale demolition pretty much destroyed the Mercato Vecchio and extended to many of the streets surrounding it. There thus took place what Florentine historians called the *sventrimento*: literally, the disembowelment (from *ventre*, belly) of the city's ancient center. For a moment, Piero Bargellini has remarked wistfully, as the encumbering huts and hovels disappeared, the age-old piazza came into view with its medieval houses and little churches. But there was no stopping the headlong urban renewers; once the pickaxes got going, down came "towers and churches and loggias and columns."

The journalist Jarro was exultant: "To have destroyed the an-

* The original is in the Cassa di Risparmio on Via Bufalini.

The Florence ghetto, before 1885

cient center of Florence was the most beautiful achievement in the service of this distinguished city within the century" (this in 1899). As against that, we have the present-day judgment on the *sventrimento* by Edoardo Dati: "the greatest crime of the past century as regards buildings"; to which Giovanni Fannelli adds his view that the destruction of the center was the greatest urbanistic blunder in a hundred years. Both these contemporary critics are reflecting not only on the wanton wreckage of historic houses (Caponsacchi, Amieri, Ubaldini), public buildings, piazzas, streets, and churches (not to mention fragments of the Roman epoch, the remains of the temple to Jupiter, bits of the old baths, and so on). They were responding as well to what was created to fill the empty space—the Piazza della Repubblica.*

The Repubblica, like its forebears, occupies the geographical center of the town, and it is in some respects—none of them artistic—the center of its life. Architecturally, it is a confused and characterless affair: a long, dark loggia, serving no obvious purpose, and a huge, gloomy archway, quite out of keeping with the visible architectural traditions of Florence, and opening onto nothing but the city's biggest cabstand. (On a typical day in 1992, one could count four tour buses in the piazza, twenty-five cabs and, ringing them about, a couple of hundred motorbikes.) Inscribed above the archway is the epigraph (in translation): "The ancient center of the city restored from centuries of squalor to a new life. 1895." Other installations include two ground-level cafes, the department store UPIM, a major bank, a big insurance company, a movie theater, and a hotel; and up above, large-worded advertisements for Campari, Fernet Branca, Stock (brandy), and the newspaper *La Repubblica*.

Despite this urbanistic mishmash, frequent foreign visitors to Florence, even while comprehending the critical reasoning ad-

---

* To perform the services of the Mercato Vecchio in its olden days, several new city *markets* came into being, and are flourishing today. The largest is adjacent to San Lorenzo; another, San Ambrogio, is behind Santa Croce; and a third is in the San Frediano district.

Vasari's Loggia del Pesce, it might be noted, after vanishing for a long spell, was reconstructed in the Piazza dei Ciompi, also behind Santa Croce, where it stands in a sort of irrelevant dignity.

vanced against the piazza, may confess to a certain tolerant affection for it. It is true that the old entrance to the forum is now the seat of UPIM (which also has its values and uses); and it is true that the buildings round about lack any sort of distinction or vibrancy. But the piazza embodies something of that civic friendliness that Henry James detected elsewhere in the city—an air of hospitality, as it were, of ungainly cordialness. In one corner is the cafe Guibbe Rosse, far from being the meeting place of literati that it once was, but a likable spot for a cappucino in the morning. And looking out from the cafe onto the piazza, one can always be grateful that the colossal statue of Vittorio Emmanuele on horseback, erected there on top of a hefty stone block amid enormous hubbub in 1890, is no longer present. It was removed in 1931 to the Cascine, where it stands in solitude, and where Giuseppe Poggi thought it should have been situated in the first place.

PART II

POINTS OF VIEW

[6]

Roman Gate and Beautiful
Outlook: The 1970s

Down in the City

In all our extensive visits to Florence, we have lived at the same
address only twice: for seven months ending in June 1986 and
again in the spring of 1989, when we occupied a quietly stylish
fourth-floor apartment in Via della Fornace, on the south side of
the river, between the old gate and the new bridge named for
San Niccolò. On all the other visits, we found ourselves settling
into a neighborhood new to us—on the right, or north, side, in
places as diverse as Piazza Santa Trinità, Via Lamarmora, Borgo
Ognissanti, and, most recently, Piazza Santa Croce; on the left
bank, on Costa de' Magnoli, Lungarno Soderini, and Via Romana.
Once, in the fall of 1969, we inhabited half of a villa named for
Boccaccio, near the village of Settignano, a few miles northeast
of the city; and another time—it is the later focus of this
chapter—we lived in the hills above the Porta Romana, at the
foot of the area called Bellosguardo.

There was nothing programmatic or principled about these constant trials of new locales. If we had had a place to return to (as
have some of our friends), we should certainly have done so. As
it was, each time a sabbatical or some other form of endowed
absenteeism seemed likely, we simply consulted with Florentine
associates and rental agents, and took what struck us as attractive.

We now count ourselves exceedingly lucky. What we have been able to experience has been a series of stirringly different points of view, each one disclosing some special aspect or historical moment or urbanistic feature of the city. I would hardly claim that the whole of Florence was finally made to appear in these various angles of vision, but a great deal of it showed up, including some of the most characteristic and compelling places. This is the Florence I want to examine, or perhaps better relive, in the pages following.

It was during the year 1972–73 that we resided in Via Romana, in an apartment at No. 51. It belonged to Signor and Signora Rossoni, a *simpatico* middle-aged couple (the husband was one of the most indefatigable bicyclists in a city of cyclists), who owned and ran the Pensione Annalena across the street. Our lodging was an oddly shaped, stretched-out affair, with a cluster of small rooms at one end (our son Nat, who passed his eleventh birthday there, slept in literally a medium-sized coat closet) and, at the far other end, down a flight of steps, a spacious living room which we rarely used. They were close quarters for a family of five, but it was, all told, a happy existence.

We engaged the apartment thanks to my mother, Beatrix Baldwin Lewis, who had been a widow for nearly a quarter of a century by this time, and had been coming regularly to stay at the Annalena—she felt at home there, and taken care of, and the cost of life in Florence was suitable for a clergyman's widow on a pension. She was eighty years old in the fall of 1972, and was perhaps the best-loved as she was the best-known figure in the little Anglo-American-Italian Annalena society. And this, despite a cheerful inability to get very far, whatever the years of trying, with the Italian language. She had something of an international background, being born in Leipzig (by chance) and spending much of her youth in Oxford, England, where her clergyman-father was a don of sorts—and given, so the grandchildren were guardedly informed, to random marital misbehavior. But foreign languages were not her specialty. Ida Giaccalone, who commanded the domestic staff at the Annalena and would become a

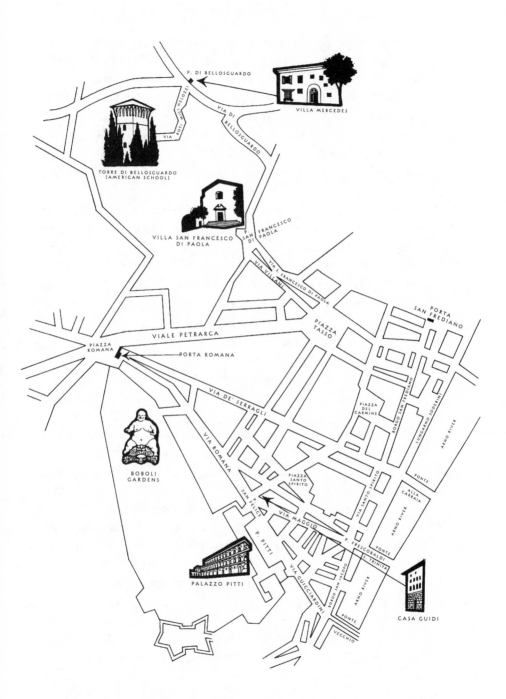

Villa San Francesco area *(upper left)*, and Via Romana area *(lower right)*

beloved personal friend, remembers the moment when Signora Lewis spoke anxiously about being in need of *dolore*. Why she should actually be in *need* of pain, *dolore*, was not clear to Ida; but what the Signora in fact was short of was *DOLLari*, dollars. Having heard the phrase "Accetto io" many times—"I accept," or simply "Okay"—my mother took to using the expression (we now use it ourselves, in family) *"accetteria."*

We were not inclined to make undue fun of such errata; control of a foreign language is always a relative matter. To curb any pride I might take in my own Italian, I had only to recall the time when my eleven-year-old niece Kate was living in Florence and attending the elite school for white-gloved young ladies at Poggio Imperiale. One beautiful starlit evening, as Kate, my mother, and I were walking down Via Romana together, Kate looked up at the sky and exclaimed: *"Ma guardate le belle stelle!"* My heart sank: not because I could not myself urge the others in Italian to look at the beautiful stars, but because of the child's flawless accent. I knew on the spot that, though I had been talking Italian, more or less, for a number of years, I could never acquire that effortlessly perfect Tuscan pronunciation.*

The Via Romana sojourn was an agreeable mixture of work, wanderings, and family activities. I had a year's full-paid leave of absence from Yale, that generous gift being a recompense for having served for six years as the Master of one of Yale's residential colleges (this beneficent leave practice has, I believe, been discontinued). Those years, the late 1960s and early 1970s, had been tumultuous ones at Yale, as on many another American campus; though Yale had the singular good fortune of being guided through them by the energetic, ever watchful, and admirably guileful tactician Kingman Brewster. The moment of freedom had arrived, anyhow, and we put Yale and Connecticut behind us without regret, and turned our attention in other directions. My personal direction, five or six mornings a week, was a biography of Edith

---

* It was essentially the Tuscan "e" that was elusive. What Kate said sounded something like "lay bellay stellay"—but even that way of transcribing the sound isn't subtle enough.

Wharton; I managed to complete a (much-too-long-drawn-out) draft of the book on Via Romana, and rewrote about half of it. The rest of the time, I joined in the explorations of the Florentine world we lived in.

Across the way, to repeat, was the Pensione Annalena, with its lovely high-walled gardens. The place was named, so we learned, for the unhappy Annalena Malatesta, the widow of a Florentine soldier of fortune, Balduccio d'Anghiari. Machiavelli tells the story in his history of Florence: how Balduccio in 1441 incurred the enmity of the *gonfaloniere* Bartolommeo Orlandini; how this latter lured Balduccio into the Palazzo Vecchio, and there had him murdered by armed toughs; the body was thrown out the window into the piazza, and the head was cut off. The twenty-two-year-old Annalena, with a newborn child, was waiting for her husband in the house on Via Romana which Cosimo the Elder had given her ten years before, when, having been orphaned, she became his ward. Now, outside the windows, came shouting: "Madonna, they have killed your husband in the Palagio de' Signori and thrown him out the window and cut off his head for being a traitor and a wrongdoer!" Two years later, the infant son died. Annalena joined a religious order, and turned her house into a home for solitary, unhappy women. It became known as Casa Annalena, and a section of Via Romana was given the name *Giardino di Annalena*. Annalena died in her private convent in 1490.

The Annalena entrance to the Boboli Gardens (the main entrance is through Palazzo Pitti) was only a step away from our building, and we enjoyed many an hour in those surroundings. The gardens, as was said, were initiated under Cosimo I, and carried out by a series of artists and landscape architects: Niccolò Tribolo (who died in 1550), Buontalenti, Alfonso Parigi the Elder (died 1590) and his son Giulio Parigi. We stood for long minutes at a time in the vast amphitheater behind the Pitti, gazing back (as Henry James had done, and following his example) toward the palazzo and the big fountain, known as the Fountain of the Artichoke, which looms up over the magnificent cortile. We strolled in the little island with the 1560's statue of Neptune by one Stoldo Lorenzi. But most of the time we made our way down to the southern end of the elaborate gardenscape, to walk about the well-tended green fields or go sit on the stone benches facing the *isolotto*—the balustraded island in the midst of a vast pool which was designed in 1616 by the younger Alfonso Parigi. (The Parigis are always hard to keep separate; but they decidedly enhanced the era of the second Cosimo.) There are pillars on either side of the *isolotto*, topped by capricorns, with another pair of fountains guarded by dolphins; dominating the enclosed island itself is a big statue of Ocean by that composer of the extra-life-size, Giambologna, and below *Ocean* appear the personification of several rivers—the Nile, the Ganges, the Euphrates. In the pool water, Perseus, or a small statue of him, is forever going to the rescue of the ever-endangered Andromeda. It is a scene studded with beguiling human artifacts, but it remains oddly restful and serene.

The area around it is made for family outings, and Eve Borsook has so exactly described what we habitually did on a Saturday or a Sunday that she may be gratefully called on:

a perfect place for solitary ramblings, picnics and children. There are shady paths, long views and occasional benches. One can parade by the grandiose monuments or play hide-and-seek in the bushes among statues of a friendlier character—bird catchers, gamesters, peasants and dogs.

Ms. Borsook's account ends where our visits drew to a close—at the Fountain of the Vintage, near the path leading back to the Annalena exit, a handy spot to pause for a drink:

Two coral-coloured stone mastiffs glumly watch a fountain . . . consisting of a farmer emptying his cask into a tub with a bare-bottomed stone child gleefully clutching the rim.

Via Romana, heading away from the river, passes a number of self-respecting, undistinguished buildings (some of them hospitals or resting places for pilgrims in far off days) and arrives at the Piazza della Calza—the "Square of the Stocking"; there used

Boboli Gardens

Porta Romana

to be a monastery nearby, the members of which wore long white head coverings like stockings. Presiding over the piazza is the Porta Romana, the most robust of the old city gates and placed at the southernmost point of the thirteenth-century circuit of walls.

The word Romana attached to both Via and Porta signals, of course, the old main road leading from Florence to Rome. There was another one in earliest times going eastward out of the city and following the course of the Arno. The modern Roman road heads more or less due south, with a slight, steady, eastern inclination, through Siena; which is why, beginning just outside the Porta, it takes the name Via Senese. The Roman gate had a battlemented tower some forty meters high when it was first built, in 1326 to 1328, on a design by Andrea Orcagna; the tower was sliced off with the neighboring towers in the early-sixteenth century. Inscriptions on the gate mark the entry through it into the city, in 1515, of Leo X (Giovanni de' Medici) and, in 1536, of the Emperor Charles V, who came to help install his son-in-law (more strictly, the future husband of his natural daughter), Alessandro de' Medici, as Duke of Florence. A Madonna and Child with Four Saints, in a fresco on the inner part of the gate, watch peacefully over the milling and swirling of automobiles in the piazza below, as cars come and go along three converging boulevards and three smaller streets. For all the noise and congestion, Porta Romana is our sturdy favorite among the surviving city gates.

Via Romana makes its northern start in Piazza San Felice, sheltering the church of that name (and *not* San Felicità, which is a little ways away near Ponte Vecchio, and which contains the several extraordinary paintings by Pontormo). Looking across the narrow piazza at the gray wall of the church is Casa Guidi, the Florentine home of Robert Browning and Elizabeth Barrett Browning from the spring of 1847 until Elizabeth's death there in June 1861.

The two were married in a secret rush in April 1846, before fleeing England and Elizabeth's despotic father, to come to Italy, where Robert had visited twice before. They stayed in Pisa first ("in a house built by Vasari," Elizabeth wrote a friend, "and within sight of the Leaning Tower and the Duomo"); then in a temporary lodging in Florence, before taking over a portion of what had been Palazzo Ridolfi at the point where Via Maggio angles into Via Romana. Eight large windows, so Elizabeth told her sister Arabel, opened "on a sort of balcony terrace . . . What a pleasure it is to have such a place to walk up and down in, when you are not inclined to go onto the streets." The place, with its windows, became known in England and perhaps even more widely in Italy when, in 1851, Elizabeth Barrett Browning published her long poem *Casa Guidi Windows.*

The poem grew out of political developments in Florence in the late 1840s. Grand Duke Pietro Leopoldo of Lorraine, yielding a little to popular sentiment and responding as well to reformist tendencies throughout Europe, had taken a few steps to improve matters in Tuscany: he granted freedom of the press, dismissed the repressive chief of police, and appointed as head of the Council a man known for his liberal views. The actions were celebrated by a large and well-organized procession, in which every phase of Tuscan society and every city in the region took part.

> I heard last night a little child go singing
> Neath Casa Guidi windows, by the church,
> *"O bella liberta, O bella!"* . . .

So, quietly, the poem begins. Eventually, after meditating on Florence and her great artists and her longing for freedom, the poet arrives at the great occasion:

> Shall I say
> What made my heart beat with exulting love
> A few weeks back?

And she goes on to describe it in exhilarated detail:

> So, one and all,
> The Tuscan cities streamed up to the source
> Of this new good at Florence, taking it

As good so far, presageful of more good,—
    The first torch of Italian freedom . . .

        How we gazed
    From Casa Guidi windows, while in trains
Of orderly procession—banners raised,
    And intermittent burst of martial strains
Which died upon the sound, as if amazed
    By gladness beyond music—they passed on!

The successive elements of society are observed as they paraded
by:

    The Magistracy, with insignia passed,
        And all the people shouted on the sun . . .
    The Lawyers passed,—and still arose the shout . . .

        The Priesthood passed, the friars with worldly-wise
    Keen, sidelong glances from their beards about
        The street to see who shouted! . . .
    The Artists, next the Trades, and after came
        The People,—flag and sign, and rights as good,
And very loud the shout was for that same
        Motto, 'Il popolo.' IL POPOLO . . .

And then came the Tuscan cities:

    Deputed representatives a-row
Of every separate state of Tuscany.
        Siena's she-wolf, bristling on the fold
Of the first flag, preceded Pisa's hare,
        And Massa's lion floated calm in gold,
Pienza's following with his silver stare.
        Arezzo's steed pranced clear from bridle-fold . . .

The new freedoms did not last very long. Within a couple of
years Leopoldo had rescinded most of them, reinstated his drably

autocratic regime, and resumed his weak-kneed fealty to the Austrian power. Elizabeth Barrett Browning responded in both poetry and prose to these disheartening events, but she never gave up her passionate belief in the Italian cause. It was the death of Camillo Cavour in 1861 that affected her most. She had pinned her faith on Cavour's political agility, and his death appeared actually to have hastened her own. She was buried in the English cemetery so called (it was founded by Swiss folk) in what is now Piazzale Donatello; and here she holds her place with Walter Savage Landor, Frances Trollope (the mother of Anthony and Thomas Adolphus, and herself a writer of vivacity and courage), Gian Pietro Vieusseux (founder of the literary Gabinetto), and other distinguished non-Florentines.

Robert described the burial in a forgivably exaggerated letter to his brother George:

She was buried yesterday—with the shops in the street shut, a crowd of people following sobbing, another crowd of Italians, Americans and English crying like children at the cemetery, for they knew who she was—the greatest English poet of her day . . .

The municipality of Florence, in another expression of the same sentiment, placed an inscription on the wall of Casa Guidi which read in part (and in translation): "Here wrote and lived / Elizabeth Barrett Browning . . . whose poems forged a golden ring / Between Italy and England."* This was the inscription that we glanced at almost daily in 1972–73, as we strolled up Via Maggio toward the river.

The wayward gestures of Tuscany toward freedom, generally unsuccessful until 1860, found a certain correspondence in Elizabeth Barrett Browning's poetry. The Florentine life-energy—that is, focusing on an ideal of freedom—summoned forth Elizabeth's creative energies not only in *Casa Guidi Windows* but in other writings of the Florentine years: "A Curse for a Nation," "The

* The inscription provided the title for the richly informative book by Giuliana Artom Treves (translated by Sylvia Sprigge), *The Golden Ring: The Anglo-Florentines 1847–1862* (1956), set essentially in the Browning years.

Dance," "Christmas Gifts," and others. The Italian experience touched and enlivened her in two deeply personal ways. There was, first, the inescapable analogy (others have commented on it) between the situation of Tuscany, historically weakened and held captive by Austria, and her own position before Robert's appearance, semibedridden and oppressed by a psychopathically tyrannical parent.* At the same time, as Elizabeth, in *Casa Guidi Windows*, went on to trace the course of Florentine art, and the great artists who had given Florence its world-resounding names—Cimabue, Giotto, Fra Angelico, and Raphael are among those evoked—she is clearly taking stock of herself as an artist in poetry, of her achievement and her promise; and, more obliquely, of the way in which the achievement is linked to a passionate devotion to freedom.

I took a special pleasure in our proximity to the Brownings during the Via Romana year, for I had enjoyed a sort of admiring association with them from a fairly early age. I could not have been more than fifteen when I stood up at a Friday morning assembly during a little program of recitations in my day school and, rigid with dignity and stage fright, gave voice to Robert Browning's "My Last Duchess" from start to finish:

> That's my last Duchess painted on the wall,
> Looking as if she were alive. I call
> That piece a wonder now; Fra Pandolf's hands
> Worked busily a day, and there she stands.
> Will't please you sit and look at her? I said
> 'Fra Pandolf' by design . . .

I was also fond of "Soliloquy in a Spanish Cloister," with its comical, growling resentment, and made a line from it a catchphrase around the school: "What's the Greek name for Swine's

---

* Elizabeth Barrett Browning, partly because of her situation, responded to cruelty and oppression wherever she saw it. The above-named "Curse for a Nation," as an example, has to do not with European politics but with the enslavement of black people in America.

Snout?" Browning's Florentine poems took my fancy from the start, and the fancy only increased when I learned something, at first hand, of their historical connections—"Fra Lippo Lippi" (we can think of that backsliding genius's *Madonna and Child* in the Palazzo Medici), "Andrea del Sarto" (I could murmur that poem's sad last line—"Again the Cousin's whistle! Go, my love"—while looking at del Sarto's gripping murals in the church of the Annunziata), and "The Statue and the Bust" (set in the Piazza S. S. Annunziata). As to Elizabeth Barrett Browning, I came to her by way of Robert: that is, through her romantic narrative poem of 1844, "Lady Geraldine's Courtship," which extolled the work of Robert Browning and drew his attention to her. The poet-narrator tells how, courting the Earl's daughter, the Lady Geraldine, he read aloud to her as they sat together on a hillside, read from Petrarch or from Spenser—

Or at times a modern volume—Wordsworth's solemn-thoughted idyll,
Howitt's ballad verse, or Tennyson's enchanted reverie,—
Or from Browning some pomegranate, which if cut down deep the middle,
Shows a heart within blood-tinctured of a veined humanity.

The New York Browning Society was taking action during our stay on Via Romana to buy the apartment in Casa Guidi and to furnish it with replicas of the Brownings' furniture. A Browning Institute was established in Florence, and Casa Guidi was made open for visitors at designated hours, by pressing a bell on the Via Maggio side. During one of our later Florentine periods, a young friend of the family, Matthew Munich, a classics-oriented student then heading for Cornell, functioned as the live-in caretaker of Casa Guidi for six months. Our intimacy with the brightening presences of Robert and Elizabeth Barrett Browning grew apace.*

* In January 1993, Casa Guidi became the property of Eton College, which engaged the Landmark Trust to help in the task of renovating and refurbishing the Casa. Casa Guidi, closed for these improvements since December 1992, is scheduled to open by mid-1994. It will serve as a study/conference center for Eton during three months of

There were other attractions along Via Maggio, as it proceeded toward Via Romana, and two of them deserve mention. One was the house built for Bianca Cappello (whose acquaintance we shall soon make more fully) by her grand-ducal lover Francesco in 1566, halfway down the street and only the shortest of clandestine walks from Palazzo Pitti. The Venetian family's coat-of-arms is displayed above the entrance—a rather stylish traveling hat, with crossed laces (the surname, of course, means "hat")—and Bianca had the walls decorated with grotesque and playful designs, still thinly visible. Near the end of Via Maggio, at No. 37, almost across from Casa Guidi, is the former home of the architect and designer of spectacles, Bernardo Buontalenti (1531–1608), one of the most gifted and decidedly one of the most appealing of the artists associated with the first two Cosimos.

It was outside Buontalenti's house that there appeared in 1575 the poet and dramatist of melancholy and abrupt disposition Torquato Tasso. Buontalenti had devised the scenery for Tasso's pastoral idyll *Aminta* (about the love of the shepherd Aminta for the maiden Silvia). The production, which took place in the newly created Boboli Gardens, was a reverberating success and made the twenty-nine-year-old author famous. So it was that one day into Via Maggio rode Torquato Tasso, to greet Buontalenti, outside the artist's house, with the words: "Are you Bernardo Buontalenti, the author of these marvelous inventions?" "I am Bernardo Buontalenti" was the reply, "but not all you say of me in your goodness and courtesy." Tasso jumped down from his horse and embraced Buontalenti closely, exclaiming as he did so: "You are Bernardo Buontalenti, and I am Torquato Tasso. Goodbye, goodbye my friend, goodbye!"* And without another word, the poet leaped back on his horse and rode off toward Porta Romana.

---

the year, and will be available for other purposes the rest of the time. It will be open three times a week for public visits. Robert Browning himself was not a graduate of Eton, but members of both the Browning and the Barrett families in this century have attended the famous school.

* *"Voi siete Bernardo Buontalenti, ed io sono Torquato Tasso. Addio, addio, amico, addio!"*

Up at the Villa

In Robert Browning's monologue "Up at the Villa—Down in the City," the foppish "Italian person of quality" who speaks the piece tells us that the city (presumably Florence in c. 1850) is the place to live, expensive as it may be:

> Had I but plenty of money, money enough and to spare,
> The house for me, no doubt, were a house in the city square;
> Ah, such a life, such a life, as one leads at the window there!

In the city, there is always something going on—"Something to see, by Bacchus, something to hear at least": the news of three "liberal thieves" being shot, a message of warning from the Archbishop, a new law decreed by the Duke. By comparison, life up at the villa is hardly human: "Up at the villa one lives, I maintain it, no more than a beast." But, alas, the city life is simply too costly:

> And so, the villa for me, not the city!
> Beggars can scarcely be choosers; but still—ah the pity, the pity!

But our personal experience of villa life in the Florence environs, particularly in the year 1975–76, was in every way more gratifying than that described by Browning's spokesman (who even disliked the sound of crickets and bees, and hated cypresses).

The villa here in question was named for San Francesco di Paola, and it stood in friendly dignity at the head of a slope looking down toward the left bank of the Arno, on the way to Bellosguardo. The five of us—the two older folk and three children, aged thirteen, ten, and eight—went there in the autumn of 1975 (directed thereto by a Yale colleague and friend, an eminent professor of psychology, who had previously lived there with *his* family).

From time to time on a Florence visit, I made a stab at keeping a journal-record of our current habitation. These entries did not accumulate into very much, but they have helped to recover the atmosphere and the look of things. One such entry, and an un-usually long one, comes from late November 1975.

Thanksgiving Weekend, 1975

We are staying in the Oltrarno section of Florence this time, on the south side of the river and not very far from the old Roman gate. We have the entire second floor of the Villa San Francesco di Paola, and from two adjoining terraces at the far end of the apartment we can see fields sloping upward to cypresses and olive trees. Until a couple of years ago, the fields were regularly plowed and tended by two young farmers, working behind a yoke of white oxen. But the *fidanzate* of the men found it de-meaning to marry farmers, so the youths are now garage me-chanics and the fields lie uncared for. "A lost generation": when Gertrude Stein used this phrase after the first war, she meant that it was hard to find a decent mechanic among the younger folk in France; but in Florence today, one has the impression that, as to skilled labor, a mechanic is about all you *can* find, and such seems to be generally the case throughout Tuscany—except dur-ing the *vendemmia*, the autumnal grape-gathering time. Tended or not, the fields make a charming vision.

Peering around in the other direction from the terrace, we catch a glimpse of the Duomo and Giotto's Baptistery; sometimes, through the branches, of Palazzo Vecchio. From the balcony out-side our master bedroom, we look down onto Piazza San Fran-cesco di Paola and, to our left, the little church of the same name. Next to it is the narrow road that climbs sharply to Bellosguardo and the American School, which the three children toil up to daily. Two minutes' walk down Via Villani—and I take personal pleasure in walking along the street named for the great four-teenth-century Tuscan chronicler—brings us to a bus stop, whence, in less than ten minutes, we can be conveyed into the heart of the city.

So we are situated in one of those happy Florentine topograph-ical settings where city and countryside gently meet and modulate into one another, where streets yield to orchards and palazzi to villas and farmhouses. Town and country are on wonderfully

View of Florence from the villa

VILLA SAN FRANCESCO DI PAOLA

The villa, front view   The loggia

good aesthetic terms here; and both the urban and the rural part of me are being not only responded to, but responded to simultaneously, in almost the same moment of perception. Elsewhere I have normally experienced either an indifference or a positive hostility between these two elements. To get back from my Yale office to our home in the Connecticut hills, a drive of twenty-five minutes, I pass through an uninspiring portion of midtown New Haven (the best of the town is not on my route), which is succeeded by a passage of increasing urban dinginess; next, a brief and indecisive suburban sprawl; and then, in scarcely more than a few hundred yards, I am in thickly wooded hills; a rural composition (and on a bracing fall afternoon, the scene is glorious) which has nothing to do with the patternless urban area I have left behind.

But about Florence, I mustn't exaggerate. It too has acquired its suburban sprawl, particularly where it bulges westward on the north side of the river—an interminable and hideously congested area that appears the uglier by contrast with the center of the city and with the graceful green hills and low-lying mountains which the suburbia sprawls toward. A distinction between town and country was once marked by the ancient circuit of walls, before that circuit was torn down a century ago; and it was this distinction (as I think about it) that paradoxically made possible the harmonious interplay of the two. All this has vanished in the blur and confusion of the northern peripheries. Our part of Florence, though, the Oltrarno, has retained the traditional harmony, that mutually enhancing awareness, between the elements.

> We tell you, tapping on our brows,
> The story as it should be,—
> As if the story of a house
> Were told or ever could be.

It is the narrator's voice speaking, in Edwin Arlington Robinson's poem "Eros Turannos." The story of this house—in the double meaning of a building and a family—is eminently worth telling, though Robinson's speaker may be right in saying that the whole story is never accessible. Our host, Harry Brewster, has set himself to write the history of Villa San Francesco di Paola and its occupants, in a yet unpublished manuscript called *The Cosmopolites*, and I have been reading it with fascination.* What strikes me is the extent to which the story touches revealingly on the social and cultural history of Florence in several epochs, and on one or two key moments of early and later *American* history as well; and how a play of radical opposites is apparent in both dimensions.

We begin with the saint himself, Francesco, anything but Florentine, having been born (1416) and bred in the little village of Paola in Calabria. He grew into a man of undoubted holiness, but also of great energy and practical wisdom, and, evidently, of very considerable charm. It was about 1440 that he founded a mendicant order known as the *minimi* (the least), to distinguish its *frati* from those of the order begun by the other Francesco, Saint Francis of Assisi, and known as the *frati minori* (the less). The *minimi* spread northward across Italy, as Francesco planted new cells in Naples, Rome, and other centers. During a month in Rome in 1483, Francesco encountered Lorenzo il Magnifico, who was in the papal city on a diplomatic errand. Lorenzo, after paying homage to the man whose spiritual accomplishments were known through the whole of Europe, presented his seven-year-old son, saying to the lad: "Giovannino, kiss your hand to the saint." Francesco embraced the boy and observed to him smiling: "Yes, I shall be a saint when you are the Pope." This remark, which comes down to us from Cardinal Bellarmin, has been taken to be not amiably ironic but prophetic; for in 1513, Giovanni de' Medici was elected Pope with the name of Leo X.

Francesco di Paola spent much of his later life—he died, finally, at the age of ninety-one—in the court of Louis XI, the most Christian and spiderlike king of France, whose confessor he be-

---

* *The Cosmopolites* was finally published in April 1994 by the English firm of Michael Russell. This deeply engrossing, trenchantly written narrative focuses almost entirely on the story of the interweaving families from the 1870s onward, as its subtitle—*A Nineteenth Century Family Drama*—indicates.

came and over whom he wielded a strong and generally good influence. During Louis's last days in the chateau at Tours, Francesco helped ward off the astrologers and other soothsayers who sought to keep the dying king in a state of nervous—and for them, profitable—alarm.

The *minimi* arrived in Florence in 1583. They came at the invitation of Bianca Cappello, the Grand Duchess of Tuscany, who was exercising such piety as she possessed in the hope of atoning for a string of questionable episodes in her earlier life. This attractive and ambitious woman was one of the most colorful characters in the gallery of adventurers, geniuses, and eccentrics in sixteenth-century Italy. I have taken much instructive enjoyment in piecing her career together in the past days: it combines so many aspects of the appealingly mixed, sometimes appallingly mixed and contradictory, configuration of old Florence. There is high melodrama—grand and illicit passions leading to extreme and carefully plotted violence—but there are other, very different but not less representative ingredients.

Bianca Cappello was the daughter of an illustrious and patrician Venetian family. In her sixteenth year (she was born in 1542), she fell in love with a young Florentine clerk named Piero Bonaventuri, who had come to Venice as errand boy for a Florentine banking house. Bianca became Piero's mistress; and when she found that she was pregnant by him, the two fled to Florence, where they were married in the church of San Marco. The fury of the elder Cappello—particularly at his daughter's marrying so far beneath herself—was boundless. He had the Venetian court pass a sentence of death on Piero, and through the Venetian ambassador to Florence he demanded that Duke Cosimo I return Bianca at once to her native city. Cosimo summoned the pair to a hearing; Piero seems to have been capable of no more than a whining plea for mercy, but Bianca defended herself with such spirit that Cosimo agreed to let them stay in Florence, providing they lived there quietly and unobtrusively.

The injunctions were not long adhered to. It may have been at the hearing that Francesco, the older son of Duke Cosimo, first laid eyes on Bianca. In any event, he soon felt a strong attraction to her; Bianca was fairly quick to respond, and in a short course of time, she became Francesco's mistress. Her husband, Piero, took the liaison complacently enough, enjoying the perquisites that went with it: a position as court scribe; a villa and farms in the country; and, on Via Maggio, just below Ponte Santa Trinità, a small palazzo elegantly remodeled and embellished by Bernardo Buontalenti. The Florentine populace looked on with its usual caustic eye; Piero became known in the city as "the golden cuckold."

Bianca's lover, Francesco de' Medici, was an individual of varied parts. He was a robust, dark-bearded, and soberly handsome man, undeniably intelligent and with a certain political acumen. But both before and after his accession, Francesco was far more interested in scientific experiment than in the art of government, and as a scientist he was a sort of erratic genius. He discovered how to adapt the Chinese method for working with porcelain, and how to make vases from rock crystal; he also invented a bombshell capable of large-scale destruction ("grandiose mortality" was a contemporary phrase for it). At the same time, the future Duke Francesco I was a most energetic libertine. Not only did he move tirelessly from one mistress to another; the author of a solidly grounded book on Florence, Edward Hutton, tells us flatly that Francesco had sexual relations with his sisters (of whom there were four) and his sisters-in-law (two). A taste for incest may in fact have been a paternal legacy. Giorgio Vasari, it is said, was at work on a scaffold painting the ceiling in one of the Palazzo Vecchio bedrooms one hot summer afternoon, when Cosimo's daughter Isabella came in, lay down, and fell asleep. Duke Cosimo then entered, and Vasari heard a sudden, single, fearful scream from the bed; and then silence. Vasari remained hidden.

To strengthen his erotic performances, Francesco, in his laboratory near the church of San Marco, invented an *elixir vitae*: a powerful aphrodisiac made of oil of vitriol. It is somehow typical of Renaissance Florence that the inventor of the most effective love potion of the age was named after Saint Francis of Assisi. Francesco's mother, the devout and beautiful Eleonora of Toledo

Duke Francesco I   Bianca Cappello

(of whom we heard mention in the previous chapter), had visited the monastery of La Verna in the Casentino, where Saint Francis received the stigmata in 1224. She prayed to the saint that she be blessed with a male child and promised, if she were, to name the infant Francesco.

In 1565, about a year after Bianca and Francesco became lovers (they were both in their early twenties), the young princeling was married by parental fiat to Giovanna (Joan) of Austria, the niece of the former Emperor Charles V and the sister of the present Emperor Maximilian II. For the Medicis, the match was politically the most advantageous yet arranged. The wedding was an extraordinarily sumptuous affair; Vasari decorated the courtyard of Palazzo Vecchio in stucco and gold, and his pupils painted views of a series of Austrian towns, to make the new Grand Duchess feel at home; the festivities lasted a week. But the marriage was a dismal failure. Giovanna, a plain-faced girl, felt humiliated at being joined—and in a region that only made her homesick— with a descendant of bankers. She felt the more so when she discovered, early on, that her husband was entirely dedicated to his Venetian mistress, Madonna Bonaventuri, and, despite her wifely protests, would continue to be so. Bianca Cappello even had the audacity to have herself made one of the Grand Duchess's ladies-in-waiting, but Giovanna quickly expelled her.

At a later date, Bianca planned and carried out a complicated and astonishing piece of deception, a Renaissance stratagem if ever there was one. Giovanna and Francesco had been married eleven years by this time, and the *Granduchessa* had produced nothing but girls, five of them; Bianca herself had had only the one child, also a girl, by her husband, and no issue of her lover. She hit upon an elaborate scheme, drawing into it a few of her most trusted servants and a bemused doctor from Bologna named Grazi. Bianca informed Francesco that she was pregnant, and the Grand Duke, seriously concerned about the succession, was jubilant at the news. The servants meanwhile rounded up three pregnant unmarried girls of the Florentine working class—Bianca was hedging her bets in the belief that at least one of the girls would beget a healthy boy child. The girls were told that a Florentine noblewoman wanted a wet nurse for her own child, shortly to be born. Bianca simulated advancing pregnancy, fattening her already statuesque figure by eating prodigiously, and keeping Francesco at a distance. In late August 1576, one of the girls, a certain Lucia, gave birth to a splendid baby boy; the infant was immediately taken from her and declared to be dead; he was then carried with utmost secrecy at night to the palazzo where Bianca was living. Bianca put on a great show of agonizing birth pangs; Francesco flew to her side and threatened to ruin the game by calling in his own physician. His mistress managed to shoo him out long enough for her maid to smuggle Lucia's child into the bedroom. When Francesco came back in, he was overjoyed to find the baby in Bianca's arms, and he agreed to call it Don Antonio de' Medici, as Bianca desired. Lucia nursed the child, thinking, of course, that it was Bianca's; but the whole truth eventually came out when Grazi, the doctor, made a deathbed confession, persuading Lucia to tell what she knew of the enterprise. Francesco was forced to disavow the child.

Piero Bonaventuri, in the interim, had been behaving in an increasingly profligate and reckless manner. He took to himself a series of mistresses and bragged all over town about his erotic achievements. The last of the series was a widow named Cassandra de' Ricci, known everywhere to have been a former companion of Francesco before the arrival of Bianca Cappello. Piero made loud public claims that he had finally revenged himself on the man who had ruined his marriage. One evening, as Piero was returning home, he was set upon, near Ponte Santa Trinità, by a group of cutthroats, and next morning his corpse was found riddled with knife wounds. At a proper moment, Grand Duke Francesco was quite willing to admit openly that he had organized the assassination (the actual murderers, whose identities were well known, were never arrested).

It was a "crime of honor," and crimes of honor were the fashion in sixteenth-century Tuscany, especially in the Medici family. The unfortunate Isabella de' Medici—who had been violated first by her father and then by her brother, but who was nonetheless refined, brilliant, and beautiful, and looked on as "the star of the house of Medici"—was strangled to death by her brutish husband, Paolo Giordano Orsini, allegedly for having entered into a liaison with her cousin, to whom she had written compromising letters. It appears, in fact, that Paolo murdered Isabella at the behest of his mistress, a creature of sophisticated ferocity worthy of the later pages of Sade. Only a few days before the death of Isabella, her brother Piero, youngest of the three surviving sons of Cosimo I, put to death *his* wife, Eleanora, by strangulation, on the charge of having an affair with a Florentine cavalier.

Grand Duchess Giovanna died in 1579. She had finally succeeded in giving her husband a boy, a sickly child called Filippo, and was again pregnant when she died as the result of a fall. It was instantly rumored that Francesco had poisoned her, as it had been said that Cosimo I personally murdered one of his daughters and two of his sons; such stories, although most probably apocryphal, suggest both the imagination of the age and the popular estimate of the reigning Medici. Within a few months after Giovanna's death, Francesco and Bianca Cappello were married, first secretly and then amid splendor in the church of San Lorenzo. To the horde of scabrous songs and pamphlets that had long circulated through Florence about the couple, there was now added the following ditty:

> *Il Granduca di Toscana*
> *ha sposato una puttana*
> *gentildonna Veneziana.*

The vigorous rhythms and stabbing rhymes of the original cannot be recovered in translation: "The Grand Duke of Tuscany / has married a whore / a Venetian gentlewoman" (the last word no doubt uttered with a snarl).

What is surprising about the relationship between Bianca Cappello and Francesco de' Medici is that, though each of them was an inordinately sensual person, there is no evidence that either was unfaithful once their liaison began. They remained passionately in love for eighteen years, and their marriage seems to have been an unusually close one. It was not long-lived, however. In October 1582 there was a large gathering in the Medici villa at Poggio a Caiano, a few miles west of Florence. The occasion was an attempt on Francesco's part at reconciliation with his younger brother, Cardinal Ferdinando de' Medici. The two had been bitterly hostile for years; but Giovanna's child Filippo had died at the age of five, Francesco had no male heir, and Bianca was clearly unproductive. It was probable that Ferdinando would succeed to the dukedom. There was banqueting, hunting, and gala celebrations. But then, one evening, Francesco was stricken with chills and fevers. Five days later, with Francesco still lingering on but growing weaker, Bianca too came down with a fever. Francesco died and, within eleven hours, Bianca followed him, murmuring at the end: "My desire is to die alongside my lord."

The Florentines, naturally, refused to believe for a minute that the deaths were coincidental; and I can't accept it either. One rumor was that Francesco, now forty-six, sought to revive his flagging sexual energies by having recourse to his *elixir vitae* and that the dose was too strong and killed him. A more popular theory at the time was that Bianca had prepared a poisoned tart with which to exterminate her brother-in-law, the Cardinal, who detested her. By a frightful mistake, Grand Duke Francesco ate the tart, and when Bianca saw what she had done, she made another poisoned sweet and swallowed it. "Malarial fever" is the common modern explanation of the two deaths; but I find it unconvincing. Edward Hutton, writing at a somewhat earlier day, says flatly that Francesco and Bianca "died of poison." I feel here the pressure of literary form: the drama of Bianca Cappello simply cannot come to its close with some meaningless country sickness. The denouement must, by all the laws of drama, be violent and swift, and the consequence of tragic error.*

This, then, was the high-born and adventurous lady, Bianca Cappello, who cordially invited monks in the order of the holy man from Calabria to come to Florence, and who helped see to their having a place for residence and worship. She persuaded her husband, Francesco, to provide the monks with a vast sum of money with which to build a church and a *convento*, or friary; and at the same time, for the same purpose, the order was given a sizable property on the Bellosguardo hillside by Alessandro Strozzi, of the famous Florentine family. (Strozzi had just returned from the Far East, bringing with him, it is said, the first artichoke to be seen in Florence: the *carciofo*, which, fried along with chicken or even potatoes, is now one of the tastiest of Tuscan dishes.) Like other wealthy Florentines, Strozzi had acquired an estate on the Oltrarno slopes; and from this, he bequeathed to the *minimi* several fields and orchards, some houses, and the site of the

---

* 1993 note: A play about Bianca Cappello, called *The Venetian*, was written by Clifford Bax in 1931 (there had been a German play and other German retellings in the late-eighteenth century). *The Venetian* was performed in London, with Margaret Rawlings as Bianca and Wilfred Walter as Duke Francesco; Cardinal Ferdinando, the most interesting characterization in the drama, was played by the thirty-one-year-old Alistair Sim.

The Venetian follows the established version of things, the author claiming that "there is very little fiction in the events of this play." The admitted purpose is to vindicate the reputation of Bianca, who had been vilified "for three and a half centuries," but who was "in reality, a fine, honest character." In the climactic scene, Bianca, driven to distraction, poisons the drink of wine meant for Ferdinando; Francesco drinks it by mistake, and Bianca, seeing what has happened, swallows the remains and dies herself.

former oratory of San Donato a Scopato. Leonardo da Vinci had been commissioned to paint a picture for the oratory; it is the unfinished but fabulous *Adoration of the Magi* in the Uffizi. During the siege of Florence in 1529, the monks of San Donato were hurriedly evacuated just before the artillery of Charles V blasted the oratory to ruins.

By the mid-1590s, the church was ready, though renovations continued well into the seventeenth century; they are by Gherardo Silvani (1579–1675), an extremely gifted and prolific, and long-lived, baroque follower of Buontalenti.* Of the friary, or place of residence, only one wing was completed, in 1593. But it achieved a certain spaciousness and it is, in fact, the building we have been living in since September. On our floor, as of 1600, monks' cells opened to right and left off the 150-foot gallery that did and does run the entire length of the building; as now high-ceilinged rooms open off it. In the early-seventeenth century, the back of the house, facing west, was embellished by Silvani with cornices and newly designed windows. Of the cloister originally planned below, one side was finished, an elegant and airy loggia of slim gray sandstone columns, well-spaced arches, and a vaulted ceiling; the whole opening onto a grassy space. A statue of San Francesco himself was commissioned by Grand Duke Cosimo III in 1695, and placed outside the church on a pedestal so high that Cosimo could see it and perhaps be inspired by it from his windows in Palazzo Pitti. The statue, moved inside the villa walls and flanked by cypresses, now looms beneath our bedroom windows.

Generations of monks lived agreeably in the San Francesco convent for two centuries, becoming rather too well known for their ready hospitality. In 1783, during the antimonastic period, the order of the *minimi* was everywhere suppressed. This building became a chancery for public records, and then, in almost total disarray, a place inhabited by local paupers. It was put up for

---

* Among the paintings in the church of San Francesco di Paola is one by an English artist, showing the meeting in Rome between San Francesco and Lorenzo il Magnifico. Not long since, a painting by Taddeo Gaddi was discovered beneath another valueless one. It was sent on a world tour and then returned to its proper place.

sale in 1874, and was bought by a young sculptor named Adolph von Hildebrand for about 30,000 lire.

December 3, 1975

That was a long entry, written at intervals over a festive holiday weekend. I needed to let a few days go by before turning from the story of the Renaissance friary to the story of the several families—English, German, and American—that have interwoven in the ancestral background of our host and hostess, Harry Brewster and his sister Clotilde Brewster Peploe. Clotilde is technically our *padrona*; Harry owns the apartment on the floor above (which is occupied by another American family).

The Brewster story goes back to an Elizabethan country squire, William Brewster, whose career was almost cut short when his mentor, Sir William Davison, became entangled in the court intrigues following the execution of Mary, Queen of Scots. Brewster himself was imprisoned for a while, before being allowed to return to his native village of Scrooby, in Yorkshire. He began to attend and then to organize meetings of the Separatists and dissidents among the left-wingers of the Church of England (like Theodore Parker in Lowell's *A Fable for Critics*, "from the orthodox kind of dissent, [they] dissented"). One of the Separatists, William Bradford, came over from his own nearby village of Austerfield to enter the Brewster household and take part in the prayers and discussions being held there; he was treated as a member of the family. With Bradford, Edward Winslow, Captain Miles Standish, John Alden, and the others, Brewster sailed on the *Mayflower* in September 1620. He brought with him his wife, Mary, and their two sons, the latter being named Love and Wrestling; other Brewster children, so Bradford reported in his book *Of Plymouth Plantation*, were left in England and came over afterwards. For four years, until his death, William Brewster served the plantation as Ruling Elder, or senior adviser on religious matters, to Governor Bradford.

There followed a hundred and fifty years of what Harry Brewster calls "quiescent vegetation"—the family seems to have taken up farming in Connecticut—until one Seabury Brewster emerged as a Minute Man in the Revolution. He was the husband, first, of Sakky Bradford, a descendant of the governor, and then of Fanny Starr. It was their son Christopher Starr Brewster who reversed the family's geographical history by going back to Europe and settling there in 1830. As I understand it, no Brewster in Christopher's direct line has been born in the United States.*

Christopher Starr came to Europe with the ambition of making his fortune as a dentist, and he was entirely successful. He spent some years in St. Petersburg as dental physician to the Czar, who knighted him. In Paris, where he arrived around 1840, he became Louis Philippe's personal dentist, and later ministered to the decaying teeth of Louis Napoleon. Christopher Starr married an English woman, Anna Bennet; their only son, Henry, born in 1850, grew to be the most distinguished figure in this phase of the family saga. Christopher died in Versailles amid the confusion and discomfort of the Prussian occupation.

To the Anglo-American strain in the Brewster blood, young Henry Brewster—or H.B. as he was called—added a German component in 1873, by marrying Julia von Stockhausen, the older daughter of the Hanoverian ambassador to Versailles. Baron von Stockhausen was himself a grandson of Baron (or Freiherr) von Munchausen, that eighteenth-century spinner of tales, and an early admirer and friend of Frédéric Chopin and George Sand. Music is a major element in this portion of the narrative. Julia's sister Lisl, a Rubens beauty who was married to a mediocre Austrian composer, became the closest "spiritual companion" of Johannes Brahms—their correspondence has been published—and a strong supporter of Brahms in the long musical war with the Wagnerites.

H.B. and Julia removed from Paris to Florence, where they established themselves in a spacious apartment on Via dei Bardi, near the river and the Ponte Vecchio. It was during the first year of their marriage that they came to know the already accomplished twenty-five-year-old sculptor Adolph von Hildebrand, the friendship arising via the young woman in an adjacent *pensione*, Irene

* Yale President Kingman Brewster was a descendant in the *indirect* line.

Schauffelen, whom Hildebrand was courting strenuously. Irene, who was the wretchedly unhappy wife of a Tübingen student, gradually yielded to Hildebrand's solicitations; a grand passion developed, and when the two were at last able to marry, in 1876, Irene was pregnant.

From my usual place at our dining-room table, I gaze across at a portrait of Irene Schauffelen at the age of fifteen; it hangs above the tallboy containing china and cutlery. The dining room is rather dim; but I have grown familiar with the charming round face, and the eyes in which intelligence mixes with humor; the well-formed bosom; the plump forearms. In her right hand, which stretches across her breast, Irene is holding one of the books she was constantly reading. There is an air about her of romantic impulsiveness, a quality which would express itself in her mature life.

The newly named Villa San Francesco di Paola, into which Hildebrand accompanied his wife, had been extensively remodeled by him: indeed, restored to architectural life after its age of neglect and decay. The essential structure of the old Renaissance friary, however, was unchanged. Hildebrand made the important decision to keep the long galleries on the second and third floor (American); but on either side of our gallery (as in the one on the floor above), walls were torn down and groups of cells converted into large individual rooms. Hildebrand raised the ceiling of his studio many feet; this, for the year, is my study, the room I am now writing in; it must be twenty-five feet high and is long and broad in proportion. Plumbing and, with the passage of time, central heating were installed. But the essential design is retained: a long walkway giving onto a series of enclosures. There is, in fact, a sort of urban cast to the apartment, and it is the only place I have ever lived in where I can literally go for a walk.

In the later 1870s and for two decades thereafter, Villa San Francesco di Paola was one of the most celebrated salons in Europe. Great musicians were particularly in evidence. Franz Liszt was to be found there, sometimes giving virtuoso performances on the piano in the *salotto* where our family forgathers of an evening. Richard Wagner, whom Hildebrand detested, was a frequent visitor, as was Cosima von Bülow, whom everyone loved. There were guests from other walks of life. William Gladstone came up for a short stay, with his daughter; Henry James, a tenant for several weeks in a roomy mansion on the Bellosguardo hilltop (and writing the novella *The Aspern Papers*), paid several visits, and was heard to say that Hildebrand was the most interesting male he had met during this Florentine stay. German royalty turned up in increasing numbers. Hildebrand was moving toward an apogee of success and fame, and commissions were pouring in from Italy, England, and, above all, from Germany; his Wittelsbrachbrunn in Munich remains today the largest fountain in Germany, and is regarded as a masterpiece.

Hildebrand's reputation was already declining at the time of his death in 1921, when neoclassicism went decidedly out of fashion. But as artistic taste circles about in its familiar way, his star seems again to be gaining ascendance; he appears to be assuming the significance in German art history that Rodin holds in France. It is being realized (I am told) that, if his work is in a degree classical, it is not so in the openly, if sometimes effectively, derivative manner of the Florentine Americans Hiram Power and Horatio Greenough. His statues and monuments, someone has said, are fundamentally ways of grappling "by means of form with the intensity, vitality and power of nature"—well-chosen words, since intensity, vitality, and power were also characteristics of Hildebrand the man. His remarkable little book *The Problem of Form* has evidently exerted considerable influence over the years—among others, on the English art critic and theorist Herbert Read.

December 8, 1975

For some time, Henry and Julia (von Stockhausen) Brewster came up regularly from the Via de' Bardi home to Villa San Francesco, and were the Hildebrands' closest friends in Florence. There then occurred a long break, due in part to the lively intrusion into all their lives of Ethel Smyth, an attractive young English woman in her mid-twenties and a musician of immense promise. She would go on to become the most distinguished and prolific female composer England has produced; she composed operas (serious, romantic, and comic—*The Wreckers* is probably the best known), chamber music, and songs; and for the suffragette movement, in which she was exceedingly and conspicuously active, she wrote *The March of the Women* (in 1911). Upon her arrival in Florence, Miss Smyth first aimed her attention at Adolph von Hildebrand, her own exuberance, joie de vivre, and wit matching his. Hildebrand began to do a bust of her, and after each sitting, as they made their way up the stone steps to lunch, Miss Smyth managed to trip and fall backwards, and Hildebrand was observed carrying her in his arms the remaining distance. Irene von Hildebrand enlisted a couple of her daughters in the task of hacking the half-finished bust to pieces, and the relationship came to an end. Ethel now turned her attention to Hildebrand's friend H.B., and they enjoyed a long association, consummated somewhat prosaically in 1895, the year that Julia Brewster died. (Much later, Ethel Smyth would become an intimate friend of Virginia Woolf.)

H.B., meanwhile, had been at work on several strange, occasionally downright baffling, yet intellectually muscular writings, which may best be called philosophical dialogues. And here the unfolding story touches upon some of my own perennial interests. H.B.'s *Anarchy and Law* (1886), for example, with its tolerant but elaborately worked out skepticism of *all* hard intellectual positions, had a strong effect on William James; traces of Brewster's antidoctrinal doctrine can be found in James's *Pragmatism* and *A Pluralistic Universe*. There was an even more vigorous thrust of mind in Brewster's *The Prison* (1891), where H.B. put forward ideas that paralleled—and maybe derived from—some of the themes in the writings of Henry James, Sr., and that first seized my imagination when I began to study the elder James many years ago. The central theme is that of identity; and when Brewster wrote that "the original quest for identity becomes a quest for freedom from the shackles of the ego," and again that "the ego must be dismantled if freedom is to be achieved," he might have been restating Henry James, Sr.'s insistence on the demolition of the self en route to true identity. And when Brewster argued that "life everlasting is not of the self but of the cosmos . . . wherein personality participates by bursting its bonds," he was virtually echoing the Jamesian image—and however strangely worded, it is enormously suggestive—of the sovereign individual taking part in a mystical, social entity he called "the divine-natural humanity."

It is not surprising, anyhow, that one of H.B.'s closest English-speaking friends in the 1890s and later was the younger Henry James. The novelist and the philosopher lunched, dined, and talked together once a fortnight during H.B.'s frequent, long visits to London; and James came often to stay with Brewster in Rome, after H.B. had settled there. Brewster's Roman residence, to James's enjoyment, was Palazzo Mattei, the original of Palazzo Roccanera in James's *The Portrait of a Lady* (written, of course, years before the two met), in which James, through the figure of Gilbert Osmond, gave his most chilling portrait of the emprisoning ego. After H.B.'s death, in 1908, at the age of fifty-seven, James wrote a friend:

I am haunted by the tragic image of our fine inscrutable Brewster, who hadn't really half done with the exquisite mystification he somehow made of life—or perhaps received from it! . . . [I] feel him such a handsome questioning cosmopolitan ghost.

In *Notes of a Son and Brother* a few years later, James reflected back on "a countryman, now no more, who spent most of his life in Italy, and who remains for me, with his accomplishments, his distinctions, his extraordinary play of mind and his early and too tragic death, the clearest case of 'cosmopolitan culture' I was to have known." The phrase there in James's quotation marks is something I want to come back to.

In the early 1900s, Christopher Brewster, the younger child of H.B. and Julia, married Elizabeth (Lisl) von Hildebrand, the next to oldest of the five daughters of Adolph and Irene, and a landscape painter of high talent; her Tuscan scenes, at once ingratiating and strong, adorn the walls of the apartment. The children of Christopher and Lisl are our host and hostess, Harry Brewster

and Clotilde Peploe; and the two families, Hildebrand and Brewster, are now one. The cosmopolitan and creative traditions of
the house carry forward. Harry is the author of a brilliant and
original set of interwoven short stories, *Where the Trout Sing*,
which has been honored in high literary places in both England
and America. The stories have to do centrally, astonishingly, and
yet encouragingly in the 1970s, with the spiritual and erotic relationships between humans and divinities, mostly in beautifully
evoked Greek settings. In addition to the history of the Villa San
Francesco and its occupants, Harry has nearly completed a novel,
set in the villa and entitled *The Perennial Encounter*.* Clotilde, who
has a dashing and delightful personality (implicit in her nick-
name Clo-Clo), is, like her mother, a notably gifted painter of
landscapes; she divides her time between Florence, London, and
Greece.

I find I have one last thought to write down, and conveniently
enough it brings me back to Florence. This city, more than any
other I personally have known, feeds the cosmopolitan personality. In part this is because Florence has hosted a cosmopolitan
community for upward of two hundred years; the roster of foreign
residents at any time since about 1770 is dazzling. But Florence
encourages the cosmopolitan temper because it first allows for
and supports the national and the individual identity. How our
daughter Sophie smiles when she tells of hearing herself and
several other co-national school friends referred to in the street
Italian of the Florentines as *"Quesdi Amerigani!"* with amusement,
tolerance, and exasperation, even as one hears the exclamation
"Quesdi Frangiesi!," or whatever.

The continuous journal of 1975 came to an end at this point.
There were other intermittent entries during the villa year, some
offering random thoughts on Florence and the difficulty of understanding it, others describing various excursions into Tuscany.
The Tuscan notations could imaginably be drawn upon for some

* This novel seems to have been permanently set aside.

future occasion. For present purposes, a bit of summarizing might be in order.

The main aim of these outings, in addition to simple enjoyment, was to enlarge our sense of Florence by getting better acquainted with its regional neighbors—on the principle of "What do we know of Florence, that only Florence know?" On all our ventures, we were conducted by Marcello Chirici—youthful (or ageless), superlative, and *Tuscanissimo* guide and cohort—driving his own car and supplying us with nuggets of information and quizzical responses along the route. In out-of-the-way little towns, Marcello would locate the best trattoria in the area through the easy technique of stopping to ask advice of a well-dressed fat man or a priest.

With Marcello at the wheel, we made the ritual fifty-mile trip to Pisa several times; and we made the run down to ever-enthralling Siena (forty-odd miles) periodically. To slightly less familiar Lucca (forty-five miles due west, and one hour on the autostrada), we went more than once: making a tour of the fifteenth- and sixteenth-century walls that enclose the town and peering up at the towers and campaniles; inspecting the *tempietto* in the Duomo that houses a treasured crucifix known as *Il Volto Santo* ("The Holy Face"), with its larger-than-lifesize figure said to have been completed by an angel when the human carver (Nicodemus) fell asleep; strolling about the piazza with its Napoleonic associations; and paying a visit to our friends, the cultivated English art historians Hugh Honour and John Fleming, at their villa in Tafori.*

At other times, I had us taken to sources of wartime memories: Rufina, a little north of Pontassieve, where I planted our mobile headquarters in the late summer of 1944; and the mountain village of San Marcello Pistoiese, to the northwest, where we moved at Christmas in the same year, and from which I launched many a

---

* Messrs. Honour and Fleming coedited the Penguin *Dictionary of Architecture* (most recent edition, 1991) and *A World of Art* (1982, 1991). Hugh Honour is the author of *The Companion Guide to Venice* (1965, and perhaps the best in that fine series), *Romanticism* (1979), and *The Image of the Black in Western Art, from the American Revolution to World War I*, a prize-winning work of 1990.

small mission on winter nights. The road to Pistoia led through the city of Prato, Florence's most bustling suburb. It is sometimes (by unkindly English visitors) called the Manchester of Tuscany; but for all its industrial display, it also offers marvelous frescoes by Fra Filippo Lippi, and a pulpit, outside the Duomo, that is one of Donatello's happiest creations. In Prato as well, in the Piazza del Commune, is an imposing statue of the hugely successful and philanthropic fourteenth-century merchant Francesco di Marco Datini, about whom Iris Origo wrote a classic historical study, *The Merchant of Prato*. And attention must also be paid to the famous *biscotti di Prato*, which, with *vin santo*, comprise a favorite after-dinner Tuscan delight.

We made numerous short forays: among them, to Vinci, Pescia, and Collodi, westward from Florence and each with its particular appeal; the birthplace of Leonardo; the town where our valued friend the literary historian and translator Rolando Anzilotti was mayor; the town which gave its name to the author of *The Adventures of Pinocchio*. We visited Badia a Settimo, Malmantile ("bad table cloth"—no one knows why), Montelupo, and Empoli; and we climbed to the hill town of San Miniato al Tedesco, so called because for more than two centuries it was the chief stronghold in the lower Arno valley of the Imperial German forces.

An important dimension of our ongoing search into the Florentine story consisted of recurring visits to Etruria, the land of the ancient Etruscans, who came across the water to central Italy, most likely from Asia Minor, sometime in the ninth century B.C. and were the overlords of Tuscany for five centuries (the Romans spoke of them as *Tusci*, from which the name Tuscany derived). An early trip into Etruria, in October 1975, brought us to the lofty town of Cortona, about seventy-five miles southeast of Florence; a place of heart-restoring tranquillity, especially in its miniature Piazza del Duomo, where one can sit and look over a waist-high rampart at the dark plain of the Chianti river valley and, to the right, at the hills, covered with gray olive trees, rising above the Val d'Arno. Cortona has its medieval and Renaissance elements, but we were more interested in the Etruscan Museum, and its much-vaunted Etruscan Bronze Lamp, locally built and dating from the fifth century B.C. Rated as the most famous lamp of its kind in the world, it is two feet in diameter, weighs 125 pounds, and is densely ornamented with crouching satyrs, open-faced sirens, and dolphins leaping in the waves.

From Cortona, we made the short drive south past Lake Trasimeno—where Hannibal destroyed the Roman legions under Consul Flaminius, who went to his grave crying, "Hannibal, Hannibal, give me back my legions!"—to Chiusi. As Clusium, in Latin, Chiusi had claims to being the greatest of the twelve Etruscan city-states, which, in the sixth century B.C., formed a loose —self-defeatingly loose and uncoordinated—confederacy. It was the home or kingdom of Lars Porsena, the Tarquin warrior who, legendarily, terrorized Rome in his finally unsuccessful effort to restore Tarquinius Superbus as its ruler.* The Chiusi museum holds wonderful examples of Etruscan art from the ninth century B.C. onward: terra-cotta funerary urns bearing the ashes of the deceased from the Villanovan (which may in fact be *pre*-Etruscan) period; bronze urns from the seventh and sixth centuries; and, from the third century B.C. (probably), an alabaster urn showing violent phases of the Oresteia myth—Agamemnon being slaughtered by Aegisthus, Clytemnestra falling beneath the blows of her son Orestes—and above all the carnage, the occupant of the urn, lying back comfortably, cup in hand, wearing a necklace. There are also, on other urns, charming scenes from everyday life: a bridegroom receiving his bride in his little house, for example, while flutists play outside.

After Chiusi came Montepulciano, at the top of another steep climb and spread out, crowdedly, along a crest. This once heavily fortified town was founded by Lars Porsena, they say, and it has

---

* The whole saga of the Tarquins is shrouded in legend, including the story of Tarquinius Priscus, the fifth Tarquin king of Rome in the late seventh and sixth centuries B.C., and that of his grandson Tarquinius Superbus the Proud, who ruled over Rome until his son Sextus committed rape upon the virtuous Lucretia—at news of which the Roman people rose and expelled the Tarquins once and for all. Lars Porsena's heroics are recorded in Thomas Babington Macaulay's *Lays of Ancient Rome;* and as we wandered through Chiusi that autumn day, I found myself remembering some lines from Macaulay which I had been required to learn at an English school in Switzerland years before: "Lars Porsena of Clusium / By the Nine Gods he swore . . ."

a diversity of appeal, beginning with Via Roma, which wriggles its way, narrow and clean, across the whole extent of the place. Here was the birthplace of the humanist and poet Poliziano, a figure of restless and uncertain genius whom Lorenzo il Magnifico took on as his son's tutor and who became Lorenzo's trusted companion (he was beside il Magnifico in the Duomo that Sunday in 1487 when the Pazzi conspirators tried to assassinate Lorenzo and did murder his brother Giuliano). But our visit to Montepulciano had, truth to tell, different aims. After consulting a stout middle-aged burger, Marcello took us to Trattoria Dina, just inside the old stone gate which is the entrance to the town proper. In this cheerful and obviously prospering restaurant, we had ravioli with cream sauce, followed by *bistecca fiorentina*, a celebrated Tuscan offering which consists of a thick T-bone steak, rubbed with crushed peppercorns and broiled over a charcoal fire, then moistened lightly with olive oil.* Accompanying the *bistecca fiorentina* —and this is what we were really after—was a bottle of *vino nobile*, the proudest feature of Montepulciano, a fine, heady, strongly flavored red wine, well-aged (five years at least). After lunch, we dropped by the *cantina* near the Piazza del Duomo, chatted with the proprietor, savored the wines, and bought six bottles of *vino nobile* (or simply *vin*, without an *o*, as it is sometimes Tuscanized). We promised the proprietor faithfully (he evidently urged this upon all visiting Americans) not to keep the wine in our refrigerator, which, of course, we had never dreamed of doing.

On a later fall morning, Marcello drove us to Volterra, about fifty miles down the *superstrada* to Poggibonsi; then west along a curving, climbing road past Castel di San Gimignano, with far vistas

---

* Marcella Hazan, in the properly named *Classic Italian Cookbook* (1973), notes that "the particular flavor and texture of a *fiorentina* cannot be duplicated with any other meat but that of Tuscan-raised Val di Chiana beef," but that "a fine American beefsteak, prepared the Florentine way, can be spectacularly good." She warns sternly against marinating the steak in oil before broiling (it will make the meat "taste of tallow"), and says that the steak should be salted "on the broiled side as you turn it . . . Moisten it very lightly on both sides with a few drops of olive oil," she concludes, and "serve immediately."

Montepulciano, panorama

Etruscan urn, Chiusi

of a countryside wilder and less fertile than the vine-covered slopes around Florence. Volterra is the handsomest type of walled and fortresslike hill town, poised above the Elsa valley, and with broad views in all directions. It "sees all the world," D. H. Lawrence said of Volterra, in the final chapter of his *Etruscan Places*.*

The "modern," or Tuscan, aspect of the town is seen in the magnificent Piazza dei Signori, containing the main palazzo, which rivals that in the Signoria, and flanked by mostly thirteenth-century buildings of church and state. Of Etruria there is a great deal: parts of the ancient city wall (the Etruscans were great builders of walls, and the Tarquin kings are said to have built the first wall at Rome, six meters high); the enormously thick arched gate, Porta a l'Arco ("a deep old gateway," says Lawrence, "almost a tunnel, with the outer arch facing the desolate country on the skew"); a complex of tombs undergoing endless exploration; the continuing alabaster industry; the Museo Guarnacci. In the Museo are more than six hundred sarcophagi, objects about three feet long and two feet high, with the effigy of the deceased (often a large head and stunted body) reclining above and myriad different scenes portrayed below. Many of them depict the departure for the underworld—on horseback, in a covered wagon, on foot, by sea. Others, and these are the more interesting, show scenes from daily life: a banquet, warriors approaching a gate, the hunt after a boar, prisoners being prepared for sacrifice (arms bound behind them) or being decapitated, a family on the move. The cumulative suggestion is of a rich, rather gracious, ritualized, and highly cultivated form of life, with a decided penchant for the brutal.

The Etruscans were conspicuous, in the centuries of their domination, for an enjoyment of life far beyond that of their contemporaries. And Lawrence makes the telling suggestion that the Etruscans, from what we know about them, are closer to the Italians of the modern age—for which, read the Tuscans—than

* Originally published 1932; published with *Mornings in Mexico*, by Penguin, in 1950; reprinted through 1974.

either race is to the old Romans. One may think of Etruscan characteristics—of joy in life, humor, an attraction to the sensual, sizable powers of creative imagination; with a "craving" (in Lawrence's words) "for symbols and mysteries" and a tolerance for the lethal—going underground beneath the hard-marching, unremittingly serious, and politically minded Romans, only to work back eventually to the surface in Tuscan forms.

As to daily life up at the villa, meanwhile, the most important figure was Giulietta Ceri, the sister of the caretaker of the estate, Piero Ceri. Giulietta was a middle-aged woman with a rather hidden personality; aristocratic of feature (it was possible to suspect a somewhat distinguished ancestry), with a large unwieldy body. She was partly crippled and, as a result, was distinctly bowlegged and walked with an effort. But she walked a lot, especially down the hill to the shrine housing a number of nuns. From these, Giulietta purchased most of the groceries she deployed in preparing our meals; for Giulietta did almost all the cooking, three meals a day, serving them too in the darkly paneled, high-ceilinged dining room. By a report which it was hard to credit, Giulietta also performed as an actress, and to considerable esteem, in the theatricals put on by her friends the nuns.

Other daily shopping was done by Nancy, mostly in the little shops that clustered at the foot of Via Villani: a *macellaio* for meat, an *ortolano* for vegetables, a *pizzicheria* for many small delectables. For the general running of the big assembly of rooms, we had the much-cherished help of Ida Giaccalone, our friend from the Pensione Annalena days. She was married to Tommaso Giaccalone, a brisk and good-natured wine merchant who had come from Sicily to settle in Florence. Ida regularly walked up to the villa from their apartment in Via della Chiesa, near Santo Spirito, and made life cheerier and livelier and often funnier by her presence. We felt at the time—and the feeling was confirmed by a memory-stirring return visit to Villa San Francesco di Paola in December 1992, and a walk down the long, dim, beautifully designed hallway and a look into the rooms giving off of it—that never had we lived in such well-tended luxury.

Every morning, the three children walked up the hill to Bellos-guardo, and what was then called the American School in Florence. It had been founded in Rome, as a tutoring school in English, in 1952, and had evolved into a proper day school before moving to Florence in 1963. Its first site there was on the eastern edge of town, near the river, and it was almost washed out (though with no fatalities) in the flood of 1966. After a period of negotiations, it was able to reestablish itself in the ancient villa attached to the Torre di Bellosguardo. Its first Florentine name was St. Michael's Day School; this changed to American School, and then—as more accurately reflecting the school's student body, staff, atmosphere, and outlook—to the American International School of Florence. The Tower of Bellosguardo belonged, in fact, to the Franchetti family, who leased it, first, to Sarah Lawrence College (for its Tuscan branch), then to the American School. In 1980, Amerigo and Michele Franchetti, returning to their native Florence, decided to open the villa, considerably re-modeled, as a hotel. It now thrives in that capacity as Albergo Torre di Bellosguardo, entertaining guests in exceptionally at-tractive surroundings, with the engaging and courtly Amerigo himself presiding. The school, in the interim, moved one last time, to Bagno a Ripoli, a few kilometers eastward along the Arno, where it occupies a Renaissance villa with a superb arcaded court-yard and a stunning view south into the Tuscan fields.

The Tower of Bellosguardo, which probably dates back to the twelfth century, was acquired sometime in the thirteenth century by the Cavalcanti family. It may have been Guido Cavalcanti, the poet and older friend (he was born in the early 1250s) of Dante, who actually built the villa that incorporates the tower; as it may have been Guido who, gazing down from the hilltop onto the city of Florence, gave the area its name by pronouncing the word *"Bellosguardo!"*—beautiful view, or, closer to the literal, beautiful outlook. The site does offer the most beautiful and comprehensive view of Florence and its enveloping hills that one can find.

Here, too, literary associations accumulate. It was to Guido Cavalcanti that Dante had written his most beguiling lyric—the sonnet that begins

> *Guido, vorrei che tu e Lapo ed io*
> *fossimo presi per incantamento . . .*

It was Dante's fantasy of being swept away by magic with his two friends; in D. G. Rossetti's translation:

> Guido, I wish that Lapo, thou, and I,
> Could be by spells convey'd, as it were now,
> Upon a barque, with all the winds that blow . . .

And it was Guido himself, a cobegetter of the medieval poetic strain known as the *dolce stil nuova*, who—after being exiled from Florence in 1300 and seeing no prospect of ever getting back to the city—wrote the lines

> *Perch'i non spero di tornar giammai*
> *ballatetta, in Toscana,*
> *va' to, leggera e piana,*
> *dritt' alla donna mia . . .*

The first line became more famous, in an English rendering, than the original, when T. S. Eliot adapted and, so to say, spiritualized it at the opening of "Ash Wednesday":

> Because I do not hope to turn again,
> Because I do not hope . . .

Eliot was speaking of a spiritual turn, or conversion, and despaired of it. Cavalcanti, altogether humanistically, was saying to his poem, his little ballad, that because *he* didn't hope to return ever again to Tuscany, the *ballatetta*, soft and gentle, must go in his stead directly to his loved one.

It was thus to the Torre di Cavalcanti, in its first designation, that the three children ascended each weekday morning; sometimes accompanied by the three children, of the same age, of Fred and Meg Licht, two accomplished art historians and intermittent Florentine residents, who occupied a cottage on the Villa San Francesco estate and provided (as they still do) the most enlivening companionship. Our children, as the results would show, received first-class academic training during their several sojourns at the American School, and to this day they speak with grateful pleasure of their teachers: Miss Brooks (Ann Brooks Cerimele), the legendary head of the kindergarten, with her classic English temperament; Miss Lo Tauro who taught third grade, who had warmth and a fine sense of humor, and put up with no nonsense; Mrs. Cantini (Sally Wickham that was), who conducted the fourth grade and was, simply, "great," in the youthful lexicon, treating her young charges as real human individuals and getting remarkable participation from all of them; Mr. Whetsel, bearded and Roman-looking (or Etruscan, according to memory), witty, stimulating, who taught a little of everything; Mrs. Merlini, Italian instructor, full of vitality; Helen Shreve, fifth-grade teacher, demanding and serious, uniquely talented in the arts of teaching, tough, fair, instantly encouraging in turn of any sign of student talent. And then, intensely there (as Henry James might have said) appeared Kevin McIntyre, the gifted, high-pressured, and admirably high-pressuring art teacher, Irish-American as ever was, and now a family friend of long standing.

The headmaster throughout these years was Horace Gibson: slight, immaculate, trim-bearded, and always firmly, quietly in control. Gibson was North Carolina-born and Florida-bred, and retained a fine soft-spoken southern civility. It was his habit every afternoon to shake hands with, and address by name, each member of the entire school, each child chanting or mumbling "Good afternoon, Mr. Gibson," in response. No few of these former students have been encountered in later years and on different continents by their onetime headmaster, and they spontaneously utter the exact same response.

———

My own literary program over these ten months was to make a start on a book about Florence: this book, as it would turn out. The year began with the publication of my biography of Edith Wharton; and with that complex task completed, I decided (as I said earlier, in the Prologue) to turn my attention to the European and Italian place where we had lived so often. As plans began to clarify, I found myself writing what was in effect a partial biography of Florence, essentially the story of its shaping; combined with a partial autobiography, personal reminiscences of life in the city.

What this meant, practically speaking, was a sort of total or life-consuming involvement unlike anything I had previously known. Quite literally, every sight we saw, every walk we took, virtually every meal we ate or bottle of wine we bought, almost everyone we spoke to: all this was or could be part of the stuff that would make up the book. The realization of such totality of experiencing, so to call it, came early. A stray journal entry in mid-November remarks the following:

Even a simple bus ride into the center carries me past strong historical and personal associations. It takes me along the Viale Petrarca, and I think of Petrarch and his writings, and the role he played in my master's essay at Chicago. We pass through the Porta Romana, the great Roman gate leading to the road to Siena and Rome, and built in 1326–28; then up Via Romana, where we lived in such close quarters but happily in 1972–73, past the Annalena on the left, where my mother lived for so many years, and, on the right, the Boboli Gardens where we spent many a playful afternoon. The bus veers left up Via Maggio and past the house of Bianca Cappello, then across the Ponte Santa Trinità, the 1560s masterpiece by Ammannati, reconstructed after its violent destruction in August 1944. Across the Lungarno and into Piazza Santa Trinità, which our lodgings looked out upon in the fall of 1957.

All of that, just to get from the villa to Via Tornabuoni. The difficulty is that, since the experience is total, almost seamless, it seems to ask for totality of response. That is not so easy to manage. Nancy and I are aware that we are looking at things in a brand-new way—really *looking* at them, taking them in, and conscious of doing so. In the past, Florence, for me, has been a site of war, and then a charming context to be casually explored between the more important and unrelated literary efforts—a long study of Ignazio Silone, an essay on Conrad, an American literature textbook, a life of Edith Wharton. Tuscany itself, in 1969 and 1972–73, was of interest primarily because of Edith Wharton connections—the monastery at San Vivaldo (where she discovered some della Robbias), La Verna, Camaldoli, and Chianciano, where we visited and talked with Iris Origo—Iris Cutting of New York that was, the much younger friend and correspondent of Edith Wharton, and an exquisite writer on literary and historical subjects (Byron's daughter; Leopardi; the Prato merchant; the war in Tuscany).

Of course we enjoyed finding out about the places we inhabited, the houses along Via Romana and so on; we did a bit of study here and there. But we hadn't tried to put things together, to see them as elements in an *insieme*. And that is the enterprise for *this* year. So much so, that items we know we have seen before, maybe often—the extraordinary murals in the vault of the Baptistery, the portrait of Sir John Hawkwood on horseback by Paolo Uccello, in the Duomo—we look at as though for the first time. But they're all part of *Fiorentinita*.

[7]

Vespucci Territory:

1987

Summertime

Summer in Florence has a bad reputation. Florence-wise friends, when told we planned to spend the months of July and August in the city, expressed alarm for our well-being and praise for our courage. The *heat*, they kept exclaiming. Sheila Hale, the author of the often knowing and witty *American Express Guide to Florence and Tuscany*, takes note of a beautiful old pharmacy on Via Cavour that was founded in the fifteenth century by the monks from nearby San Marco: "Their specifics," she writes, "include an anti-hysteric, which might come in handy if you are visiting Florence in August." We had lunch in the third week of July at the Or-ologio, a particularly nice trattoria on the south side of the river, and asked Franco, the gentlest and kindest of waiters (we had come to know him the year before), if the place would be closing soon. Yes, said Franco with a kind of violence. He pressed his hands together, then yanked them apart in a savage ripping motion, to indicate desperation and imminent collapse. Without an immediate period of *riposo*, he said, he would not survive.

The heat can be oppressive at times. It seems to get caught in Florence's topographical curvature; one walks perspiring and mostly in the morning; local nerves do get frazzled after a while. But except for a mean little spell toward the end of our stay (a spell washed away by a tumultuous *temporale*), the temperature rarely rose above 90 degrees Fahrenheit during our 1987 summer. It was hotter in Rome and Naples, according to the daily reports, and murderously hot in Calabria. New Yorkers were much worse off than we were, so we read. And anyhow we are among those who feel about Florence as Cole Porter did about Paris, and love it when it sizzles.

In fact, no few of our Florentine acquaintances speak fondly of the summer here, and of August as their favorite month. The city empties out delightfully, and, as it does, things close down all over town. The majority of the restaurants, like the Orologio, close for up to a month, as they do in other Italian cities and with an annual clang in Paris. Many food stores are shut, as are a number of luxury shops. The streets become invitingly vacant. Nor are the tourists any sort of menace. We counted twenty-one tour buses one morning, lined up on the Lungarno stretching eastward away from Ponte alle Grazie, and the newspaper informed us that the number of tourists had increased a good deal since the previous summer, when varieties of fear and foolishness had kept Americans out of Europe. But tourists were hardly visible in most parts of the city.

As in some surrealist movie, they tended to tramp about on the Ponte Vecchio and the street running north from it; to cluster at the entrance to San Lorenzo's New Sacristy and the Medici tombs; and to push together in thickets around the Duomo. The line of people waiting to get into the Uffizi stretched most mornings in snakelike fashion halfway across the Piazza Signoria; but the depressing spectacle was caused in part by the Uffizi authorities, who instructed the ticket takers—as a symbolic protest against some ministerial action—to delay matters by scrutinizing each ticket with care, turning it over and back and peering at the stamp. Elsewhere, the casual visitor was rarely in evidence; and elsewhere was where we lived.

We lived in a quite remarkably spacious and high-ceilinged apartment on Borgo Ognissanti, a street at the edge of the "historic center" of the city that departs from Piazza Goldoni and Ponte

Borgo Ognissanti area

alla Carraia and runs parallel to Lungarno Vespucci and the river. An official of the American consulate generously put it at our disposal when he took his family back to Texas for home leave. This was our tenth stay of any duration in Florence, and never have we inhabited rooms of such airy vastness. Henry James, after inspecting similar large chambers in several old Florentine palazzi in 1873, commented with almost unmixed approval on "the echoing excess of space" he observed in them; and thought that "the spaciousness of some of these ancient drawing-rooms is that of the Russian steppes . . . Such quarters," he ventured, "seem a translation into space of the old-fashioned idea of leisure." Leisure was certainly a requisite just to get around in the place. It took a measurable amount of time for one of us to walk across the apartment—shouting would have been useless—to summon the other to the telephone.

The apartment occupied much of the second floor (European style: fifty-nine steps up, or ascend by the hard-breathing little elevator) in a building known as the Palazzo della Marescialla. The name goes back to the early-seventeenth century and one Eleanora Dori, who married the lowborn Florentine Concino Concini, and who in time became the confidante of Maria de' Medici, the Queen of France. The latter, the daughter of Francesco I, the second Medici Grand Duke of Tuscany, had married Henri IV, and had helped bring things Florentine to Paris and the French court. After the king's death, Concino Concini became a special favorite of the widowed queen, who made him governor of Picardy and Normandy and gave him the title of Marshall (*Maresciallo*). Concini and Eleanora were profiting happily from their situation until the new king, the adolescent Louis XIII, vexed by their influence with his mother, decided to get rid of them. The *Maresciallo* was assassinated in front of the Louvre in 1617, and a few weeks later the *Marescialla* was beheaded and then burned as a witch.

Long before this, Eleonora Dori, in status-seeking moves in Florence, had renamed herself Poponelli and then Galigai. The palazzo bears the coat-of-arms of the illustrious Galigai family—

crossed chains—to which the *Marescialla* had no claim whatever.
A satirical verse about her circulated in Florence. In rough translation:

> Now Dori, now Poponelli, and now Galigai,
> What in hell will you ever be satisfied by?

It is a beguiling neighborhood, both in its ongoing life and its
history. Fashionable shops along Via de' Fossi down the way,
offering *antichità*, neoclassic statuary, ceramics, and exquisite silk,
give way, upward on Ognissanti, to the food stores: the *ortolano*
(for fruit and vegetables), the *macellaio* (for beautiful cuts of veal
and beef), the *panificio* (for bread), the *alimentari* (cheese, *prosciutto
crudo*, staples), the *latteria* (for milk). Shopping, as all foreign
residents in Florence come to discover, is a daily exercise in neighborliness, a round of visits and talk. Our excellent wine merchant
delivered on call from the other side of Ponte Carraia, bringing
up heavy cartons of mineral water, that indispensable summer
item, and such assorted wines as the occasion called for—especially, that year, a marvelous 1985 Cacchiano red.

On our way to the *panificio* and the *ortolano*, we walked through
Florentine history, as represented in this quarter-mile by the
church of Ognissanti, built in 1256 by the Umiliati, a colony of
Lombard monks who founded the wool industry, which was the
basis of the city's wealth, and of all the wealth it gave rise to, for
two centuries. The Umiliati had charge of Ponte alla Carraia, near
at hand, the oldest of the great medieval Florentine bridges. They
rebuilt it in 1269, and, as was said in an earlier chapter, it took
its name—"cart road"—from the *carri* which hauled wool across
it to the section of San Frediano, where most of the wool workers
lived. The church itself has an early-seventeenth century baroque
facade and a modest square-topped bell tower from the thirteenth
century.

Inside, at one of the altars to the right, is a Madonna of Mercy,
an early painting by Domenico Ghirlandaio which displays members of the Vespucci family (donors of the chapel and Ghirlandaio's "guardians") and, among them, the youthful Amerigo,

Vespucci family, with Madonna of Mercy

looking alert and watchful. Next door to the church, and with its own entrance, is the former refectory, which contains a Last Supper of Ghirlandaio, at once serene and dramatic, with glimpses in the background of a gracious garden with abundant foliage and skylarks in flight. It is a variant of Ghirlandaio's *Last Supper* in the Convent of San Marco, and students of the artist may be reminded that this is the one without the cat.

Ognissanti is Vespucci territory. The family, from Peretola, a few kilometers west of Florence (the name seems derived from *vespa*, the word for "wasp," and in our day for a motor scooter of arguable charm), made their original fortune in silk, though they also went in for wool and banking. They had their houses on Borgo Ognissanti, directly across from our palazzo; Amerigo was born in one of them in 1454. Another of them was made into a hospital in 1388 by the prosperous silk merchant Simone Vespucci, and when the hospital was enlarged in the later sixteenth century by Grand Duke Ferdinand I and given its present name of San Giovanni di Dio, it absorbed all the Vespucci holdings.

San Giovanni di Dio is now a day clinic offering varieties of services.

The *quartiere* of which Ognissanti is a part is called Santa Maria Novella, for the church of the same name. Via de' Fossi at its far end opens into the piazza over which the church presides. William Dean Howells, in *Tuscan Cities*, tells of coming to Florence for the winter of 1882–83 with the notion of writing about it. He took lodgings for the family in Piazza Santa Maria Novella, and soon was wondering "why I should have thought of writing of the whole city, when one piazza in it was interesting enough to make a book about."

Howells was aware that the twenty-one-year-old Longfellow had lodged in Piazza Santa Maria Novella in 1828, in virtually the same building as the Howells family, on the west side of the square; and that Boccaccio (to whom Longfellow later paid tribute as a master teller of tales) had set the opening of the *Decameron* in the church. He was even more conscious that Henry James had spent a productive period, completing *Roderick Hudson*, in rooms overlooking the piazza from the south end, on Via della Scala. It was from this address that James had written Howells in the spring of 1874 to say that Florence now seemed to him an old literary masterpiece of which one turned the pages with constantly renewed pleasure.

James, after another stay in Florence, in 1877, recorded visiting the church of Santa Maria Novella—always, for James, the best of the Florentine churches—bearing in hand a copy, just acquired, of Ruskin's *Mornings in Florence*. He "looked about for a while at the beautiful church"—lingering under the multitiered frescoes of Ghirlandaio in the choir, and no doubt pausing before the Trinity of Masaccio and, in the Strozzi chapel, the frescoes of Filippino Lippi—and then sat down to peruse the Ruskin essays. There he learned that he had been all wrong in his enjoyment of "the good old city of Florence" and most of its art works. "I had taken great pleasure in certain frescos by Ghirlandaio in the choir of that very church; but it appeared from one of the little books that the frescos were as naught." (Ruskin had said that the paintings were "simply—good for nothing.") "I had much admired

Santa Croce and had thought the Duomo a very noble affair; but I had now the most positive assurance that I knew nothing about them." Finally, wrote James, it was with Ruskin himself that he "lost patience . . . not the stupid Brunelleschi, not the vulgar Ghirlandaio." He lost patience with the view that there is rigid truth and unforgivable error in the human response to works of art; with the "apocalyptic terminology" that suggests a kind of damnation in not seeing things correctly; with the total absence of any portion of *joy* in the aesthetic experience.

The piazza's irregular shape is punctuated by two imposing stone obelisks, by Giambologna (1608), set on the backs of two bronze turtles. The obelisks served as goal posts for an annual chariot race that was one of the chief public spectacles introduced by the Medici dukes. One of the spectators seated in the grandstands in June 1581 was Michel de Montaigne, who found the event extremely stimulating. The chariots made three turns around the square, and the Strozzi charioteer, to the cautious enthusiasm of the crowd, was declared to have arrived at the post an instant ahead of the Grand Duke's man. Montaigne thought the verdict plainly wrong, but wrote that he "liked this spectacle more than any other I saw in Italy." Some two hundred and fifty years later, James Fenimore Cooper, who had been in Florence for the winter and spring of 1829, gave his own account of the *corso dei còcchi* (carriages). He felt that the effect of the whole scene was impressive: the parade of guards on horse and foot, the well-dressed populace, the balconies "garnished by tapestry and fine women." But the race itself seemed to him a bumpy and unskilled performance. "One may witness the same any fine evening in New York," he said, "between two drunken Irish cartmen who are on their way home."

The great railway station behind the church—it too is called Santa Maria Novella ("FIRENZE S.M.N." is the sign that greets you as your train is pulling in)—was the scene of chaos and distress on the last weekend of July. A new and independent union known as Cobas—the word comes from *comitato della base*, and means essentially a union directly representative of the workers —brought about a nationwide strike of railway employees. Al-

A chariot race in Piazza Santa Maria Novella, 1744

most 80 percent of all local trains across the country stopped running for twenty-four hours, more than 60 percent of all long-distance trains came to a halt, and there was no movement of freight at all. The entire system was paralyzed. It was, of course, one of the most heavily scheduled weekends of the summer for Italian and foreign travelers, and among the untold scores of thousands left stranded were those many seeking to escape the literally killing temperatures of Calabria. The Florence station, when we looked in on it, was a sea of despondently milling stranded passengers.

The strike was in protest against a contract recently proposed for the railroad workers by the ministry of transport in Rome, which offered a modest pay increase to take leisurely effect over a three-year period, and some slight reduction in the number of hours per week. The terms were rejected by the Cobas, who rallied a quite unexpected majority of workers to the cause. In the wake of the strike, charges and countercharges filled the air, accusations of lying, wild exaggerations. But what impressed the American onlooker was the almost total absence of concern for the public welfare, for the interests of the average citizen. This was true of the Cobas as it was of the ministerial spokesman; and not less so of the large established unions (CGIL to the left, CISL to the right, UIL somewhere in the middle), as they regarded the affair with skeptical eye. There were vague references to the need for union self-discipline; but these seemed to be old refrains, an accepted part of the *spettacolo*, the histrionics, of the process.

I felt the same lack of concern, the same fundamental indifference (*menefregismo*—fuckyouism, in American—is the earthy Italian word for it), to the well-being of the citizenry during a series of strikes by the Florentine bus services earlier in the summer. Buses stopped running for an entire morning, or for two hours at several different periods during the day. The strike times were announced in advance by the Florence newspapers, but the resulting inconvenience was enormous; on five separate days over a two-week stretch, the life of the city was thrown into calamitous disarray. And during all the heated public discussion of the strikes and the issues that lay behind them, I failed to hear a single note of genuine anxiety about their effect upon the city's people.

This indifference causes one a peculiar pang in Florence, for it was here that the very notion of the public welfare first came into being, at least on the European continent: *la cosa pubblica*, the public thing, as understood by the *Primo Popolo* and the *Secondo Popolo* in the thirteenth century. The edict ordering Arnolfo di Cambio to prepare models for the cathedral enjoined him that, like all other works commissioned by the Commune, his should "correspond to the noble soul which is composed of the souls of all [the Commune's] citizens united in one will."

The force, one might say the allure, of that principle persisted into the sixteenth century, when it gradually lost all vitality and died under Medici rule. If there are faint signs of a revival today, as some would like to claim, they are not to be found in the sphere of the public services. It does not altogether become an American in the 1990s to complain about the decline of the public sentiment in other countries; but even the most chastened American can feel a spurt of good national feeling when he is made to undergo the miseries of the Italian postal system.

Matters were not so bad during the summer of 1987 as they were during a long stay a good many years ago when, in the course of a months-long postal strike, tons of mail (so we heard) were routinely destroyed, dumped into the sea, thrown into the furnaces. But it is, without competition, the worst delivery service in the Western world; even an Italian government report not long back described the "disservice" as intolerable. (Edith Wharton arrived at the same finding before the First World War.) Anything larger than an airmail letter can be held up indefinitely. A visit to the storeroom in the station where packages accumulate from incoming freight trains is enough to make your hair stand on end. There is obviously no plan on the part of the attendants— as they sit about and smoke and laugh—for sorting and distributing the items in the foreseeable future.

A small clasp-envelope packet of letters and bills, all of some urgency, was sent to us from America at the end of June. It reached Florence in a fortnight, but no action was taken about it for another two weeks. We were then informed by a notice that we could pick the thing up at the office on Via G. B. Foggini. No one we consulted locally had heard of the street; in our *quartiere* post office, the clerks fell to arguing good-naturedly over its whereabouts. We finally located it on a large-scale map: several miles away on the southwest outskirts of town. We proceeded to the general area but failed to hit upon Via Foggini after several tries. Finally we approached an aged woman who was buying vegetables. She had lived in the neighborhood for years, she said, but still wasn't sure which street was Foggini. She thought it was the one veering off to the left. We peered through binoculars: she was right. *"Mille grazie!"* we said fervently. *"A voi!"* ("Thanks to *you!"*), she replied with quavering, ancient courtesy. We went on, paid 250 lire for some inexplicable charge, and collected our packet.

In "Casa Alvisi," an essay in his collection *Italian Hours*, Henry James wrote with tender nostalgia about another American resident in Italy—in Venice, but with Florentine connections—during the late-nineteenth century. This was Katherine De Kay Bronson, originally of New York, who "sat for twenty years at the wide mouth . . . of the Grand Canal" in Venice, as James put it, offering choice hospitality to a steady flow of visitors. Both William and Henry James took their ease in her drawing room; and Henry, while staying in the guest house at the back in 1887, sketched out *The Aspern Papers*. The visitor to whom Mrs. Bronson became most attached was Robert Browning: "Nothing in all her beneficent life," James recorded, "had probably made her happier than to have found herself able to minister each year, with the returning autumn, to his pleasure and comfort." One of our most luminous experiences in that summer of 1987 was coming to know Katherine De Kay Bronson's granddaughter, the Marchesa Nannina Fossi.

She was ninety-one years old, and Henry James would have doted on her: gracious, easy, quick-spirited, brightly interested in everything; and the very embodiment of what James called "the visitable past." Katherine Bronson's daughter Edith married Conte Cosimo Rucellai, a career naval officer and a descendant of the age-old Rucellai family in Florence. (Connections proliferate: Edith Wharton, stopping over in Florence in 1903 to visit Florentine villas and villa gardens, spoke of going out to see Edith Rucellai, whom she had known as Edith Bronson in Newport.) An offspring of this marriage, in 1896, was our treasured new acquaintance, Nannina Rucellai. She would eventually marry Marchese Piero Fossi, a writer and student of the Italian past.

She is named for Nannina de' Medici, the daughter of Piero di Cosimo ("the Gouty") and the sister of Lorenzo the Magnificent, who was married in 1466 amid an extraordinarily sumptuous display to Bernardo, the son of Giovanni Rucellai. The latter, with a combination of shrewd financing and tactful diplomacy, brought the fortunes of his already three-hundred-year-old family to their peak. It was for Giovanni Rucellai and at his expense that Leon Battista Alberti, in the 1470s, designed the portal and the singularly beautiful upper facade of Santa Maria Novella, the religious center of our *quartiere*. As for Nannina de' Medici, she can be seen, at about age thirteen, riding horseback with her sisters in the procession in Benozzo Gozzoli's "Journey of the Magi," on the wall facing the altar in the chapel of the Palazzo Medici, built for her grandfather Cosimo by Michelozzo.

On the evening of June 24, the day of San Giovanni, the patron saint of Florence, we watched a stirring display of fireworks over the Arno, joining the crowd on Ponte alla Carraia (the same bridge which collapsed under the weight of people observing a similar spectacle in 1304). On a brisk Sunday morning we witnessed a parade, coming down Lungarno Vespucci toward Ponte Santa Trinità, of the Bersaglieri, the celebrated Alpine regiment of many historic encounters, with its zestful regimental chorus and its plumed headgear. Thanks to old friends, part-time residents in Florence who took us in their car, we made several little tours of southern Tuscany. On one of them we went to San Quirico, southwest of Siena in the Val d'Orcia, to see an open-air exhibition of sculpture by Constantino Nivola, a powerfully gifted contemporary Sardinian artist (he was an American citizen for some years; it was Nivola who, in the 1960s, added robust sculptures to the courtyards and walls of Morse and Stiles, the new Yale residential colleges then being constructed by Eero Saarinen). We went on to Pienza, the charming little town created and named for Pope Pio II, the fifteenth-century humanist scholar Enea Silvio Piccolomini; its piazza, with flanking views of Val d'Orcia, is one of the loveliest in Italy. Thereafter we took supper in the lofty hill town of Montepulciano, the home of the *vino nobile*, whose quality we proved once again.

For the rest, in Florence, we made the old rounds, dropping in on the familiar monuments and places, and finding them as before, in the Jamesian language, friendly and sociable and sane. We visited—to name a few once again for the poetry of their names—the Bargello and the Badia; the library in San Lorenzo with Michelangelo's dramatic staircase; the church and the square of Santissima Annunziata, probably the most satisfying single space in the city (or rather, it used to be: see ch. 8); Orsanmichele, the statuary outside (what is left and visible of it), the tabernacle of Andrea Orcagna within; Palazzo Medici on Via Cavour, where, again, we paid special attention to the breathtakingly beautiful

Madonna and Child of Filippo Lippi and the far-flung ceiling fresco the *Apotheosis of the Medicis,* by Luca Giordano (1680s).

There was, in this season, an artistic errand to give point and direction to our wanderings. In the past few years, Nancy has become increasingly interested in the work of Bronzino, the painter much favored by Duke Cosimo I, and she had agreed to give a talk on the subject that fall to a New Haven group. We spent a succession of mornings going about in search of this artist, whose active career, mostly in Florence and Tuscany, extended from the 1520s to his death in 1572. Like other *studiosi,* we had the repeated and frustrating experience of discovering that this or that art work was inaccessible, had been removed for *restauro,* or was in a room or a portion of a church that was itself blocked off during the long work of *restauro.*

There remained a great deal to see. Most compellingly (these items were mentioned earlier) there is the little chapel in Palazzo Vecchio that Bronzino decorated for Eleonora of Toledo, the strong-minded, unhappy wife of Duke Cosimo: biblical scenes of great sweep and power, rich with historical and political symbolism. Amid the glowing frescoes by Pontormo, Bronzino's teacher and associate, in San Felicità, the small church near Ponte Vecchio, at least one of the four Evangelists was painted by Bronzino. The Uffizi contains seventeen pictures by Bronzino, many of them gathered into a single *sala,* number 18. The majority of them are portraits, including one of Eleonora with one of the children, and another of Duke Cosimo: a sternly handsome face, this latter, with an intently concentrated sideward gaze, and giving the impression of vigorous emotions held in check—hardly the face curiously made out by Howells in the Bargello bust of Cosimo by Benvenuto Cellini: "a terrible face . . . its ferocity . . . is something to appal us still."

We paused at length before the portrait of Lucrezia Panciatichi, the painting which Henry James transferred in imagination to the country house Matcham in *The Wings of the Dove,* where Millie Theale is brought to see it, on the grounds that it resembles her. Millie looks at the portrait through tears, and perhaps, James

Lucrezia Panciatichi, by Bronzino

writes, it was the tears "that made it just then so strange and fair . . . the face of a young woman, all magnificently drawn, down to the hands, and magnificently dressed; a face almost livid in hue, yet handsome in sadness and crowned with a mass of hair rolled back and high that must, before fading with time, have had a family resemblance to her own." The lady in question was a very great personage, Millie thinks, only she was "unaccompanied by a joy." Few of Bronzino's figures *are* accompanied by a joy; it was part of his genius to portray the contained sadness that experience brings to the human visage. But they are incontestably alive, and their vitality added appreciably to ours during the passing summer days.

L'idea di Firenze

The Gabinetto Vieusseux, one of the city's most admirable institutions, is engaged in a mammoth effort to collate the work in and related to Florence of foreign writers and artists in the nineteenth century; and an involvement with this undertaking kept the present writer occupied on a number of summer mornings. The Gabinetto was founded in 1819 by Gian Pietro Vieusseux, from a Swiss commercial family, who, on his travels, discovered in Florence a cosmopolitan ambiance very much to his taste. For the furthering of it, he opened a *gabinetto*—a salon or reading room—which made available periodicals from all over the world and became a meeting place for foreign visitors. (Dostoyevsky was astonished to come upon a Russian review there, one he had seen nowhere else in Europe; Howells passed many an hour in the Gabinetto.) For a dozen years, until it was suppressed, Vieusseux published a review called *Antologia*, to which the leading literary figures of the day contributed. He also initiated the *Archivio storico italiano*, a semiannual publication of rare or unknown historical documents, of which the guiding spirit was Gino Capponi, the great political leader and historian of the Florentine state.

The Gabinetto Vieusseux, which occupies part of the massive and famous Palazzo Strozzi, now houses a library of 500,000 volumes, and it is active on any number of cultural fronts. Among these is the attempt to piece together *l'idea di Firenze*—the idea, or image, of Florence—as it variously appeared in the writings and art work of foreigners in the city from about 1790 to 1915. The task is the province of a section of the Gabinetto known as the Centro Romantico, itself begun in 1973, and it is being carried out under the direction of Maurizio Bossi, the Centro's youthful, intense, and brilliant coordinator. There was a three-day conference on *L'idea di Firenze* in December 1986, held in the Gabinetto's elegant little auditorium on the ground floor of Palazzo Strozzi; papers were read on the Florentine envisionings of a series of foreign observers—English, French, American, Austrian, and German—in the *ottocento*; Sir Harold Acton and the English art historian Francis Haskell were among the participants. In the present stage of things, a huge bibliography is being compiled—it may run to two thousand titles—of writing of every literary sort on any significant aspect of Florence during the era. An assembly of photographs, a *fototeca permanente*, of art works depicting the scene is simultaneously under way. All this material will eventually be drawn together in a volume of perhaps thirty-five comprehensive essays collating and interpreting the offerings that project the multifarious Florentine idea of a century ago. A large parallel study of Florentine craftsmanship in the nineteenth century is also moving ahead in the Centro Romantico.

My contribution was to identify American literary visitors, draw up lists of the relevant texts, and summarize the Florentine images in them. They were a goodly host, the Americans—in no particular order or selectivity: Longfellow (who wrote a sonnet in Italian about the Ponte Vecchio), Cooper, Emerson (Brunelleschi's dome was "set down like an archangel's tent in the midst of the city"), Charles Eliot Norton, Lowell, Hawthorne (the tenant in 1858 of Villa Montauto in Bellosguardo, which became the Apennines castle in *The Marble Faun*), Mark Twain (who denounced Titian's *Venus* in the Uffizi as "the foulest, the vilest, the obscenest picture the world possesses"), Constance Fenimore Woolson (among her several relevant writings, her long short story of the 1890s, "A Florentine Experiment," is a minor masterpiece which, properly scripted, would make a superb television drama), Frances Alexander (Ruskin's "darling Sorella," who became internationally famous for her *Roadside Songs of Tuscany*), Howells, William James, Henry James, Edith Wharton.

For those of us on the American desk in this campaign, the fundamental interest was, of course, the *contrasting* ideas about Florence that the Americans, between them, can be seen to provide. Hawthorne, for example, riding to Florence from Arezzo in June 1858, saw the city from far off as in a dream or an allegory: because of haziness in the atmosphere, he wrote, "Florence was little more distinct to us than the Celestial City was to Christian and Hopeful, when they espied it from the Delectable Mountains." For Howells, as has been said, Florence was almost nothing but its living human actuality. He grew bored with what he called the dreary farce of old-mastering, and in a moment of engaging and suggestive rashness declared: "I would rather have a perpetuity of the *cameriere*'s smile when he came up with our coffee in the morning than Donatello's San Giorgio." (The comment brings to mind the lines of e. e. cummings: "A pretty girl that naked is / Is worth a million statues"—sound enough in its way, as someone has said, but not a useful principle for anyone preparing an exhibition of sculpture.) Henry James dealt with Florence in both his longer and his shorter fiction, in superlative letters to the family and in his travel writings.

A passage from "The Autumn in Florence," in *Italian Hours*, shows James's special mode of impressionism, his delicate, pleasurable mingling, or interbreeding, of the human and the aesthetic that places him, in this spectrum, somewhere between Howells and Hawthorne.

He has been trying to find the right words to say what it is that "infuses so rich an interest into the general charm" of the city. What he comes to, as he wanders hither and thither over the weeks, is "the sense of one of the happiest periods of human Taste"; and it is this that settles upon his spirit. He goes on:

The memorials of the past here address us moreover with a friendliness, win us by we scarcely know what sociability, with equal amenity, that we scarce find matched in other great aesthetically endowed communities and periods.

Here is a portion of what I had to offer at the December 1986 conference:

During his visit to Florence in the spring of 1874, Henry James was at work on his first novel, *Roderick Hudson*. Most of that story is set in Rome, but toward the end several of the main characters come to Florence to spend the summer in the Villa Pandolfini: "at the top of the hill," says the narrator, "which sloped straight from one of the gates of Florence." This is Villa Mercedes in Bellosguardo, to which James had made several excursions. On

Villa Castellani, by Frank Duveneck

Villa Castellani (Mercedes): another view

one of these, in the late 1870s, he encountered two old Boston friends, Francis Boott, a composer of some gifts, and his daughter, Elizabeth. They had been coming to Florence and living there for thirty years. Boott's finest work was religious in nature: we can mention the *Mass* and the *Miserere*, composed in Bellosguardo and much influenced by the church music he was hearing. Elizabeth, thirty-one years old, was an attractive young woman who aspired to be a painter. Father and daughter, varyingly transformed, figure centrally in Henry James's novel *The Portrait of a Lady*, where they inhabit a very dark version of Villa Castellani (later Mercedes).

In 1880, coming to Florence for a few days, James found Elizabeth Boott studying art with a young painter from Cincinnati, Ohio, named Frank Duveneck. James found Duveneck rather crude in manner, but pronounced him "much the most highly developed phenomenon in the way of a painter that the U.S.A. has given birth to." This was a surprising statement, if we consider simply the American painters who preceded Duveneck in Florence. To name only the most accomplished, one thinks of: Washington Allston, who came to Florence in 1804 and here painted a lovely Madonna and a head of Dante's Beatrice; Rembrandt Peale, of the prolific Peale family, who had a studio in Piazza della Signoria (then, in 1829, Granduca), where he painted elegantly costumed figures; Thomas Cole, who arrived in 1831 and who loved to stroll along the Arno and study the views from the bridges—one of his finest works was the highly imaginative and colorful *View at Sunset from the Ponte alla Carraia*; George Inness, the poet-painter of the Tuscan landscape who, in the wake of his Florentine experience (in the 1850s), went on to become America's greatest landscape painter; and, above all, John Singer Sargent, who was born in Florence and spent the first twenty years of his life here, roaming the galleries and exploring the gardens and doing the first of the portraits (one of Vernon Lee among them) which would establish him as his country's supreme artist in that genre.

Frank Duveneck belongs in that company, if not at the head of it. His picture *The Italian Girl* is an undoubted masterpiece. His portraits, which had suffered a little from the bravura style and heavy brushstrokes he had adopted during his student days in Munich, now became more clearly and delicately rendered. He and Elizabeth Boott were married in 1886, and his large portrait of her has a gentle glow of beauty. Nor should one forget Duveneck's moving effigy for his wife's tomb in the Allori cemetery on the way to Galuzzo. There were also engaging studies of Tuscan settings and genre scenes in Bellosguardo and elsewhere. Duveneck went back to Cincinnati after Elizabeth's death in 1888, and remained there, much honored and celebrated, for the rest of his life.

But Duveneck's most valuable performance may have been as a teacher of painting, in which role he was quite exceptional. In 1878, he began his own painting classes in Munich, with about thirty young students, many of whom had come with him from America. He brought the group to Florence in 1879 for a two-year stay, with frequent visits to Venice. In Florence they created a kind of sensation, as one result of which they entered American literature as "the Inglehart boys" in William Dean Howells's novel of 1885, *Indian Summer*. The hero of that novel, Colville, first hears of them as "a score of young painters" who worked "under the lead of a singular and fascinating genius . . . They made the greatest excitement everywhere, and had the greatest fun." Colville later encounters them in a trattoria (in real life, in Via Guelfa) all talking at once, shouting their opinions about painters and tobacco and causing "a jolly uproar."

It was during his residence in Florence in 1882–83 that Howells heard about the "Duveneck boys." William Dean Howells was forty-five at this time, and was emerging as one of the most distinguished and influential figures in his American literary age: in the view of some, he divided the leadership of that age with Henry James. He was really without rival as an analyst in fiction of the drift of American social history in his time. He had, as well, a long-standing association with Italy. In the 1860s he served as American consul in Venice, an experience he thoroughly enjoyed. He took every opportunity to travel about the country; and in 1865, he published the fruit of these travels, a collection of sketches called *Italian Journeys*, a book warmly praised in a review by the young Henry James.

Howells came to Florence in the late fall of 1882 with the frank intention, as he said, of writing about it. He lodged with his family in the Hotel Minerva in Piazza Santa Maria Novella, pleasantly conscious that Longfellow had preceded him there. What Howells did write about the city was a long discursive essay, "A Florentine Mosaic," which constituted the first half of his volume of 1886, *Tuscan Cities*.

The more immediate literary consequence of the visit was the novel *Indian Summer*. This brilliant work—the astute critic Van Wyck Brooks calls it "perhaps the most perfect of all [Howells's] novels"—is set entirely in Florence, beginning on Ponte Vecchio and ending with a marriage feast in a palazzo on Lungarno della Zecca Vecchia. The story has to do with a middle-aged American, Colville, who on a visit to Florence encounters an old friend, the widowed Mrs. Bowen. For about 250 pages, Colville deludes himself into thinking that he is in love with Mrs. Bowen's youthful ward; but he recovers his senses in time to realize that it is Mrs. Bowen whom he really loves and to take a lead role in the marriage party just mentioned.

These not very electrifying events take place on a Florentine scene that has been observed with marvelous clarity and accuracy. We move amid familiar sights and places: the Boboli Gardens, Via dei Bardi, the statues outside the Uffizi, Palazzo Vecchio, Via Cavour, Piazza San Marco. We read the papers in Gabinetto Vieusseux and take an ice at Giacosa's. We hear of early Florentine history, and the way the city's architecture expressed Florentine character in different periods. Ingredients such as these, far from being guidebook notations, help create the reality—the human and moral and aesthetic atmosphere—through which the fictional characters move and come together.

The emphasis in *Indian Summer* is of necessity upon the American characters and their destinies. In "A Florentine Mosaic," the emphasis is rather on Florence itself, and the Florentines. As we consider this latter essay, it may be illuminating to compare the Florence we discover in it with the Florence we find in various sections of Henry James's *Italian Hours* (1909)—in "Italy Revisited," "The Autumn in Florence," and "Florentine Notes." Howells indeed seems to invite such a comparison. The narrator in *Indian Summer* openly calls our attention to James, and to other and earlier Americans in Florence. There is an allusion, for example, to Longfellow's Italian-language sonnet "Ponte Vecchio." One of the book's characters remarks that "Hawthorne used to live in a villa just beyond the hill over there"—pointing vaguely toward Bellosguardo, where Nathaniel Hawthorne spent the summer of 1858 in the forty-room Villa Montauto. And at one moment in the story, two of the characters fall to wondering fancifully whether they may be thought to inhabit a novel of Howells's or of Henry James's.

For Howells, Florence was first and last a *human* phenomenon. "Italy is above all lands the home of human nature," he wrote in *Tuscan Cities*; and human nature never expressed itself so clearly and attractively as in Florence. This is what he sought even among the venerable monuments of the city. "I could not pass a church door," he said, "without the wish to go in, not only for the pictures or statues one might see, but for the delightful natural human beings one could always be sure of." As to statues and pictures, Howells was not deeply interested; purely aesthetic emotions, he confessed, were beyond him.

With his family, Howells could watch the drama unfolding from the windows of their hotel rooms. There was the brave spectacle of military troops, infantry or cavalry, passing across the piazza. There was a funeral, with the coffin bearers in white robes carrying torches; and a priest, with his retinue, coming from the church with the Host in his hand, on his way to administer the last unction to some dying person in the neighborhood. And there were slighter things, simple manifestations of the human which brought Howells more pleasure than any work of art.

On the largest scale, Florentine history was a drama; and as he led the reader through long stretches of it—from the early times to the reign of the Medici dukes—Howells rejoiced in the still-living dramatic character of the great moments. Having rehearsed the story of the slaughter of Buondelmonte on Easter morning 1215 and the start of the Guelph-Ghibelline warfare, Howells remarks, "After six centuries the passions are as living, the characters as distinct"—that is, in the Florentine accounts of such events—"as if the thing happened yesterday." The grand motif of Florentine history, in Howells's view of it, was the valiant effort over several centuries to secure and maintain political freedom for the citizens. For Howells, who in this regard was very much an American, the gaining of political freedom was the highest possible human achievement. And it was just the struggle for freedom that Howells believed had been betrayed and defeated by the Medicis.

Howells had no kind words for any of the Medicis, not for Cosimo the Elder and certainly not for Lorenzo the Magnificent, who was the worst of all. "No touch of sympathetic poetry relieves the history of that race of demagogues and tyrants," he wrote in summary. "From the first Medici to the last, they were nearly all hypocrites or ruffians, bigots or imbeciles; and Lorenzo, who was a scholar and a poet, and a friend of scholars and poets, had the genius and science of tyranny in supreme degree."

The Florence of Henry James, in *Italian Hours*, is less easy to identify. We come close to it perhaps if we say it is more than anything else a *personality*. The actual city is palpably present: the yellow Arno and the houses along it; the great palazzi, especially those of the fifteenth century, "sombre and frowning"; the Boboli Gardens; Via dei Bardi, Via Maggio; the churches—the Duomo, Santissima Annunziata, Santa Croce, and, above all, Santa Maria Novella ("the church in Florence" that was "really interesting . . . beyond all others"); the countryside, Bellosguardo and Vincigliata. Unlike Howells, Henry James was a dedicated and, indeed, an extremely cultivated observer of painting and sculpture. The galleries of the Uffizi and Palazzo Pitti figure prominently in his discussions; and as we have noted, James has many things to say, admiring and even loving, about particular artists—Fra Angelico, Filippo Lippi, Ghirlandaio, Botticelli ("alone among the painters of his time," James felt, Botticelli "strikes us as having invention"; he allowed his artistic power "to sport and wander and explore on its own account"). But all these elements—places, artists, works of art—were absorbed into something larger: a being, a presence, a personality. It is what, at the end of "Florentine Notes," James calls "the eventual human soul of [the] place."

It is a lovely phrase, and we understand its meaning when we perceive James's habit, throughout his Florentine commentary, of mingling the aesthetic with the human.* This had always been James's practice, and would continue to be in all his later travel writings. But it is peculiarly and beautifully adapted to the evocation of Florence—to the evocation, as we might say, of the essential and enduring Florentine reality. Thus, James speaks of the "friendliness" and "sociability" of the palaces and churches of Florence; and records his impression of "an abiding felicity" in the "old Florence," of "saving sanity, of something sound and human." Similarly, Giotto's bell tower expresses a "temperate joy"; the Duomo, for all its hugeness, gives a sense of "geniality" and a "feeling for life"; Fra Angelico and the other painters of the *quattrocento* are "gladly observant." The Jamesian tendency to fuse the aesthetic with the human found its perfect subject in what endured of the old Florence.

Accordingly, when James spoke of *history* as related to Florence, he was not referring to the great and terrible dramas, the passionate individual conflicts that so interested Howells. James meant rather some human emanation from the past that has mysteriously survived, something faint but unmistakable. He received an overpowering impression of history in this elusive sense, one afternoon, when he stood in the Boboli Gardens, with his back to the amphitheater and in front of him the great palace with its two rectangular arms. He thought of all that had come to pass there, on that spot, during the long occupation of the Medicis; and in this Jamesian meditation the Medicis assumed a radically different aspect from that in the hostile vision of Howells.

He was struck, James wrote, by "a sense of *history*" that took

---

* Bonny Macdonald develops this idea at expressive length in *Henry James's Italian Hours: Revelatory and Resistant Impressions* (UMI Research Press, 1990).

his breath away. "Generations of Medici have stood at these closed windows . . . and held *fêtes champêtres* and floral games on the greensward, beneath the mouldering hemicycle. And the Medici were great people!" What remains of all that now, James went on, "is a mere tone in the air, a faint sigh in the breeze, a vague expression in things." The "deep strain of experience" was nonetheless ineffaceable. "Time has devoured the doers and their doings, but there still hangs about some effect of their passage." There and everywhere in the old Florence, there remained what that old Florence had brought into being above and beyond its palaces and churches: the eventual human soul of the place.

Before closing, I should acknowledge the suggestive fact that the Florence that emerges in Henry James's *fiction*, as against his travel writings, is a decidedly darkened version of the actual city. It has become gray and shadowy; it is autumnal rather than springlike. To be sure, the actual Florence, for James, was most herself and most attractive during the waning days of autumn. "The decline of the year," he wrote in an early article called "Autumn in Florence," was the best of times for the visitor to move through "these many-memoried streets and galleries and churches." Old things and places, he thought, tended to "give over their secrets most freely in such moist gray melancholy days."

But in the fictional image-making, all the friendliness, the openness, and the charm seem to disappear. This is compellingly true of *The Portrait of a Lady*, where James is at work evoking something ominous, something false and corrupt beneath the surface of charm and sanity. The actual Villa Castellani was a warmly hospitable place, as James described it, with a sunny terrace and a view of "the richest little city in the world." In the novel, the villa has become cold, impersonal, self-enclosed, secretive. And in the imaginative atmosphere of the novel, as Gilbert Osmond's evilly negative personality begins to affect everything, we inhabit a dwindling autumn that is giving way to the chill of winter. The dark human propensities, James suggests, may appear in Florence as easily as anywhere else, and the city of Fra Angelico and

Ghirlandaio may also contain a portion of quiet horror on a not too distant hilltop.

L'idea di Firenze, the volume containing the thirty-five papers read at the December 1986 conference, was published in September 1989 by Centro Di in Florence. The essays cover an authoritatively broad range of cultural history, from the Napoleonic epoch down to late-nineteenth-century historiography, with particular inquiries into English, French, Austrian, German, and American writers and artists active in Florence and responsive to it, and the interrelation between Florentine enterprises (the Bargello, as an example) and foreign models or derivations.

Francis Haskell, in a brief but telling introduction, argues that "the idea of Florence"—that is, the special appeal of Florence for foreign visitors in the nineteenth century—was notably different from that of Rome or Venice or Naples. It began much later in time—it is in fact, Haskell says, "a recent phenomenon"—and it was a good deal harder to come by. "For many visitors, it seemed as natural to admire the Colosseum or the Pantheon as to become spellbound before a beautiful sunset; but the sensibility necessary to comprehend San Miniato or the Baptistery was something that had to be acquired." For this reason, a good part of the attraction of Florence lay in the very effort "to recover a sense of the past." In addition, Florentine painting in the fifteenth and sixteenth centuries, Haskell writes, seemed to endorse and encourage a set of virtues—diligence, discipline, a certain staunchness—that pleased the Victorian temperament.

There was also what Haskell describes as the special impact of Florence. It had not only a unique significance in itself, something very much worth the grasping after; the straining attempt to understand it was, at the same time, somehow *self*-enlarging— Florence seemed thereby to confer a special dignity upon its devotees and students.

It is a rich atmospheric pressure which the student's own efforts help to beget, and are a part of. Countless *stranieri* in Florence can testify to the phenomenon, in whatever language or idiom the experience gets formulated. This writer can testify to it. And meanwhile, for me personally the pressure increased as I went ahead preparing my contribution to the book about "the idea." Between 1987 and our return to Florence in the spring of 1989, and with the help of two skilled research assistants at Yale, I drew up a fairly complete bibliography of American literary visitors to Florence over the long period stipulated. I presented it to Maurizio Bossi soon after our arrival in March of the year, and he declared himself speechless—*senza parole*—at such a job actually being done.*

---

* I was guided along the way by Nathalia Wright's *American Novelists in Italy* (1974), a model of its kind; and gladly acknowledge, as does Professor Wright, the help of the groundbreaking work in the area, *Come gli Americani Scoprirono l'Italia*, by Giuseppe Prezzolini (Milan, 1933), which traces the story of discovery up to 1850.

In addition to those writers mentioned earlier in this chapter, the bundle I delivered included twenty-five names, with specific texts identified and summarized. Among those were Henry F. Tuckerman (d. 1871; *The Italian Sketch Book*, 1835); Thomas Bailey Aldrich (d. 1907; poems); John William De Forest (d. 1906; *European Acquaintances*, 1858); Margaret Fuller (d. 1850; *Memoirs*, 1852, and *At Home Abroad*, 1856); Richard Watson Gilder (d. 1909; a number of poems); Charles Eliot Norton (d. 1908; *Notes of Travel and Study in Italy*, 1859, and *Letters*, 1913).

[8]

The Santa Croce

Neighborhood: 1992–93

The Piazza

Of the four *quartieri* that historically have composed the city of
Florence, the one named for the church of Santa Croce has perhaps the clearest outline: centering, as it does, on the great thick-
bodied church itself and the vast piazza, endlessly alive, spread
out in front; bordered at its base by the river and the Ponte alle
Grazie, and extending in all other directions to well-defined
limits.

The actual geographical boundaries of the old *quartieri* have
pretty much disappeared, and indeed Grand Duke Pietro Leopoldo in 1785 redivided the city into *terzieri*, thirds, for fiscal
reasons—a division that never caught on in the local vocabulary.
But the major portions of Florence do retain distinctive personalities, and each, in a certain perspective, seems to be a world of
its own. Our vague awareness of this grew into a clearer and
firmer sense of the matter during a 1985–86 stay, when we were
lodged in an apartment on Via della Fornace, on the south side
of the Arno, not far from Porta San Niccolò (the only old city
gate, incidentally, which still rises to its original height). Our rear
windows looked onto the river and across it; and in a brief journal
entry in March 1986, I commented on the situation:

We have a river apartment this time. It faces the Arno from a goodly height above (we're on the fourth floor, American, and you have to climb sixty steps to get up to us), at a point up river from Ponte alle Grazie and not far from the much newer bridge of San Niccolò off to the right. Looking out from our bedroom window, we can see, to the left, the spire and massive eastern flank of Santa Croce. Directly across is the big graceless headquarters building of the carabinieri, with the Porta della Zecca Vecchia standing solitary guard nearby.

What we are mainly conscious of, from our vantage point, is the river life. On this particular Sunday morning, pleasantly sunny with a drift of haze, Florentines, singly and in pairs, are energetically sculling between the little falls, a hundred yards downstream, and Ponte San Niccolò. Two pairs of red-shirted oarsmen seem to be practicing for some future race, rowing hard into a swarm of single scullers (I counted fifteen), who sought to scramble out of the way.

On the opposite bank, several fishermen have stationed themselves a dozen yards apart and are casting their lines into the river. They evidently spent the night there; a little red tent can be seen in front of some bushes; and we imagine that they were up at dawn.*

Santa Croce and its environs, seen from that window, was "way over there"; the river and its busy life lay in between; and when we visited the area occasionally—perhaps to get some ice cream from the Vivoli *gelateria* or to look at art books in the excellent Salimbeni bookstore farther along Via Palmieri—it was decidedly and stimulatingly an excursion into a different world. But, of

---

* This extremely well-designed and cozily inviting two-floor apartment belonged, as it still does, to Guido and Anne Calabresi, friends of nearly thirty years. We share a devotion to Florence, and have met there frequently; our two sets of children attended the American School together. In recent years, the Calabresis have made use of their Via della Fornace apartment whenever Guido has been able to snatch a few days away from his duties as Dean of the Yale Law School, and when Anne can escape her municipal commitments and give time to her ongoing book about Tuscan *contadini* and their continuing use of ancient forms of agriculture. Twice, when the apartment was free, we have been their fortunate tenants.

The view described above is the one presented in the frontispiece of this book.

CAFE RIVOIRE

LOGGIA
DEI LANZI

PALAZZO
VECCHIO

PIAZZALE
DONATELLO

VIALE ANTONIO GRAMSCI

P.
GHIBERTI

PIAZZA
BECCARIA

VIA FIESOLANA

VIA SANT' EGIDIO

VIA DELL' ORIUOLO

P.
SALVEMINI

VIA PIETRAPIANA

P.
DE'
CIOMPI

VIA DELL' AGNOLO

BORGO DEGLI ALBIZI

VIA DEL NEGHISSOLI

VIA PALMIERI

VIA VERDI

VIA DE' PEPI

VIA DE' MACCI

VIA BONAROTI

VIA GHIBELLINA

VIALE DELLA GIOVANE ITALIA

VIALE GIOVANNI AMENDOLA

VIA GHIBELLINA

P. S.
FIRENZE

PIAZZA
S. CROCE

VIA DI SAN GIUSEPPE

VIA DEI MALCONTENTI

BORGO ALLEGRI

PIAZZA
DELLA
SIGNORIA

P.
PIAVE

L. PECORI GIRALDI

VIA DEI NERI

VIA DEI BENCI

LUNGARNO DELLA ZECCA VECCHIA

PONTE S.
NICCOLO

L. D. ARCHIBUSIERI

L. MEDICI

L. DIAZ

L. DELLE GRAZIE

ARNO RIVER

ARNO RIVER

PONTE
ALLE
GRAZIE

PORTA DI
GIUSTIZIA

BADIA

BARGELLO

S. FIRENZE
TRIBUNAL

VIVOLI'S
ICE CREAM

S. CROCE AND
PAZZI CHAPEL

Santa Croce quarter

ARNO RIVER

PONTE ALLE
GRAZIE

VIA DEI BARDI

LUNGARNO SERRISTORI

VIA DEI RENAI

VIA SAN NICCOLO

VIA SAN NICCOLO

PORTA S.
NICCOLO

LUNGARNO CELLINI

VIA DELLA FORNACE

PONTE S. NICCOLO

PIAZZA
FERRUCCI

Via della Fornace area

course, each of these entities, experienced from within, is not only a specific place of residence and of activity; it is also a neighborhood. None is more so than the urban sector dominated by the church of Santa Croce, where we spent six months from the early fall of 1992 to the early spring of 1993.

The apartment was again high up, on the fourth floor (American); happily there was an elevator, for otherwise each ascent would have required a climb of nearly seventy steps. Many was the time that we gaped with incredulity when some delivery man, ignoring the elevator with Florentine bravado, hefted a huge carton from home or several cases of wine from our local *vinaio* all the way up the stairs, almost at a run. (*The Stairs of Florence*—someone should write a book with that title, perhaps a sequel to Mary McCarthy's *The Stones of Florence*. Stairs are what confront you everywhere, at public monuments or private dwellings; witness the daunting flight of steps that leads up to the Uffizi galleries.)

The building itself, to give it its most familiar name, is Palazzo Antella; it occupies about half of the southern side of the piazza and is one of the most resplendent edifices in the city. It seems that, in the second half of the seventeenth century, a wealthy mercantile family called del Barbigia built a mansion on the site, incorporating several old, perhaps medieval, houses belonging to the Ricoveri clan. One feature of the del Barbigia palazzo was the line of stone projections—designated in English by the phrase "corbel courses" and in Italian by the word *sporti*—set in place (in 1565) to sustain the overhanging second story and the stories above. It was an old Florentine architectural device; in fact, the Palazzo Antella *sporti* replaced wooden ones, said to have been "old and ugly," of the Ricoveri houses. But the usage was discontinued when Duke Alessandro de' Medici declared his opposition to it, as an impediment to light and movement.

In the first years of the seventeenth century, Costanza del Barbigia married Niccolo dell' Antella, of a family that played an important role in the political and cultural life of Florence. The palazzo was part of Costanza's dowry, and before long her husband acquired the adjoining house of Filippo Gondi (just then passing through bankruptcy) and commissioned Giulio Parigi to unify the two buildings. Niccolo served as the Grand Duke's representative at the Accademia del Disegno (originally founded by Cosimo I in the 1560s), and was in touch with the best painters in Florence. In consultation with Parigi, he oversaw an extraordinary enterprise: the decoration of the newly enlarged facade of the palazzo by thirteen painters (some say twelve), working uninterruptedly for twenty days. They produced a fabulously colorful display, covering every available inch: single figures and pairs, human, animal, and symbolic; graceful, heroic, portentous; in every kind of garb. Among the painters, the Val d'Arno artist Giovanni di San Giovanni received the greatest acclaim, and it was said that thereafter no great work of fresco painting was undertaken in Florence that was not assigned to his brush (an entire *sala* in Palazzo Pitti now bears his name). The frescoes virtually faded away over the next several centuries, but they were restored in part in the 1920s, and a more thoroughgoing job was completed in 1990.

The palazzo by this time had passed from the dell' Antella family (which died out in 1696) to the del Borgos and della Stufas, and in the late 1920s it came into the hands of the Cinelli family. The most striking member of this latter clan was Delfino Cinelli, a writer of great charm and power, whose semiautobiographical and artfully evocative novel *Castiglion che Dio sol sa* (1931) bespoke Cinelli's deep love and knowledge of the Tuscan countryside, as well as his uncommonly resolute and clear-headed antifascism (because of which he spent his last years in the United States, dying there in 1942). Palazzo Antella was inherited by Cinelli's daughter Federica, whose marriage to Sallustio Piccolomini (named for the Roman historian Sallust, but known to all as Bandino) brought into the family a line of descent going back to Enea Silvio Piccolomini, the humanistic Pope Pius II, whose comely Latin writings I encountered in graduate school, and whose beautifully refashioned little hometown south of Siena, renamed Pienza by and for him, makes so rewarding a visit. Contessa Federica Piccolomini, a superlative padrona, rents out a number of apartments in her palazzo for shorter and longer periods, and it was in one of them that we took up our stay.

It consisted of a fairly large space, neatly divided into a living room and a dining room (both amply furnished), with an artfully designed raised fireplace; a comfortable main bedroom; an in-between-room, usable for a guest or guests; a back bedroom, where once (we guessed) a governess or maid had slept; two bathrooms; a well-equipped kitchen down the hallway, with a table where the two of us took our meals; and an alcove of sorts which served as my work space. Here we lived from October to April, liking it very much; and being spoiled, in the later months, by Rita Meiners, a Florentine woman married to an electronics expert, who came in twice a week to clean and converse, and collaborate in the preparation of delectable Tuscan dishes. Another Florentine friendship developed; and in the winter, Rita and her husband, Fausto, drove us down to the castello, which is their real home, below Greve in the Chianti country, for an enchanting, long day of Tuscan vistas and hospitality.

All the windows in the apartment, six of them, looked onto Piazza Santa Croce. It is unique in Florence now, this urban opening, the only piazza that truly functions as a piazza in the great tradition. Piazza Santissima Annunziata used to be such a space; and with its cluster of attractions—Brunelleschi's Innocenti, the loggia facing it, the portico of Michelozzo's church, Palazzo Grifoni, Giambologna's equestrian statue of Grand Duke Ferdinand I, and Tacca's fountains—it has the makings of one of the handsomest squares in the world. But the Annunziata has fallen on bad days: cars and motorbikes crowd in and around it, blotting out its features; bottles and plastic containers and other debris litter its surfaces; drug-ridden derelicts sleep on the loggia steps. (One hears, though, that a doughty sixty-year-old, Gino Bandini, sweeps the place clean every morning before going off to his work of grooming horses on a farm outside of town; he is becoming a local saint.) Santa Croce too was a parking lot until recently; pictures of it submerged under automobiles make one's heart sink. But now cars are forbidden to park even briefly at the sides or the ends, until seven in the evening; and the piazza has come back into its proper life.

People walk across it endlessly, moving briskly toward some destination or, in a leisurely fashion, looking about to enjoy the stalwart buildings that surround it. They walk singly or in pairs or threesomes, or occasionally in tourist groups of as many as forty or fifty picture snappers, these latter, taking photos of the church or the piazza or this building; we gaze down at them as they peer up at us through their lenses. Children and teenagers hurry across on their way to school; *bravi ragazzi* they seem to us, all of them, with their lively morning faces and the hefty book bags on their shoulders. Young mothers or fathers go by, pushing a baby carriage, sometimes with one or two very young children in tow. We were interested to observe that we could fairly well distinguish the nationalities of grown-ups seen from above—as between Italians and non-Italians at any rate, and the Americans in particular (from their physical posture and gait, pitch of voice, rhythm of laughter). But the three-year-olds and four-year-olds might be any nationality on earth, as they dashed away busily for a few yards, then came rushing back, then set off on another twenty-yard excursion. Men appeared at an early hour each morning taking their dogs for an airing; we grew to recognize the special bark of the brown-haired spaniel and the dark-haired police dog. Dogs have no nationality either.

The space in front of the church of Santa Croce has been the scene of a more public kind of activity since the Franciscan friars preached here to the Florentine populace in the thirteenth century. *Giostra*, joustings, and *calcio*, soccer games, were held here from the fifteenth century onward (the marker indicating the midpoint of the football field, mentioned earlier, is almost directly below our window). Christopher Hibbert has given a dramatic account of the joust that took place in February 1469, in which Lorenzo de' Medici won the top prize, and eighteen Florentine nobles played the part of the knights (the whole affair, needless to say, is a ritual reenactment of an earlier medieval display):

Preceded by heralds, standard-bearers, fifers, trumpeters, and accompanied by pages and men-at-arms, the knights paraded through the piazza to the enthusiastic cheers of their thousands of supporters. All of them were magnificently clothed and most had elaborate armour and helmets especially made for the occasion, displays of beauty being more highly regarded on these occasions than demonstrations of reckless courage and strength.

None of the knights looked finer than Lorenzo de' Medici . . . His white charger, which was draped in red and white pearl-encrusted velvet, was a gift from the King of Naples; another charger, which he rode for the jousting, was presented to him by Duke Borso d'Este of Ferrara; his suit of armour came from the Duke of Milan.

The tournament was in honor of Clarice Orsini, shortly to be married to Lorenzo; it cost 10,000 ducas, and was the subject of Luigi Pulci's poem *La Giostra di Lorenzo de' Medici*.*

The tradition was continued in the nineteenth century when masked balls and other social ceremonies took place here. It is very much alive today. Soon after our arrival, we watched a vigil with candles on the steps of the church, convened to protest a recent surge of racism in Italy; and there was a similar meeting a bit later to announce and encourage some strike or other. Soccer is played or practiced at all hours in the piazza and by all ages: in groups of three or four, and sometimes with what looks like a complete team getting ready for a weekend *partita*. Four-year-olds kick and chase and tumble enthusiastically, already showing a natural aptitude. The big lights in the piazza are kept lit all night, and it is not uncommon to hear the cries and the thud of soccer practice on that stone-hard surface at three in the morning.

Early in October, we were treated to a spectacle of skill and daring in the piazza that clearly descends from its *giostra* ancestry.

---

* Christopher Hibbert, *The Rise and Fall of the House of Medici* (1974), Ch. IX. The author also gives an account of the tournament held in 1475 to celebrate Giuliano de' Medici ("twenty-two years old, tall, dark-haired, athletic and universally admired"), who had his standard designed by Botticelli and his helmet by Verrochio. This event inspired Poliziano's *Stanze della Giostra di Giuliano de' Medici*, that writer's "earliest literary masterpiece."

Jousting in Piazza Santa Croce, sixteenth century

Preparation for football (soccer game), Piazza Santa Croce, 1744

Piazza Santa Croce

"Midfield marker" for soccer games   Somersaulting automobile in Piazza Santa Croce, 1993

It took shape gradually. There was, first, a gigantic steel stand or easel set up at mid-piazza one afternoon. Next, a small compact automobile—a Golf Cabrio, as we learned—appeared alongside the structure, eventually to be hoisted up to the top girder and hung there almost vertically. Small crowds were gathering at this stage, moving about the strange sight to inspect it from all angles; and as the onlooking Florentines pointed their fingers, cocked their heads, addressed one another in puzzlement or disbelief, they reminded us of nothing so much as a group of observers in a painting, say, by Ghirlandaio or perhaps Masaccio, conversing in wonderment together as they looked upon some miraculous happening or angelic appearance. In the piazza, on the third day, there arrived television trucks, camera crews, klieg lights; and finally the truth became known.

It was the makings of a Saturday night live sequence of a weekly television program called *Scommetiamo Che?—Would You Like to Make a Bet?*—wherein a panel of guest stars (Peter Ustinov showed up on one of these programs) place bets with the master of ceremonies that such and such an undertaking will or will not be accomplished. In the present instance, the bet was for and against the possibility that a forty-two-year-old Florentine commercial agent named Andrea Anderlini could make his Golf Cabrio swing over completely, three times, on the easel, purely by the power of the car's motor; and that he could hold the machine stationary in midturn by the power of his brakes. Andorlini was a pretty good investment: he had appeared on *Scommetiamo Che?* the year before, whisking away a long tablecloth (attached to his car) on a table set for thirty people without breaking a single glass or plate.

On this particular Saturday night, we watched from our windows, occasionally glancing back at our television set, while Andorlini—cheered on by several thousand persons hugging the piazza's sidelines (among them Andorlini's wife and eleven-year-old son) and awaiting the technological miracle—made the car spin up and over three times, holding it horizontally in place for some timeless moment, his hand raised in triumph. Afterwards, Andorlini, though showing no ill effects, confessed that he experienced a brief fright when he saw the car rapidly losing water and oil.

The piazza is dominated by the church, as it has been for almost seven hundred years. The polychrome marble facade, with its sculptures, was not put in place until 1863 (the bell tower dates from about the same time), and it has come into a good deal of head shaking. "Hideous" is the word used by the often pungently accurate editor of the *American Express Pocket Guide*. In fact, the *facciata* is based on a neo-Gothic design of the seventeenth century; and as with other (far from all) "modern" additions to the Florentine cityscape, one can—after living near it and looking at it day after day—develop a certain affection for it. We could not resist telling each other, about the church, that we'd grown accustomed to her facade, it almost made the day begin. The monumental statue of Dante, it can be added, was set up in the middle of the square when it was inaugurated in 1865, on the six hundredth anniversary of the poet's birth. It was out of place there; by this midcentury, it loomed up distractedly amid the sea of parked cars, and in 1988 it was moved to where it better belonged, at the top of the steps on the northern side of the church.

About the interior of the church, John Ruskin spoke with customary disdain: "The ugliest Gothic church you were ever in," he wrote in *Mornings in Florence*; it had "no vaultings at all"—and so was not even a Ruskin-style Gothic building—and "the roof of a farm-house barn." He wondered if it could really have been designed by "the renowned Arnolfo," but then he looked with favor on some of its individual features. Among those latter, as we have said, are the extraordinary contributions, in the chapels and along the walls, of Giotto, Agnolo Gaddi (his *Story of the True Cross*, c. 1390, around the high altar, was a main inspiration for Piero della Francesca's version of the legend of Santa Croce in Arezzo), Michelozzo, Donatello, and others; and the gallery of tombs and memorials of great Florentines—(in order) Michelangelo; Dante; the tragic poet Alfieri (by Canova); Machiavelli; Ugo Foscolo the Risorgimento poetic champion; the two humanist chancellors Leonardo Bruni and Carlo Marsuppini; Galileo; Gino

Church of Santa Croce, with Pazzi Chapel

Santa Croce: *The Death of Saint Francis*, by Giotto (Bardi Chapel)

Capponi, the nineteenth-century statesman and historian. Santa Croce became for us in these months a religious and historical treasure-house where we could drop in from time to time, perhaps to gaze again at some particular art work—for example, in the Bardi di Vernio chapel at the far end on the left, Donatello's *Crucifixion*, with the realistically agonizing and sweat-covered Christ, an early masterpiece which the testy and competitive Brunelleschi dismissed by saying that Donatello had "crucified a peasant [*contadino*]," which he had brilliantly done. We could also, when asked, provide easygoing guidance through the temple for visiting friends.

The Quartiere

In no other place of residence in Florence have we lived in such intimate touch with the city's historical past, and in so many of its expressions. Every day of the week, except Sunday, I went down in the *ascensore* at 7:30 a.m., walked across the piazza to the little newsstand on the northwest corner, and there collected the daily *International Herald Tribune* and the local paper, *La Nazione*. (The two together cost 3,600 lire, an average of $2.60, within the fluctuations of the exchange.) This excursion took no more than four minutes, especially since the amiable news vendor usually spotted me coming through the square and had my papers ready in hand; but each morning it comprised a memorable little tour. A glance to the right took in the church of Santa Croce, with the billowy statue of Dante in front and, on the south side, the entrance to Brunelleschi's Pazzi chapel, with its modest dome. Walking ahead, with a few other figures moving past in both directions and several *signori* walking their dogs, I could catch a glimpse of Palazzo Vecchio, rearing up handsome and friendly, among the rooftops. I went past Palazzo Serristori, on the west side of the piazza facing the church: an interesting construct of Giuliano da Sangallo in the late 1460s, with the first floor (Italian) jutting out over the ground floor, above stone underpinnings. Closer by, on the edge of the square, was the elaborate and intricately worked marble fountain, the most recent (1968) replacement of what was originally, centuries ago, a public wash-basin. A few more steps and I could make out the thin Badia tower and the rectangular battlemented Bargello tower, seemingly inches away from each other. And then, on my way back, news-papers under my arm, I could examine once again the long fres-coed facade of Palazzo dell' Antella and, sometimes, just under the roof, the light shining in our kitchen. Breakfast should be almost ready.

That tiny morning event set a pattern: wherever we went from our Santa Croce home, on whatever domestic or social or profes-sional errand, we brushed up against the historical. We went around the corner to Piazza Peruzzi, for example, to arrange for a fresh supply of wood and kindling for our apartment fireplace, and thereby entered one of the most picturesque piazzas in Flor-ence, though one now deconstructed by the scores of cars crammed day and night into its small area. The Peruzzis were a highly regarded banking family in the early Florentine days; they went bankrupt, with several other families, during the ill-fated transactions with King Edward of England in the fourteenth cen-tury; but they continued to take part in city activities until well into the modern period, the last conspicuous member being Ubal-dino, who died in 1891, and who had much to do with the founding of the Kingdom of Italy.

Our wood supplier was a lively character. On our first visit to him, he flew into a rage at the mere mention of our address, Piazza Santa Croce 22; he almost literally leaped off the ground in his fury, and exclaimed in a thick voice that never again—"*mai, mai, mai!*"—would he deliver wood there, that he had tried to, by agreement, a few days before, and there was *no one there to receive it*. He had dumped the wood inside the palazzo door and had left. But he calmed down after a bit, and brought us several big baskets at a time throughout the winter. Our fireplace was an aesthetic and practical gem; and the fire that burned in it regularly was, as Frank Lloyd Wright said it should be, "the heart of the house."

After our negotiation in the *legnaia*, we would usually stroll back along Via de' Bentaccordi, crossing Borgo dei Greci and then

Via dell' Anguillara to Via Torta, and so out to the piazza. That is, we followed the vast curve of the ancient amphitheater, which filled that great space outside the eastern wall of the Roman city. It was a gigantic construct, of more than Yale Bowl proportions, and was, as Marcello Vannucci has said, the glory of the city. Florence, writes Professor Vannucci, was anything but a secondary outpost to Rome.

It possessed an amphitheater hardly inferior to the Colosseum, where there were held spectacles—above all, gladiatorial—that aroused great enthusiasm in the big crowds that hurried in from the nearby countryside to watch them, and that came in such numbers as to remind one a little of a Sunday crowd in a modern stadium. We may well believe that the most popular athlete, the idol of the crowd . . . was honored as much as was the Emperor and perhaps more.

The old palazzo of the Peruzzi was built on the ruins of the amphitheater. We walked around the whole affair many a time, marveling at its sheer bulk—broken as it is now, of course, by two cross streets. The last phase of it is on Via Torta, a word that means "twisted" or "curving," as descriptive of the ancient sportive oval.

One place to pause on the way back from the wood store is the corner of Via dei Bentaccordi and Via dell' Anguillara, where a plaque tells us that Michelangelo Buonarotti "spent his childhood in this house." The plaque fumbles Michelangelo's birthplace a little, giving either the wrong village or the wrong region;* but it seems true that at the age of five or six, after his mother died, Michelangelo was brought in from Settignano, where he had been in the charge of a wet nurse, and joined the rest of the family on what his father in a public declaration called "Via da Bentachordi." It was only a decade or so later, in 1490–92, that Michelangelo was executing such youthful marvels as *The Battle*

---

* Michelangelo seems to have been born on March 6, 1475, in the town of Caprese, near Arezzo, where his father, Ludovico, was mayor.

of the Centaurs and *The Madonna of the Stairs*, works which, with others, may be seen at the Casa Buonarotti, the property on Via Ghibellina, a few blocks away, that Michelangelo bought in 1508 and later gave to his nephew Ludovico. (It became a public museum in 1858.) It is generally thought to be altogether fitting that when Michelangelo died in Rome in 1564 (at age 89), and his body was brought back furtively to Florence, he should have been buried in his old parish church of Santa Croce.

We made our way periodically up Via Verdi to the big post office at the corner of Via Pietrapiana: going there to mail our letters (no sensible person drops letters in the red mailboxes, from which, so one hears, they are collected only on whim), and also to pay bills. One of the peculiar arrangements of Italian life requires you to stand in line at the post office at stated times to pay the rent, or the electricity, or some other household account. Via Verdi runs north from Piazza Santa Croce; it is a continuation of Via de' Benci, which itself starts from the river and the Ponte alle Grazie. The route carried us past Teatro Verdi, which, with a capacity of three thousand and despite its name, caters mostly to operettas and musical comedies (*My Fair Lady*, in some strange mix of languages, played there in the fall of 1992). The post office was designed by Florence's premier architect, Giovanni Michelucci, in his last years (he died not long ago at age 100). It is rather disdained by local commentators—it looks like a stranded ship, said one of them. It is four stories high, and the middle portion bulges and overhangs; but its long ground-floor corridor is not uninviting.

Via Verdi ends at Piazza Salvemini, a busy intersection named for the fiercely freedom-loving professor of history in Florence, Gaetano Salvemini, who escaped from Italy in the 1920s and taught at Harvard from 1933 through the war years. As I have mentioned, I stumbled into his small lecture course on the history of Florence, and listened, fascinated, as Salvemini, beard bristling, spoke of the conditions and aspirations of the wool workers and the craftsmen in the Florentine thirteenth and fourteenth centuries. He came back to Italy after the war's end; and began his first discourse at the University of Florence with the words: "As I was saying in my last lecture . . ." Salvemini died in Sorrento in 1957, at the age of 84.

Three streets spray west from Piazza Salvemini toward the Duomo area; on each, we often had something to search out or take care of, and each had its special historical appeal. On the northernmost of these, Via Sant' Egidio, and beyond a shop that sells the most charming terra-cotta ware in the city, is the hospital of Santa Maria Nuova: not very thrilling architecturally—though both Buontalenti and Giulio Parigi contributed to the *loggiata*, in the early 1600s—but one of the great hospitals in Italy and perhaps in the world. It owes its origin in part to the generosity, in the late 1280s, of Folco Portinari, one of the town's leading citizens and the father of Dante's Beatrice.

Next, Via dell' Oriuolo angles away from the piazza. Its slightly tongue-baffling name is a Florentine version of *orologio*, the word for clock or watch; and it seems related to the name of the mechanism that makes the hourly bells ring, for example, in Palazzo Vecchio. Along this street, and past two indispensable resources (for shoe repair and leather-goods repair), is the Museo di Firenze com' era—Museum of Florence as It Used to Be—a differently indispensable resource for many students, including this writer. It was founded as a museum of Florentine history around 1950 on premises long occupied by the Oblate Sisters; it has a lovely garden in front, and an attractive interior courtyard. Inside, it offers treasures of sketches and prints of the city, its features, and some of its leading citizens from the fifteenth through the nineteenth centuries, with the classic maps of the city and the eighteenth-century prints of Giuseppe Zocchi.

Finally, there is Borgo degli Albizzi, the very sound of which wakes up some echoes. The Albizzi were, it will be recalled, the most tenacious of the enemies of the Medici family and especially of Cosimo the Elder; they almost got him assassinated and that generation of the clan spent the rest of its days in furious exile. The street that memorializes them has another good shop for terra-cotta and other items, and a long row of self-respecting palazzi.

Returning to our piazza from this part of the *quartiere*, we liked to wend our way down Via Palmieri, which runs parallel to Via Verdi, though it is much narrower and darker. It begins in the piazza of San Pietro Maggiore, a title which serves to distinguish the square from others named for the Apostle Peter. There is something likable about this irregularly spaced piazza, entirely free from cars as it is, and with a nice medley of the historical and the contemporary: the high arch, which is all that remains of the original (1630s) large and impressive loggia of the church of San Pietro, which can itself trace its ancestry back to the year 1000; a lean brownstone medieval tower; the smaller archway that once led to the north-circling city wall; several other palazzi of note; a discreet-seeming restaurant, a pizzeria, and a Grana Market—one of a chain of eight stores in the town that among other things sells the best Tuscan and Italian cheeses.

At Via Ghibellina, still heading south, Via Palmieri gives way to an area called Isola delle Stinche. We used to come over to this place from other parts of town (as I've said), especially from across the river at Via della Fornace, to visit the *gelateria* of Vivoli; but now we came also to look about the old Isola. It was the name of a huge prison-house built in the 1290s—on land confiscated from the defeated and detested Uberti—to contain prisoners of various kinds. The prison building was in effect a fortress, surrounded by a moat filled with water (Via Verdi, on the eastern side, used to be called Via del Fosso, that is, a ditch, or moat); so that the great edifice was indeed an island, an *isola*. The name "Stinche," unappealing to Anglo-American ears, comes from the name of a castle in the Chianti belonging to the Cavalcanti: Le Stinche. The first occupants of the prison had been captured there, so that the new place was known as "The Island of those seized at Le Stinche," and then, for short, "The Island of Le Stinche." Six centuries later, the ancient prison was taken over, remodeled, and brightened up as the Teatro Verdi, in honor of the recently (1901) deceased opera composer.

Vivoli's *gelateria*, meanwhile, continues to display thirty different kinds and combinations of ice cream, among them chestnut, hazelnut, blood orange, and many varieties of chocolate and mint.

"The taste," says one customer, who has known Vivoli since she was eight years old, "is different from anything you get in America."

Of an evening, at intervals, we walked in a quite different direction, going past and behind our church into the web of streets where three of our favorite restaurants in Florence (or anywhere else) could be found: in no particular order, the restaurants named Dino, Cibreo, and La Baraonda. This is the Sant' Ambrogio section, containing both the church and the big marketplace of that name. For us the area began just to the left of the church (as one walks east), with the newly inaugurated Largo Bargellini, in memory of the Florentine who was mayor of the city at the time of the 1966 flood, and who died in 1980, in his nineties. He was exceptionally well-versed in the history of Florence, and wrote frequently about it; though he might perhaps (it is no less honorific) be called a learned journalist rather than a scholar. He was the editor in chief of the six-volume compilation *Le strade di Firenze*, which informs one of every point of interest in every street in the city and immediate suburbs, with excellent little biographies of those for whom the street is named (for instance, and simply in our own neighborhood, Verdi, Salvemini, Albizzi, Palmieri, Neri, Pazzi, San Giuseppe). During the flood, as has been recorded, he behaved with energy and steady good sense.

Largo Bargellini continues a couple of blocks, crossing Via Pinzochere (another name of tortuous linguistic descent, probably referring to the grayish color of the gown worn by widows and maidens associated with the Franciscan order, and about whom scandalous and unproven tales abounded). At a certain point Largo Bargellini changes to Via San Giuseppe, but after two more blocks it changes again to Via dei Malcontenti. The whole stretch used to be known as Via dei Malcontenti—literally, "the discontented ones"—but that was a derisive, ironic title bestowed in ancient times by the Florentines upon the wretched folk being led down in chains to the Porta di Giustizia and the gallows erected there. They came from the Bargello—its tower is clearly visible from anywhere on the fateful street—or the Isola delle Stinche: down Via dei Neri, over Borgo Santa Croce, across the square, and then down the long stretch of Via dei Malcontenti to the awaiting gibbet, where they would be hanged for some criminal offense. Today the *via* ends at Piazza Piave, overlooking the river; the old city gate has disappeared, but there is still standing the tower of the old minting workshop, Torre della Zecca Vecchia—"solitary and indifferent," in the words of one observer (in *Le Strade*), "despite all the traffic which swirls around its feet." Capital punishment, incidentally, was abolished in Florence in 1782, largely through the influence of the Milanese jurist Cesare Beccaria and his treatise of 1764 *Dei delitti e delle pene* (*Of Crimes and Punishments*). The sturdy tower of Piazza Beccaria, honoring him, looks down the *viale* toward the place that once held the scaffold, and beyond it to the river.

The *malcontenti* may have been assisted a little, spiritually, or they may only have been cast into greater gloom, by a company of brethren—Compagnia dei Neri, named for their black hoods —who received permission in the mid-fourteenth century to build a chapel along the route and to chant a Mass for the Dead as the prisoners shuffled by. But in the Florentine topography, a happier note was struck at an earlier moment on the narrow street that leads away from the present Via San Giuseppe, toward the church of Sant' Ambrogio. The street is called Borgo Allegri, "the happy ones." Cimabue had his workshop there, and, according to Vasari, when the visiting King Charles of Anjou was taken to see Cimabue's *Madonna* around 1280, an enormous crowd of citizens followed along and were so excited by the painting that they carried it in triumphant procession down the street—"which thus," says Vasari, "they called Borgo Allegri . . . and it has retained that name ever since."* Elizabeth Barrett Browning, in *Casa Guidi Windows*, speaks of "Cimabue's Virgin" and says that:

---

* Sober scholarship would have it that the street name derived rather from the Allegri family, which lived hereabouts from the 1340s onward; it too fell afoul of Cosimo the Elder, but it also produced the painter Antonio Allegri, known as Correggio. But many prefer the Vasari version.

A king stood bare before its sovran grace,
A reverent people shouted to behold
The picture, not the king, and even the place
Containing such a miracle grew bold,
Named the Glad Borgo from that beauteous face.

We ourselves, returning from this area, preferred to walk back along the Glad Borgo, buoyed by the recent meal and the mild awareness that both Cimabue and, a century and a half later, Ghiberti had their studios here.

The route we followed most often on our sorties took us up Borgo dei Greci (past the hospitable palazzo-home of Ubaldino and Emilia Peruzzi, a social and literary center of special popularity during the days of *Firenze Capitale*), then across the quietly busy Piazza San Firenze, and up the slope to Piazza della Signoria—there, perhaps, to look in at Pineider's across the square for some stylish notepaper, or to take coffee or tea at Rivoire's cafe, or to go for lunch or supper in the comfortable atmosphere of Cavallino's restaurant on the northern edge. Or simply to pass through to other errands on Via dei Calzaiuoli and the streets beyond.

It was Piazza San Firenze that particularly caught our attention, and our fancy, in these months. We had not taken it in on previous visits; but now what had seemed only a vague confusion of styles gradually sorted itself out (it is a quintessential Florentine experience) into an arresting historical pattern. The structure for which the piazza was named is a tellingly complicated affair: a *seventeenth*-century church on the left (as you face it), eventually paired with an *eighteenth*-century oratory on the right; the two of them united by a single facade in the 1770s, with a boldly formed palazzo thrust in between and two authoritative angels with trumpets up above. The palazzo and the oratory are now the seat of the Tribunale, the chief law court of the city. The whole mammoth, oddly coordinated building, as it now stands, is thought to be the strongest example in Florence of baroque architecture.

Directly across the way and in almost total contrast is the Palazzo Gondi. It was stylishly designed, probably in 1490, by Giuliano da Sangallo, for his friend, the merchant Giuliano di Lionardo Gondi, who was returning to his native Florence after a long and profitable career in Naples. With its three arched portals on the ground levels, and its perfection of symmetry and contained force, it is a model of Renaissance beauty and severity; and it is frequently coupled with Palazzo Strozzi (early chroniclers, in fact, dated the Gondi palace the same year that Palazzo Strozzi famously took its start) as the ideal representative of its kind. In 1870, the nearly four-hundred-year-old building underwent a perhaps necessary operation, when Giuseppe Poggi was called on to cut away the southern flank to permit the street running alongside (now Via de' Gondi) to be widened. Poggi's new facade seems a bit cool in context; but seen from a certain distance and the right perspective, the palazzo has a renewed integrity and charm.*

In this piazza, we came to feel, the *quartiere* of Santa Croce reaches its fulfillment. The towers of the Badia and the Bargello seem to stand there, together, in particular and long-enduring familiarity. As one's eye moves about the piazza, indeed, it perceives the thirteenth-century Badia and the fifteenth-century Bargello; then, the exemplary Renaissance private home and the exemplary eighteenth-century religious shrine facing one another, with a nineteenth-century addition on the side. "Only in Florence," writes the editor of *Le strade di Firenze*, "is it possible—pausing in the midst of a piazza like this one, full of unpredictable surprises—to make out with such assurance the passage from one epoch to another, from one style to another, from one manner of taste to another."

And to tell the truth, the Piazza della Signoria, when we arrived there on these outings, was a recurring disappointment. It is being restored to death. As of January 1, 1993, the following restorables greeted the gaze of anyone entering the square: the towering

---

* The present occupant, Marchese Gondi, whom we encountered at a small lunch party, proved to have his own very considerable charm, to be a witty and effervescent person in his eighties, bubbling over with anecdotes and given to a speech that shifted in rapid mid-sentence, or even mid-word, from English to Florentine.

equestrian statue of Duke Cosimo I, done by Giambologna in the 1590s, was encased in a sort of gigantic wooden box, entirely invisible; the Loggia dei Lanzi, that great gathering place for community and art, was shut away behind a wire fence and scaffolding, its pillars draped with plastic bagging; the pavement of the Piazzale degli Uffizi, between the two long wings of the gallery, was torn up; the palazzo across from Palazzo Vecchio—it is an undistinguished product of the 1870s, but in its massive way it dominates the square—was swathed in canvas bandages from top to bottom, its facade blanked out; the entrance to the Cassa di Risparmio on the northern border was obstructed by an ugly wooden structure; and to the right, some more scaffolding.

What began in the city as a response to a very serious need for the restoration and bolstering of some of the public buildings developed first into an obsession, and then into a kind of hysteria. (Something of the same, I am told by the well-informed, has happened with regard to painting; Michelangelo's *Holy Family*, now half-hidden behind plate glass, is a disconcerting case in point.) Enterprises without system are being carried out by agencies (again, so one hears) not adequately equipped for the job. The Loggia dei Lanzi, meanwhile, is probably ruined for good, its statues lurking behind the metal and plastic, never again to be truly accessible to the visiting observer.

Similar restorative goings on, of course, are occurring in other Italian cities—in our most recent view, in Venice and Bologna. But there, at least, one senses a certain sequence and timing to the work; you do not find an entire priceless section of the town under wraps; nor is the process of uglification so intense. As to Florence, it must be admitted that the Piazza della Signoria is improved in one respect: during our previous stay, four years earlier, its whole pavement was ripped up and open (in successful search, it seems, for some ancient relic and bones buried beneath it). And there are undeniable instances of completed restoration: as an example, the Brancacci Chapel in the Carmine, with the frescoes of Masaccio and Masolino, which opened to view at last in 1992. That job took an unconscionable amount of time, years more than were truly necessary (while finances were squabbled over). It is now a high-style commercial venture; one enters it no longer through the church but through side doors and across courtways, and after paying several thousand lire per ticket. But the frescoes, restored, are thrilling; no other word suffices.* Beyond that, one can only applaud, and thank the urban powers for it, the marvelous new tidying up of the Piazza del Duomo, standing out now clear and distinct for the first time in one's memory, liberated from that desecrating swarm of parked vehicles which has been a source of revulsion for visitors from John Ruskin onward. Cathedral and bell tower and Baptistery and the spaces around them: each and all together have recovered their true nature.

The Neighborhood

The residents of the Santa Croce *quartiere* are not the most vigorous, among Florentines, in praise and defense of their urban region. That honor goes without question to the inhabitants of San Frediano, the zone named for the ancient church and the Borgo so designated, itself part of the Santo Spirito *quartiere* in Oltrarno, and including the Carmine and the grand old Porta San Frediano. The San Fredianini—in their local habitation, they have earned a local name—express themselves in a spicily slangy dialect of their own creation; and to cross the river into their area, says Eve Borsook, "is to cross into alien territory." The Florentine novelist Vasco Pratolini has given the section permanent fictional life in *Le ragazze di San Frediano* (1951) and the still better-known earlier work *Cronache di poveri amanti* (*Tales of Poor Lovers*, 1947). And when the municipal authorities, in the fall of 1992, threatened

---

* An article in *La Nazione* for April 5, 1986, announced that "within about a year . . . there will be completed the most important restoration in the history of Florence: that of the marvelous chapel of the Carmine, the fundamental testimony of the early Renaissance created by Masaccio, Masolino, and Filippo Lippi." The work was being financed "without limit" by Olivetti, the article continued; and its completion would give courage to anyone "who trembles for the conservation of the Giotto of the Scrovegni Chapel in Padua, the Piero della Francesca in Arezzo, the churches of Assisi, the tabernacles of Florence." The article went into persuasive detail about the extraordinary difficulty and complexity of art restoration, and the many challenges and questions that the Florentine authorities had not yet faced up to.

to bar all traffic and parking on a stretch of Borgo San Frediano, the protest that resulted had a strong patriotic tone: here was another sign, it was said, that San Frediano was "a city forgotten, depressed, provoked into rebellion." It had been (in an effective Italianizing) *"snobbato"* by the lordly denizens of the other side of the river, on Via Tornabuoni and Via della Vigna Nuova, who were carelessly endangering the quarter's livelihood.

But the San Fredianini are only an extreme version of sectional pride. The Santa Croceans exhibit something of the same quality, and it shows up especially in the somber pleasure they take in recalling the flood days of November 1966, how horrifically they were inundated, how grievously the whole area suffered—particularly Piazza Santa Croce—and how heroically they fought back and survived. A marker on a building opposite our palazzo showed that the water surged there to a height of fifteen feet.

It rained almost unceasingly during the first eight or ten weeks of our stay in Palazzo dell' Antella. At times the rain came down with such force that one could scarcely believe it possible. There were occasional fits of lightning, followed by thunderclaps that, during the night, sounded like avalanches taking place in the piazza. And during the day, walking about—that essential Florentine activity—became a problem. I noted in my journal for October 21: "It is difficult enough at any time to walk along these narrow streets or on three-foot-wide sidewalks. But to walk along with a raised umbrella is almost impossible. You have to push your umbrella higher (so that it doesn't function properly), or slide it sideways to grate against the wall, or step off into the puddles and the oncoming cars." By late October, it was obvious that we were experiencing that every-quarter-of-a-century-or-so torrent and flooding that was spoken of after the 1966 *alluvione.*

The papers grew full of flood stories and memories, talk of alarms and alerts. "Thousands crowd the bridges, paralyzed with fear" ran the typical lead-ins; and there were allusions to *finimondo,* the end of the world. We walked around to Ponte alle Grazie every so often, and saw little sign of the panic alleged. People crowded onto the bridge, certainly, but they seemed to be looking down at the swollen heaving waters rather with interest and excitement. An official estimate in early November, after a day and an evening of blindingly heavy rain, declared that Florence had undergone the heaviest rain in a single month in 180 years, and perhaps longer: more than two feet. And from conversations with Florentine acquaintances, we were made to realize, as never before, how profoundly traumatic the 1966 flood event had been to almost everyone in the city. It was something all the more terrible exactly because it *did* occur so relatively soon after the frightful war-summer of 1944. Little wonder that Florentines today, particularly those who live near the Arno, cancel all appointments and dig in, whenever big rainfalls come and the river begins to rise.

The daily household-supplying in this most neighborly of Florentine sectors was, if anything, even better for morale than it had been in the places along Via San Niccolò (as it slopes upward and then down into Via de' Bardi), in the Via della Fornace days, or on Borgo Ognissanti. Via dei Neri was our shopping street. It begins near Ponte alle Grazie, a couple of hundred yards from our palazzo, and proceeds westward three or four blocks to Via dei Leone, in the undershadow of Palazzo Vecchio. At the final corner, there is a good-looking, high-arched loggia, designed in the early-seventeenth-century—for what was already a four hundred-year-old grain market—by Giulio Parigi, at the request of Duke Cosimo II. The latter's bust, bearing the arguable title "To the Father of the Poor" (*Egenorum Patri*), occupies a niche on the wall.

The street is not named, as one might suppose, for the medieval Florentine Black partisans (*Neri* being the plural of "black"), or even for the once well known sixteenth-century Neri family. It is instead a respelling (no one knows why) of the name Nori, a family devoted to the Medicis, whose most famous offspring, Francesco Nori, gave his life for Lorenzo—literally hurling himself in front of his friend—during the 1487 Pazzi assault in the cathedral. The Noris once had homes on this thoroughfare, as did the Davanzatis and the Rusticis.

For us, though, Via dei Neri was the way of the shops, the

best in Florence (many others would agree). There were nearly threescore stores and small establishments of all kinds from one end to the other. These included four clothing stores (one, for young people, was called Piccolo Slam); five general food stores (*alimentari*); four places to buy meat or chicken; five bakeries and bread stores; two places specializing in fruit and vegetables; one milk shop; two shoe stores; two leather stores (the real leather market was on the adjoining Borgo dei Greci); five jewelry stores; five places for household furnishings; two dry cleaners; two barbers; a florist; a record shop (*Dischi*, it said); a pharmacy; a travel agency; a photography shop; two bars; and four restaurants.

By choice and necessity, we were particularly regular customers at the Gastronomia Giuliano, whose *pizzicheria* was near our end of Via dei Neri. It was run by the brisk and amiable Giuliano, with his kindly wife, Luigina, their son, Mario, and Mario's friend Giovanna. Here we bought *prosciutto*, available in four or five different grades; roast pork; *vitello tonnato; lasagne* (some of the best you ever ate); individual portions of Russian salad; salmon and tuna mousses; items from a whole case of prepared dishes; olives; and the occasional bottle of ordinary wine. *Babbo* Giuliano and *Mama* Luigina took a warm personal interest in our needs (as in those of their other friends and customers), our little supper parties, our food experiments, and, in the Christmas season, the arrival and presentation of our children from America. On our farewell visit, in the last days of March, Luigina embraced both of us and begged us, with tears in her eyes, to tell our American friends back home that not all Italians were thieves and evildoers, like those just then being taken to prison across the land for bribery and corruption.

On the opposite side of the street, a bit farther along, was the bakery, the *forno*, conducted by Renato Zanetti and his mother. The *signora* became a special friend, and a visit to her shop always entailed a lively conversation—about bread, family, weather, personal activities, public happenings. We bought all our bread at the Zanettis—many differently shaped loaves, each with its own Florentine name; breadsticks, cookies, and other delicacies. *Signora* and son also prepared wonders of bakery: *ramerini*, big breakfast rolls made of sweet dough, with fresh rosemary and big-seeded raisins; *fritelle*, sweet fritters; *scacciate*, flat white bread, baked with olive oil and salt; *budini*, cakelike pudding (as its name suggests).

Elsewhere on Via dei Neri, we made almost daily purchases at the *ortolano*, where Andrea and Massimo Zoccali offered the freshest of fruits and vegetables from all over Italy, in all weather; at the *rosticceria* presided over by Mario (there was an informal *trattoria* at the back), where, by phone-call arrangement, hot servings of roast chicken and potatoes would be ready for us to take back; and just beyond it, at the butcher shop of Anzuini and Massi (*Carne e Salumi*). We gave our custom, once or twice, to the shoe store named Mazzoni, after looking for weeks at its fine display (mostly running shoes) in the front windows; and at Lorenzetti's, the excellent men's shop at the far end of the street, I acquired and (for a friend) we had made several perfectly tailored shirts.

Via dei Neri, obviously, represents a way of life. By comparison: the shopping center nearest our Connecticut home is dominated, in fact, is overwhelmed, by a gigantic building called the Super Stop & Shop. It contains no bars, restaurants, or barbers, but otherwise it holds almost everything one can find in the sixty-odd shops spread out on Via dei Neri. Plaques high up across the front announce a bake shop, a pharmacy, cards and books, health and beauty, a fish market, a cheese shop, and a florist; and inside, you come upon a butcher shop, a dry cleaning establishment, endless open bins of fruits and vegetables, "Hot Food to Go" (roast chicken, fried chicken, potatoes, and quite tasty-looking pizzas), a film-development counter, a money-machine, and a check-cashing corner. There are twenty-three numbered checkout counters. The greater part of the stadiumlike interior is given to mammoth four-tiered structures, eighteen of them in all, each one stretching about 160 feet across the building from side to side, and packed dense, front and back, with items. The bake shop, at the south end, as an example, displays three long glass-enclosed shelves of cakes; four long shelves of rolls and "specialty breads"; thirty-six six-tiered shelves of baked goods, with such related items as ice cream and sherbet; open piles of different loaves of bread and cookies. The so-called butcher shop is actually four very long shelves, one above the other against the back wall, each with about fifteen trays of packaged meat, each tray holding on average some forty packets. There must be more than five thousand packages of meat and sausages and the like when the shop opens every morning.

An all-purpose market of this kind under a single colossal roof is a great practical convenience, needless to say, and especially for busy working people who come by on their way home, and have about twenty minutes to get supplies for the next few days. Costs are realistic. Everything edible, except fruit and vegetables, is carefully packaged, and hence invulnerable to germs. You get almost no human help, to be sure, as you wander about among the packagings, though there is a digital machine near the entrance, which, on fingered request, flashes a map of the place and shows you where to find whatever it is you're looking for.

This is a way of life that inevitably destroys any other competitive mode. Stores of individual appeal have been mostly driven out of the Woodbridge shopping center, outmarketed by the Super Stop & Shop and the resulting immense rise in rents. A cafe-cum-delicatessen (an American *pizzicheria*) has vanished; a first-class stationery store, where we have done business for twenty years, has given up; an electrical supply shop has disappeared; a clothing store of quality moved to another mall ten miles away. The entire complex has been remodeled in the Hollywood-Swiss style of the Stop & Shop, with little white pointed roofs; and in place of the stores departed, there is now an unprepossessing array of outlets for cheap goods—cheap economically and in most other ways. What is totally missing, and is unimaginable, is the human interchange on Via dei Neri, the talk about food and cooking and recent experience, the enhancement of life thereby granted.

For certain needs and desires, we had to go farther afield than Via dei Neri. That street has no book shop (unlike the Super Stop & Shop, which has a little alcove of best-selling hardbacks and paperbacks). For books in the Santa Croce neighborhood, we went to the Paperback Exchange, at the end of Via Fiesolana, an extension of Via Verdi, where a knowing and helpful couple made

Friends in the Santa Croce neighborhood:
(top left) Giuliano and family; *(right)* Signora Zanetti and son, *fornaio*;
(middle left) *pizzicheria* offerings; *(right)* Andrea and Massimo Zoccali, *ortolano*;
(bottom) restaurateur Gino with Lewis daughters

available the works of the major English and American fiction writers, many shelves of mystery stories (I always looked there first), and an invaluable section of books on art history and dictionaries of art and architecture. Another reason for going to the Exchange was the proximity of the restaurant Acquacotta: here, on our first return visit in October, the manager, Beppo, prepared a mushroom dish which was almost out of season but which he recalled as a favorite of ours—making it as a gesture of welcome, of *"ben tornato."* For more copious literary offerings, both English and Italian, we went over to Seeber's on Via Tornabuoni, an old-time favorite with a rather stiff atmosphere; and for a still more generous collection of English-language texts, we liked the BM bookshop in Borgo Ognissanti (across the street from our lodgings in 1987), with an especially agreeable and conversable manager.

For the big art books, there was—in our neighborhood—Salimbeni's, in Via Palmieri; the learned owner, with the famous Florentine name, once lived in our palazzo. And in Piazza de' Mozzi, just across Ponte alle Grazie, is Centro Di, which probably has the best array of art books in Florence; its publishing house brought out *L'idea di Firenze*, the book based on the 1986 conference at the Gabinetto Vieusseux.

To get film developed, we made a point of walking to Nonnino's on Via Sassetti, behind Piazza della Repubblica. The efficient woman in charge is another friend of some years; it was cheering just to visit there, and the walk back has special attractions— Via Sassetti with its dignified facades; Via Davanzati and the fourteenth-century Palazzo Davanzati, its interior completely restored to late-medieval domestic life (something unique in the historic center); and down Via Condotta into Piazza San Firenze.

For wine and liquor, finally, we dealt, as we have done for close to twenty years, with Renzo Salsi, whose *bottiglieria* of *vino e olio* on Via de' Serragli we first came to know when we lived on the next street over, Via Romana. This too is a family enterprise: Signor Salsi shares the main labors, and the stalwart son does much of the heavy work when big orders are to be delivered. Salsi—stocky, soft-spoken, expressive, humorous—knows the Italian wines, from the Tyrol to Sicily and Sardinia, as well as anyone we have consulted, and his taste and judgment are superb. Here again is a Florentine shopkeeper with whom commercial expertise and human intercourse are inseparable. On a day in late November, according to a note, after considerable discussion with Salsi, we ordered twenty bottles of wine, including eight *fiaschi* (double size) and twelve bottles of assorted red and white wines, two of Chianti Classico among them and two from Sardinia (recommended by Fred Licht, who has frequent engagements in Sardinia); plus a bottle of Vodka and some tonic. The total price, delivery included, was 177,000 lire, which on that day was about $125.

A different and recent addition to our quarter was a place called CarLies, tucked away on Via delle Branche, a lane that leads off Piazza Peruzzi. As well described in a March 1991 article in the Chicago *Tribune* (by Lisa Anderson), it is "Italy's first American bakery," a shop "whose ovens daily perfume the Florentine air with the exotic scent of chocolate chip cookies, muffins and carrot cakes." Apple pie, cherry pie, cheesecake and, by constant demand, brownies are likewise to be found there. *"La prima pasticceria in tutto Italia di dolci americani,"* so *La Repubblica* put it; *"il paradiso dei mitici 'brownies,' vere e proprie bombe morbidissime di cioccolato"* (the key phrase there, identifying the "mythical brownies," might be translated "very soft and rich confections").

CarLies was founded in 1988 by Elizabeth Nicolosi and Carmel D'Arienzo; the name conjoins their first names, in reverse order. They are two young college graduates (Smith and Wellesley) from New York, of Italian descent; they had spent their junior year in Florence in the Smith College program. The idea of opening an American pastry shop in the heart of Florence took hold gradually. There was no precedent, and there were virtually no guidelines; the mind darkens at the thought of the bureaucratic jungle they had to prowl through, and with only a smattering of Italian: health codes, work permits, building permits (the site chosen had been little more than a garbage dump since the flood), licensings of all kinds. But CarLies was in working order within one miraculous year.

The customers were mostly Americans at first. Students and teachers from the American School took to dropping in at the end of the day; and word spread to the several hundreds of Americans engaged in study across the province. Then the Hotel Excelsior, the graciously high-toned mansion on the river, began to serve CarLies's cheesecake at afternoon tea. "Our clients are often Americans, and it's something nice to give them," remarks the hotel's director of banquets (as quoted by Anna Maria Biondo in the Detroit *News*). By Nicolosi's calculation, Italians now provide 70 percent of the shop's trade.

Ms. Nicolosi has, within the year, become the sole owner of CarLies. She is a dark-haired young woman, thirty years of age, outspoken and outgoing, deeply attached to her Italian background. Her mother came from the small village of Campagna, in the province of Salerno, five kilometers below the town of Eboli, where Christ stopped (and went no farther), according to Carlo Levi; Elizabeth spent summers there as an adolescent, and goes back regularly to visit with her great-aunts and uncles. Her father's family home was not far from Messina, in the village of San Fratello.

Despite CarLies's location on an obscure back street, en route to no visitable urban site, its profits have increased steadily: upward of $250,000 in 1992. The future is yet more promising.* Elizabeth Nicolosi has a flair, verging on genius, as an entrepreneur; she also has a talent for friendship, as it might be said for neighborliness, and has performed with notable skill in the difficult art of community-making among Americans in Florence.

Restaurants are more important in our Florentine lives than they are at home. It is not only that Florence contains so many *ristoranti* and *trattorie* that could be ranked between *discreto* and *ottimo*, between two stars and four; the top-flight inquirer Christopher

---

* In early 1995, CarLies products were selling in New York, at Bloomingdale's and Trump Tower, and in East Hampton at Jerry Della Femina's Red Horse Market. In a nice reversal of the usual course of influence, customers in the eastern United States were expressing pleasure at discovering items "from the bakery in Florence." Negotiations are also under way to place CarLies products in Shanghai.

Cowie, in *Eating Out in Florence*, lists some two hundred establishments that could be so judged. (And—a telling point—every visitor to Florence, after a stay, has his or her startlingly different inventory of the eight best places.) Beyond that, eating out, like shopping, is a vital phase in the multitextured experience of living in and into Florence. Going there at noon or of an evening, along a new or a familiar route, meeting the *padrone* and *padrona*, sensing the atmosphere of the moment, inspecting the menu and listening to word of the specialties, checking the *vini* and the prices, absorbing the meal and taking part in the conversation it encourages, and, later, walking back home: this, no matter how often or after how many months, remains an event to be savored.

In our Santa Croce zone, the restaurant we grew most fond of—the one that best embodied the spirit of the neighborhood—was called I Che C'è C'è. It was on another side street, Via Megalotta, which ambles away from Borgo dei Greci, not far from CarLies. The name, as decoded by its chef and owner, Gino Noci, means "What you find, you find"; his son Iacopo translates it more literally as "What there is, there is." Either phrase is apt. An air of easy hospitality pervades the place; in the words of Christopher Cowie, it is "a restaurant as public house"; where good friends meet, eat, and drink together, catch one another up on the latest news. At lunch, the long central table is filled with companionable local people—lawyers from the Tribunale in Piazza San Firenze, artists and writers, good-spirited Florentine folk from nearby, chatting and laughing and calling out.

Gino Noci took over I Che C'è C'è in 1989; it had been running for twenty years, on and off, without making any particular mark. Before that, he had been the head chef at the Monnalisa Restaurant, a cavernous place up beyond San Lorenzo, capable of seating five hundred guests; Gino rather enjoyed catering to such a throng. From 1974 to 1982, he worked as a cook in another restaurant in the same area, owned by his father; and in the earlier 1970s, he was a waiter at Buca Lapi, the venerable locale off Via Tornabuoni that occupies the cellars of Palazzo Antinori and serves wines from the Antinori farms. But Gino traces his start as a serious would-be restaurateur to his service in London in the

late 1960s, waiting on the tables of two high-class Parisian restaurants there and closely studying the French cuisine. A *cucina
mista*—Tuscan, French, international, but with Tuscan predom-
inating—characterizes I Che C'è C'è.

As the name suggests, you get what's ready that day (though,
of course, special requests are attended to). On an evening in
November, we went with a visiting American friend, and the
moment we sat down we were given an aperitif of gin, vermouth,
and white wine (perfect, of its kind). We were then served a mix
of antipasti: delicious *crostini*, variously with artichokes, mush-
rooms, and liver pâté; *misto di mare* (squid, shrimp, etc.); and
other offerings; plus a bottle of white wine. Then came *penne
strasciate alla Fiorentino* (macaroni in meat sauce), and, finally,
lombata di manzo (grilled beefsteak), accompanied by a Chianti.
For dessert: the relative newcomer and ever more popular *tira-
misu*—ladyfingers soaked in whiskey, covered with a rich custard
sauce and heavy cream, layered with grated chocolate (the cheery
title means "Pull me up").

Gino joined us over the *espressi*. He is a tall, husky man, with
active hawklike features, a dark mustache, and a piratical grin.
He chatted and reminisced and advised on living and dining in
Florence: a splendid show, funny, original, energetic, a fine histrionic Florentine version of the host in an English pub. Gino
explained how to make "champagne" out of white wine: add
some barley and sugar, and let it ferment for two months. We
were all invited to the third birthday party of I Che C'è C'è later
that month, and there was talk of a special Christmas dinner.
(The bill, with a good tip included, ran to 185,000 lire, about
$140.)

The two of us were on hand for both those festive occasions. The
Christmas party was all the more memorable, since two of our
offspring, with companions, had come back to their old school-
city for ten days, and we made a table of six at I Che C'è C'è.
Gino and his own family, as might be imagined, made the most
of ours, with hugs and greetings and exclamations.

Christmas is an exhilarating time in Florence. The city is the right size and has the right shape for it; it possesses the right temperament; the rising holiday ill-temper so common in the U.S. is scarcely visible in Florence. Florence indeed seems to coalesce around the colorfully lit-up streets: Por Santa Maria, as it stretches up from Ponte Vecchio toward Piazza Signoria; Via dei Servi, as it runs its assured way from the Duomo to Piazza Santissima Annunziata. *Babbo Natale* (Father Christmas) is much in evidence, and roasted chestnuts (from the Casentino) are for sale on street corners. Music—symphonic, religious, popular (the locals love "White Christmas")—greets you as you go about your shopping.

On the Sunday before Christmas, we all went to a concert in Palazzo Vecchio. We sat on folding chairs in the vast, enormously high-ceilinged hall, which was unheated; looked up at the Vasari paintings overhead; and listened happily to a medley of classical and Romantic music (Rossini was featured, it being his 200th birthday), and a Christmas group—"Silent Night" (in Italian), "Jingle Bells," "White Christmas," and a nicely sung chorus of "How High the Moon." Between numbers, we murmured to each other about Christmases past in Florence: Christmas Eve gatherings at I Tatti—in 1969, when Myron and Sheila Gilmore entertained us so beautifully, and in 1985, when Craig and Barbara Smythe were our cordial host and hostess; and concerts provided by the American School, and held in the church of St. James. From those days, there returned to memory the Italian carol that so took our fancy—

> *Tu scendi dalle stelle*
> *O re del cielo*
> *E vieni in una grotta*
> *Al freddo al gelo.**

Its tender melody and lilting rhythm haunt us yet.

For dinner on Christmas day, Gino Noci and his family-crew

---

* You come down from the stars
  O King of heaven,
  And come into a cave
  Of freezing cold.

served an assortment of antipasti; then several different pastas delivered simultaneously; then a choice of roast chicken, roast lamb, veal cutlet, or beefsteak. Fried artichokes, peas, and new potatoes were on the table, and there was a dessert of *pandoro* with chocolate (*pandoro* is a sweet risen bread, a Veronese Christmas invention, a descendant of the famous Veronese bread named for Christmas—*natalizia*). The wines were Chianti and Vernaccia; and the fee was 60,000 lire per person. The place was packed to its 48-seat maximum; the din was intense, highly good-humored, unending, and bilingual; and Gino Noci moved about among his friends and neighbors, greeting most of them by name. As an interplay of the Dickensian and the Santa Crocean, presided over by the one-time Londoner and quintessential Florentine, it could hardly be bettered.

Among the other places we favored, the most modest was Tavola Calda, on Via Palmieri; the phrase is usually translated "Snack Bar," but Tavola Calda is better than that, its busy, friendly service providing very satisfactory *lasagne* and *vitello milanese* to take out or eat on the premises. And there were the three enjoyable restaurants, clustering on Via Ghibellina and Via de' Macci. In keeping with the history-laden nature of the *quartiere*, all three have a special historical aspect to their *cucina*. At the well-known Cibreo on Via de' Macci, owned and run by Benedetta and Fabio Picchi, you find Tuscan country dishes like *pappa al pomodoro* (tomato, garlic, and bread soup) and the quite remarkable *collo di pollo ripieno* (chicken neck stuffed with sausage). At the restaurant called Dino—run by Dino Casini with his wife and two younger children, in a fourteenth-century palazzo on Via Ghibellina—the specialty is dishes drawn from recipes the Medicis used at their banquets, like *stracotto del Granduca* (beef flavored to the Grand Duke's taste with garlic, rosemary, almonds, pine nuts, mint, and cinnamon). A block away on Via Ghibellina is La Baraonda, where the managers, Duccio and Elena Magni, insist on Tuscan authenticity in their dishes and their cooking methods. Their key reference book is the classic nineteenth-century text by

Pellegrino Artusi, *La scienza in cucina*.* Among the personal favorites: *polpettone in umido* (meat loaf cooked in seasoned tomato sauce) and *rognoncini di vitello al vino bianco* (veal kidneys cooked in parsley and white wine).

We did not fail to go outside the area to Harry's Bar, where Leo Vadorini's greeting was more voluble than ever, and the staff and offerings even more memorable. And we went often to Cavallino's, on the edge of Piazza Signoria (it seemed the right place for a New Year's Eve dinner for eight); curiously avoided by tourists, who perhaps think it too obviously in a touristy spot, but where again we find ourselves with old friends. There is no point, meanwhile, in naming eating places that disappointed: where you were hurried to a table half occupied by strangers and jammed against the wall; or where the service was ostentatiously poor or the food second-rate (we walked out of one place not far from our piazza, after waiting one hour for the first menu item), or where the prices outraged. It is possible to come upon a poor restaurant in Florence, much more than it used to be. But with two hundred pretty good restaurants, there is little cause for discontent.

E pòi: *Last Words*

One of the persistent traditions among Florence lovers is the complaint that the city has deteriorated badly in the last ten, twenty, thirty years. Henry James, coming to Florence for the first time in the fall of 1869, listened to Florentines describe "the change for the worse, the taint of the modern order, bitterly lamented by haunters, admirers, lovers." Survivors of "the golden age"—for so the epoch of the Grand Duchy was regarded in some quarters—had seen the effect upon Florence of becoming the national capital, had seen

* The complete and well-worded title is *La scienza in cucina e l'arte di mangiar bene*. In *Celebrating Italy* (1990), Carol Field speaks of "Pellegrino Artusi, the great gastronomic writer . . . who addressed his cookbook to the middle class of the newly unified Italy." Artusi came from Romagna. *La scienza in cucina* was last reprinted in 1985.

the ancient walls pulled down and the compact and belted mass of which the Piazza della Signoria was the immemorial center expand . . . into the ungirdled organism of the type, as they viciously say, of Chicago.

James felt that such objections were pointless, and that in Florence one had "to try at least to read something of the old soul into the new forms." Even the big new *viale* and the piazzas along it (he thought) had a certain charm, if only because Florence had "flung an element of her grace" over them. "They are Florentine." But James too, some decades later, would say that Florence had lost some of the appeal it originally had for him.

Among English-language writers, John Ruskin was the most emphatic in declaring Florence to have gone to ruin. The wreckage of Florence, he wrote in *Mornings in Florence* (mid-1870s), "is now too ghastly and heartbreaking to any human soul who remembers the days of old." Those desperate words, as Henry James remarked after quoting them, alluded to the fact that the Piazza del Duomo had become "the resort of a number of hackney-coaches and omnibuses." James agreed that "a cab-stand is a very ugly and dirty thing, and Giotto's Tower should have nothing in common with such conveniences"; but he found Ruskin's rhetoric, here as elsewhere, absurdly exaggerated. Even so, we ourselves, returning to Florence in the 1970s, were repelled by the motor-cycles flung six deep against the cathedral walls and around the Campanile and the Baptistery, and said sadly that Florence in some respect was no longer the beautiful old city we had come to know in the 1950s. All the more did we cheer, on this last visit, to discover a Duomo area entirely cleared of vehicles and splendidly spruced up.

Something about Florence makes one alert to anything in it that irritates or offends, and to say or repeat that things used to be better. The city may well have a genius, as James contended, for "making you take to your favour . . . everything that in any way belongs to her"; but by the same token, it makes you resentful of any aspect or development that spoils the beautiful impression. In the 1990s, the motorcycle traffic had finally, for us, become intolerable. *Il motociclo*, said a commentator in *La Nazione*, is the curse of Florence. The streamlined machines are no doubt useful conveyances for some members of the citizenry, in a city where parking is so difficult; and it is nice to see middle-aged individuals, male and female, spinning along toward their place of work. But the headstrong younger drivers are the menace. They pay no attention to traffic rules, speed the wrong way down one-way streets, leap through red lights, career around corners without looking, and hurtle across white-marked safe passages.* Several friends were knocked down by these criminally negligent drivers, and one was hospitalized. And the motorcyclist behaves with preposterous machismo. In the Santa Croce neighborhood, at least, we did not happen to see a cyclist rear up on his back wheel and make bouncing dashes at a pedestrian, cackling with pleasure, as we used to see them do around Piazza Poggi (one young woman was knocked down and nearly killed); but they clearly exult in their violent sallies and freedom from regulation.

But the quality of life was most impaired, in these months, by the endless series of strikes. They had been tedious and disruptive enough in our Borgo Ognissanti summer; but now they seemed to invade the very marrow of existence, and from the first moment. The day after our arrival, we went to our trusty shipping agent, Fracassi, to arrange the pickup of the half-dozen boxes we had dispatched from America (and which contained the books and documents for the work we were anxious to get back to). They were held up in Customs, we were told; there was a strike of Customs workers; and another week passed before the things were delivered. We went next, as directed by our *padrona*, to an office of the Minister of Finance, in Piazza dell' Indipendenza, to get the card of the *Codice Fiscale*, in effect a residence permit. That office, we were told apologetically as we gazed at the locked

---

* There are, of course, several grades and sizes of motorcycles in Italy; here they are being treated as all of the same kind.

entrance door, was closed because of a strike; as it was when we spent a second morning on the same errand.*

These were minor, even semicomical, vexations. The city looked more seriously disorganized on a different occasion, which should have been a time of pride. The urban authorities decided in mid-fall to launch an antismog campaign, and to this end they decreed that no traffic—except for medical emergencies—would be allowed in the city center on a stated series of days between 8:30 a.m. and 12:30 p.m. and between 2:00 p.m. and 6:00 p.m. It was an admirable project, one that promised to set an example for the rest of Italy; but when the first morning came, it turned out that the traffic police—the *vigili*—had gone on strike, so there was no one to enforce the no-traffic regulation. The elements in the city power structure seemed to have been wholly out of touch with each other. After two more useless days, the *vigili* came back to work; but even as they were efficiently handing out huge fines to automobile lawbreakers, the motorcyclists—not included in the ban—were leaping along the half-empty streets, racing their motors excitedly, and spreading fumes all through the town center.

As always, the big unions called for strikes of transport workers at the busiest times of the year, to cause the greatest inconvenience and unhappiness. Buses stopped running from 9:00 a.m. to 12 noon with maddening frequency, and hordes of citizens were unable to get to work. Nor were these stoppages ever clearly explained. Motives for strikes went virtually unmentioned in the press, and there was little indication later that anything had been accomplished. In Florence (as to a degree elsewhere in northern Italy), striking has simply become a reflex action; a move without much meaning in an obscure power game. It is perhaps a modern expression of the old Florentine zest for litigation; but if so, it is an impulse that has lost its original character. And in fact it is in America that the habit of litigation has taken over, with suits for enormous damages being now the instant response to a grievance.

Americans, friends who have lived and worked in Florence for

---

* The process, when we got in at last, was surprisingly unbureaucratic and courteous; and it was interesting to learn that women in Italy are identified on official documents by their maiden name—e.g., Lindau Nancy.

thirty years, are of the opinion that what has most deteriorated in Florence, during this time, is the quality of civility. Bad manners in public interchanges are, admittedly, encountered more often than they used to be. We have walked out of a stationery store and a bakery on Via Verdi after being rudely neglected or barked at for fifteen or twenty minutes; we cannot recall ever doing that before. But as against all these considerations—motorcycles and strikes and rudeness—we think of our friends and neighbors on Via dei Neri, of our enlarging Florentine family, and we know that, outside of the United States, there is no place on earth we would rather live.

Politics dominated the larger public scene in the Santa Croce period. There was the American presidential election in November; and a fortnight before the day, we went to the United States Consulate on Lungarno Vespucci to hand in our absentee ballots (which, we were promised, would be mailed off promptly). The coverage of the campaign in *La Nazione* was depressingly inadequate: ignorant and ill-written articles with a vaporous right-wing bias (Bush, they intoned, was universally recognized as one of the great figures in twentieth-century history; Clinton was a mediocre nobody). For American political news, we relied on CNN television every morning; it came to us from England, and included Dan Rather's broadcast of the previous evening. We counted even more on phone calls from home: one of them woke us up on November 3 (it was 1 a.m. in New York) with word of the outcome.

In Italy, it was the year of *Tangentopoli*, Kickback City—the steady, relentless exposure of bribery and corruption throughout the interlocking worlds of business and government (the coined Italian word seems to come from *tangente*, a "share"). Hardly a day went by without headline news of this process; it was part of the breakfast ritual. The whole thing started, as Italy-watchers will recall, when a man named Luca Segni, who had the cleaning concession in a Milan nursing home for the elderly, complained to a magistrate that he had been forced to give back half of his profits to one Mario Chiesa, the director of the home. In Italy, police investigations are mostly under the judiciary; and the magistrate in question, forty-two-year-old southern-born Antonio di Pietro, set up electronic surveillance: the resulting film showed Chiesa pocketing a bribe of seven million lire ($4,300) from Segni. Chiesa was arrested by the carabinieri, and soon was turning state's evidence—and opening up what became a tale of billion-dollar bribery in high financial and political places. Italians are wearily knowing about corruption, but this story has filled them with horror and disgust.

There are special conditions in Italy that made the grotesque operation possible. One is that the government—that is, the political parties that rule by coalition—actually controls 50 percent of the economy, including banking, steel, manufacturing, and public works. So if a construction company wishes to secure a contract, say, to build a third lane of the Milan-Venice highway or a new phase of the Milan subway system, it must agree to kick back—to return—a solid percentage of the fees to "the government." The company in turn prolongs the work and increases the cost, so as to ensure its own proper profit. One obvious consequence is a rise in the national public debt (which has risen, experts say, by $73 billion since 1980).

The vigilant pursuit of the wrongdoers, under the direction of the new national hero di Pietro, has led to the investigation of thousands of politicians and businessmen, with some seven hundred persons sent to trial. *Le maniche*, handcuffs, was another term one heard or read with ringing regularity. Internationally known names—Bettino Craxi, Andreotti, Fiat—came into scandalous prominence; and the process has gone on.

Another important factor has been the long-standing if fairly well concealed relationship between the Christian Democratic Party and the Mafia: a relationship based on the Mafia's ability to deliver the votes, especially in southern Italy, which helped keep the Christian Democrats in power, in alliance with the Socialists and other anti-Communist groups. Standing in vigorous, unchanging opposition, in former days, was the strongest and perhaps the smartest Communist party in Europe. All this unraveled with the virtual end of the Cold War in 1989 and the fragmenting of international Communism. The need for Mafia support and elaborate cover-ups disappeared.

Several outside observers have expressed the belief that the whole complex development is proving healthful for Italy, and we ourselves came to the same view. The overall investigation was given the title Clean Hands, *Mani Pulite*; and there is something positive and hopeful in the line of procedure from Kickback City to Handcuffs to Clean Hands. But the immediate *political* horizon could hardly be cloudier. The Christian Democrats and the Socialists have virtually disappeared; the Communists are ex-Communists, calling themselves the Party of the Left; neo-Fascism is busily on the rise; and a television magnate managed to buy himself into temporary power.

Reflecting on all this in the newspaper *La Repubblica* (March 2, 1994), Umberto Eco, renowned cultural commentator and novelist, suggests that recent developments are mainly fierce new gusts of winds against the very idea of "state." "Our country has never been able to become a national state," he said to an interviewer. "Italy has never wanted a state, it has been the country of communes and corporations." Changing the metaphor, Eco suggested that "Italy has never succeeded in finding a paternal image . . . It has always been a confederation of uncles, with an indulgent mother, the Church." Even the Medicis, he said, were uncles. But: "The father is *the Law*. Our country is unable to identify itself with the *Law*. And without doing that, you have endemic *tangentopoli*." As to the future, Eco describes himself as a person of tragic optimism.

The political scandals, as it happened, had relatively little impact upon the daily round of life in our *quartiere*, or, so far as we could tell, elsewhere in the city. We heard many references to it, of course, and exchanged sighs, groans, raised eyebrows, and a phrase or two of contempt or bewilderment (and then there was the tearful solicitation of *Mama* Luigina in Giuliano's *pizzicheria*). *La Nazione* made as much as it could out of grossly improper local or regional doings, like the work on the dam near Pontassieve that cost several times what it should have and took years more than needed. There were probably other carefully mismanaged public works in Tuscany (it is an open question whether the restoration in the Carmine suffered from the national disease). But life in Florence, as we went our ways, seemed to go on with its familiar Florentine tang and accent.

And our own life was not greatly affected by it: that is, our personal experiencings, our walks, our taxi rides, our shopping, our work and the sightseeing and book buying and interviews connected with it, our social visits and visitors, our conversations in both languages.

As to the social life, it was quietly active, perhaps a trifle more so than in Connecticut. Friends, academic and otherwise, made a point of coming through Florence on their Italian travels; we toured the Santa Croce area with them, took them to restaurants of our own advising or arranged small supper parties in our apartment, and even accompanied them on an occasional trip. (With one of them, an art historian of rising eminence and a remarkably companionable individual, we drove down past Arezzo to Monterchi to see Piero della Francesca's *Madonna del Parto*, that proudly pregnant and yet incalculable figure; then to Borgo San Sepolcro and the Museo Civico, where we looked long at Piero's *Resurrection*, the vigorously emerging Christ, the heavily sleeping soldiers, the fading foliage, the planes of distance—one of the greatest paintings in the world, says Aldous Huxley, and we could only agree.) Our younger ones having come for the Christmas season, two of them came back in February to go to Venice with us for the Carnevale—three days of marvelously ornate eighteenth-century costumes and masks in Piazza San Marco, and festivities along the twisting streets and the canals, tea and cakes at Florian's, dinner at Harry's Bar.

There is in Florence no single distinct American community that a visitor can be taken into, but rather fragments of several. A community of sorts is formed out of the American School and the church of Saint James; gatherings are arranged at the church where American students in Florence can meet one another, and more permanent friends can reconvene. These are warming affairs. The Center for Renaissance Study in the former Berenson villa, I Tatti, has its own community; much of it changes annually, but we count two members of the regular staff, Flavia Superbi and Eve Borsook, as among the friends we most value in the province. And Harry and Clotilde Brewster, when in residence at Villa San Francesco di Paola, continue to represent the American-Florentine society of great former days.

On the English side, there are vestiges of what has been the largest and most vital "foreign" community in Florence, and we felt fortunate to be reintroduced to some of it, by our *padrona* and others. Sir Harold Acton was for years its most conspicuous and admired figure; many visits have we exchanged with this distinguished literary personality (*Memoirs of an Aesthete*, 1948; *The Pazzi Conspiracy*, 1979)—at his Acton family home, Villa La Pietra on Via Bolognese, or in our lodgings at Villa San Francesco or elsewhere; and many the evening we all spent together at the British Institute, one or the other of us delivering a talk. But in 1992–93, Sir Harold was seriously ailing and inaccessible.*

E pòi—"and then"; it is the Italian version of *et puis*—there is what we think of as our own community of Florentines: Leo Vadorini and Renzo Salsi from earlier sojourns; Gino Noci, Giuliano and Luigina, Signora Zanetti, Rita Meiners from the most recent one. Our *padrona*'s name should be the last one invoked —it brings with it so much Florentine and Tuscan history and literature in its run of syllables: Federica Cinelli Piccolomini.

---

* Harold Acton died on February 26, 1994, at the age of eighty-nine. For us, the disappearance of that commanding, engaging presence means the loss of a main portion of our Florence. In an editorial of early March, *The New York Times* reminded the reader that "nobody could write a book about [Acton's] generation of British writers, artists, trend-setters and general gadabouts without mentioning him." He made a memorable appearance, it was recalled, in Evelyn Waugh's *Brideshead Revisited*, under the name of Anthony Blanche, reciting poetry through a megaphone from his study to passing oarsmen. The *Times* article spoke of his leaving his Florentine estate and an endowment of $25 million to New York University, and ended very suitably: "What he could not leave was his charm, his humor, the sheer fun of him."

Acknowledgments

Notes on Maps and Illustrations

Some Scholarly and Literary Sources

Contemporary Guidances

General Index

Index of Florentine Place-names

Acknowledgments

These acknowledgments refer in fact only to individuals who in one way or another actually contributed to the making of this book. Over the years we have come to know a great many Florentines, native and foreign-born, and count a goodly number among our friends. They will understand, I hope, that if I do not list them all here, I have them in mind and memory.

My first acknowledgment, as before, is to Nancy Lewis, very much the co-begetter of the book: the co-observer of the scenes described and the sharer of the experiences recorded, in the period since 1950. Her understanding of people and places, her discriminating judgment, her ability to summon up choice recollections—these qualities, along with her unfailing *gentilezza* and her patience, have made it all possible. Nathaniel Lewis, Sophie Lewis, Emma Lewis, also as before, have helped greatly, supplying correctives and additions through their own keen angles of vision and their varied and particular memory-framings.

Quite a few of the friends to whom I am indebted—for wisdom or advice or instructive companionship—have appeared earlier in the narrative. Guido Calabresi and Anne Calabresi have been cherished Tuscan neighbors, as they have been Connecticut neighbors. We have met together in Florence, traveled together (to Ferrara and elsewhere), done errands for one another. They are an essential part of our Florence.

With Meg Licht and Fred Licht, the relationship was born in Florence (more than twenty years ago), and it has continued to flourish there, though it has also expanded back home. What I personally owe the Professors Licht for insights into Florentine cultural history is scarcely to be reckoned. Fred Licht educated me especially in the more recent history of Florence: the 1966 flood, the heroic efforts at preservation, the extent of damage, even some surprising happy consequences; twentieth-century Florentine architecture, the building of Ponte San Niccolò, the entire career of Giovanni Michelucci. Meg and I conducted a seminar on the history of Florence in Calhoun College at Yale in the early 1980s; or, rather, I served as the attentive Teaching

Assistant in Meg Licht's brilliant course of study. On several occasions as well, I was able to hear her lecturing to groups of students in Florence, as she led them about the historic center, from site to site. Beyond that, the Lichts are always the best imaginable company.

Horace Gibson, former headmaster of the American School in Florence, and Kevin McIntyre, former art instructor in that school, have been crucial presences in the city (and in their hospitable home in Piazza Pitti). Kevin McIntyre is indeed a key presence in the text itself, with his carefully designed maps of several of our neighborhoods. For these, I remain immensely grateful.

From a much earlier time, I remember with pleasure the spirited help of Delphine Jenkins, perhaps the most distinctive and enjoyable American resident in Florence in that epoch (and the original, incidentally, of "Auntie Mame"). To her son, the gifted composer Newell Jenkins, we also owe a debt of gratitude.

For the finding of our successive Florentine homes, we are indebted to many. For nearly twenty years we were the fortunate clients of the rental agent Natasha Abranovna (with whom we also consorted at Leland's Tea Room). It was Natasha who negotiated domiciles, for anything from two months to a year: in Piazza Santa Trinità, on Costa dei Magnoli, on Lungarno Soderini, in Piazza Nazario Sauro, on Via Lamarmora, and at Casa Boccaccio.

I am glad to express again our gratitude to Harry Brewster and Clotilde (Brewster) Peploe, owners of Villa San Francesco di Paola, where we occupied the wonderfully designed *piano nobile* in 1975–76. (Yale colleague William Kesson and Marion Kesson, former tenants there, recommended it to us.) Harry Brewster's fine contributions to my knowledge of sixteenth-century Florentine sociopolitical and erotic history are spelled out in my Chapter 6 above.

To Robert Geis, former Cultural Affairs Officer at the U.S. Consulate in Florence, we owe special thanks for his making available to us, in the summer of 1987 (when he and his family were on home leave), the spacious Consulate-owned apartment on Borgo Ognissanti. Our friendship with Bob and Anneliese Geis, and their winning daughter, Alexandra, dates from that time and continues. Outings with the Geises in southern Tuscany were memorable occasions; as of now, they have become outings in North Carolina and Texas.

We first heard of Palazzo dell' Antella through Francis Thorne and Ann Thorne, who had lived there in years past. The rental contract was efficiently arranged by Kit Fattorini. From the moment of our entrance into the apartment on the *terzo piano* in October 1992, we enjoyed a life-enhancing association with its hostess, Contessa Federica Cinelli Piccolomini. The Contessa too has been introduced in these pages; here let me add only that no *padrone* or *padrona* we ever encountered in our Florentine stays has been more thoughtfully hospitable, or has added so much (in part, by making available the fictional work of her father Delfino Cinelli) to my knowledge of things Tuscan. Let me also express my gratitude, for help and advice, to Manfredi Piccolomini (currently professor of Italian at CUNY).

Among those who have helped in the running of these places of residence, I should name once again Ida Giaccalone, housekeeper in several of them (most notably, in Villa San Francesco di Paola), and Letizia Lawley, who had charge of our firstborn in the mid-1960s, and who helped improve our command of Italian-Tuscan speech.

Others have added important information about Florence and Tuscany, and per-

Acknowledgments

spectives on them. Ulrich Middledorf (as I said in my prologue) introduced me to medieval and Renaissance Tuscan painting; and later, as head of the German Institute in Florence, he guided my researches into the long and wildly varied history of the Guidi clan. The late Harold Acton, both in his books and in person, offered glowingly rich insights into the whole subject. On many an excursion in the 1960s and 1970s, our friend and driver Marcello Chirici provided nuggets of local information or regional folk wisdom.

The British Institute Library, on Lungarno Guicciardini, was as helpful as could be in locating and lending relevant volumes of historical study. It is one of the most inviting places in the city.

Likewise the staff at U.S.I.A., on the opposite side of the river on Lungarno Vespucci, were helpful in several kinds of ways; I should especially name Sergio Era, a friendly guide to Florence but no less so to his native Bologna (where his rating of restaurants is impeccable). Among the U.S. Consuls in our Florence days, I should name Merritt Cootes and Robert Gordon for their kindness and hospitality.

For the work that went into my part of *L'idea di Firenze* (see Chapter 7), I am happy to record my appreciation of Maurizio Bossi, Director of the Centro Romantico at the Gabinetto Vieusseux. Maurizio's cordiality, enthusiasm, and encyclopedic knowledge of nineteenth-century Florence were inspiring. As to the gathering of information about American writers in Florence during that century, I am much indebted to my young Yale assistants, Barbara Lassonde and Glenn Wallach.

The sources for the *illustrations* in the book are indicated in the section following, "Notes on Maps and Illustrations." But I should also speak of the kindness and thoughtfulness I met on all sides in locating and procuring the pictures. The personnel at the Alinari Archives on Via della Vigna Nuova were charmingly efficient; visits there were a great pleasure. At Art Resource, on Bleecker Street in New York, I was particularly beholden to Derin Tanyol, who found print after print for me; and who, if any given print was lacking, promptly arranged for it to be sent over from Florence. Art Resource is exactly what its name declares; and a treasure for those turning to it for help. At the Museo di Firenze com' era, meanwhile, Signora Leone was kindness itself; after meditating my pictorial needs, she dug through the archives to come up with exactly the right materials. Signora Leone also gave me a guided tour of the old building, with its courtyard, and provided documents rehearsing its history.

Marc Adams, expert photographer and teacher of photography (and currently a resident in Tuscany), supplied the author's picture on the dustjacket, and took a number of shots of the remains of the old Arnolfian wall-circuit, from which I selected one. Our transactions with Mr. Adams were another source of enjoyment during 1992–93.

During much of the process of acquiring pictures, I was fortunate to enlist the skillful assistance of Aurora Savillo. She has been particularly helpful in the matter of securing permissions to use a number of the pictures—almost all of those that do not derive from Alinari or SCALA. Signorina Savillo's own training in art history, and Tuscan history in general, has been indispensable.

I am enduringly grateful to the John Simon Guggenheim Memorial Foundation for a grant which made possible the 1975–76 visit to Florence and Villa San Francesco di Paola. The groundwork for the book was laid during that fellowship year, the first chapter was written, and much of the rest prepared in outline.

Acknowledgments

A version of Chapter 3, under the title "A Knowable City," appeared in the January 1993 issue of the *Yale Review*. I am grateful to the editor of this strikingly reanimated periodical, J. D. McClatchy, for valuable editorial suggestions and for permission to reprint.

In the preparation of the manuscript, Daniel Avery has been the key person. He has printed and reprinted chapter after chapter, revision after revision, adding his own cogent comments and queries on the material passing through his computer. He also took a key part in preparing the Index. It was a great good fortune to have his assistance.

Jonathan Galassi, editor in chief of Farrar, Straus & Giroux, is one of the distinguished editors of the day, and was the ideal editorial overseer of this book. He knows Florence and its history intimately (he was even an occupant for a spell at Villa San Francesco di Paola), and is thoroughly conversant with its language and cultural folkways. Mr. Galassi has succeeded William Arrowsmith as the chief English translator of both the poetry and the prose of Eugenio Montale. On no few occasions, he has rightly questioned my method of proper naming, or has added a reference of his own from Florentine traditions. For me, this has been an uncommonly gratifying author-editor experience.

Notes on Maps and Illustrations

FRONTISPIECE

View from the terrace of our apartment on Via della Fornace, April 1989. Photograph by Bruce Avery; courtesy of Dr. Avery. See Chapter 8, p. 275.

The picture was taken during a visit with us by Dr. Avery, Dr. Shirley Avery, and their son, Andrew Avery. Beyond the river and the energetic Sunday morning scullers, and above the stretch of Lungarno, we see the Duomo, with the Campanile, and, to the left, the spire of the Badia. Immediately below the Duomo is the spire of Santa Croce and the outline of the church: the dominant feature of our 1992–93 neighborhood.

PROLOGUE

page

13 Piazza Santa Trinità. Museo di Firenze com' era. Etching by Giuseppe Zocchi (1711–67), the most gifted of the "panoramic" artists who appeared in early- and mid-eighteenth-century Florence. Zocchi's volume of twenty-four views (*vedute*) of the principal streets, piazzas, and buildings of Florence was published in 1744.

Here we see, to the left of the piazza, Palazzo Bartolini-Salimbeni; beyond it, facing the fountain, is Palazzo Spini. Farther along is the bridge of Santa Trinità, and in the shadow to the right is the church of Santa Trinità. In the middle of the square is the so-called Column of Justice, a granite column erected to celebrate the acquisition by Duke Cosimo I of absolute power. A statue honoring the elder Cosimo as *pater patriae* is among the stucco figures at the top of the column.

13 View of Lungarno: Ponte alla Carraia and above. Museo di Firenze com' era. Etching by Giuseppe Zocchi (see previous note). Directly across the river is the broadly spaced Palazzo Corsini. To its left, and in fact fronting Piazza Goldoni, is Palazzo Ricasoli, attributed to Michelozzo but probably not begun until 1480. To the far right is Palazzo Spini.

Notes on Maps and Illustrations

20 Map of Tuscany. Courtesy of Veronica Soell, Yale University Printing Service.

25 The Roman city, with its wall superimposed upon contemporary Florence. From *Le strade di Firenze*, courtesy of Casa Editrice Bonechi.

25 The 1175 wall-circuit. From *Le strade di Firenze*, courtesy of Casa Editrice Bonechi.

31 Ponte alla Carraia; Archivi Alinari.

31 Ponte alle Grazie, in its earlier form. Courtesy of Archivi Alinari.

32 Ponte Santa Trinità, the older one, in a painting by Domenico Ghirlandaio. Scala/Art Resource, New York.

This is a fragment of a painting in the Sassetti chapel in the church of Santa Trinità. The picture is known as *Resurrection of the Boy of the Spini House*. In portions of the painting not shown here, the boy is seen falling from a window of the Palazzo Spini, and then restored to life by the saint and seated upright in the middle of the piazza. Various recognizable Florentine figures are clustering about, marveling and rejoicing at the miracle.

32 Ponte Santa Trinità today. Archivi Alinari.

35 Arnolfo presents his plans for the wall-circuit to the Priors of Florence, painted by Giorgio Vasari in the early 1560s. Scala/Art Resource, New York.

Vasari, author of the first great work in art history, *The Lives of the Most Eminent Architects, Painters and Sculptors* (1st ed., 1550), was also a historian of Florence in his painting. Many of his best pictorial recordings of Florentine history adorn the ceiling of the Salone dei Cinquecento, the Republican Council Hall (initiated in 1495) in Palazzo Vecchio. This picture of Arnolfo offering his design for the wall-circuit is among them.

The imaginary setting is a hillside on the south bank of the river, and several of Arnolfo's main architectural accomplishments—the Cathedral (next to the Campanile), Palazzo Vecchio, and the church of Santa Croce—are visible in the background, as though already completed. The depiction of the energetic musicians at the lower right, meanwhile, with their tambourines and drum, accurately reflects the popular enthusiasm for Arnolfo's undertaking.

35 The Second Communal circuit of walls, designed by Arnolfo di Cambio in 1284; see Chapter 1, p. 32, and Chapter 3, p. 95. From *Le strade di Firenze*, edited by Piero Bargellini and Ennio Guarnieri, 1977. Courtesy of Casa Editrice Bonechi.

Arnolfo's circuit is here superimposed on a map of contemporary Florence. Circled numbers indicate the various city gates, among them (4) Porta Pinta, (6) Porta San Gallo, (9) Porta al Prato, (11) Porta San Frediano, (13) Porta Romana, and (16) Porta San Niccolò.

Key monuments in the urban design may also be located. The Duomo, with the Campanile, is more or less in the center. On a line to the left of it is the church of Santa Maria Novella, near the big stylish railway station. Below the Duomo, a little to the right, is Palazzo Vecchio, and on a line with the Palazzo, farther to the right, are the church and the piazza of Santa Croce.

The four medieval bridges are clearly visible, with the modern bridges of Amerigo Vespucci and San Niccolò to the west and east, respectively. On the south side of the river, we see the vast complex of Palazzo Pitti; above it, a little

Notes on Maps and Illustrations

to the left, is the church of Santo Spirito; behind it are the Boboli Gardens; and beyond the Gardens is the Fortezza di Belvedere.

39 Ponte Vecchio. Archivi Alinari. The view is from above Vasari's corridor as it disappears into the Uffizi, on the right bank. Beyond Ponte Vecchio, we can see Ponte Santa Trinità and Ponte alla Carraia, and in the farther distance, dimly, Ponte Vespucci. On the left bank, one can make out the spire of Santo Spirito and, beyond it, the church of San Frediano in Cestello.

39 Ponte Vecchio in 1944, with the approach dynamited. Museo di Firenze com' era. This view, by Carrado Pogni, shows the wreckage caused by German explosives in the summer of 1944, when the other bridges were destroyed and areas on both sides of the river laid waste.

45 *The Florence Flood of 1844*, by an anonymous painter. From *Firenze di una volta*, by Piero Magi (1973). Courtesy of Casa Editrice Bonechi.

This stirring tableau is seen from Ponte alle Grazie, with the flood waters pouring up Via de' Benci, past Via dei Neri on the left, and curving around to the right toward Piazza Santa Croce. Citizens with torches, rafts, barrels, and poles attempt to save the desperate situation.

CHAPTER 2

60 *Guadralda Refuses to Kiss Emperor Otto IV*, by Vasari and Giovanni Stradano. Scala/Art Resource, New York. The tableau is on the ceiling of the Room of Guadralda, in the apartment of Eleanora of Toledo in Palazzo Vecchio. Guadralda faces the Emperor, with her obsequious father, hand outstretched, in between. The male figure to the right, with his arm curved in front of him, is probably intended to be Guidoguerra IV, the Emperor's henchman and future husband of Guadralda.

77 The town of Poppi, seen from the plain below. Archivi Alinari.

77 Saint Francis of Assisi, below the monastery of La Verna, receiving the stigmata in 1244; by Domenico Ghirlandaio. Scala/Art Resource, New York.

The scene here is highly imaginary: Saint Francis in fact received the stigmata—the scars on hands and feet, and the body wound—while praying by himself in a grotto hidden away on the mountainside. The representation of La Verna as it came to be, however, is very faithful.

CHAPTER 3

82 View of Apparita. Museo di Firenze com' era.

101 Church of Santa Croce: facade, prior to the marble facade installed in 1863. Archivi Alinari.

101 Church of Santa Croce, interior. Archivi Alinari. Directly across is the memorial to Dante, executed by Stefano Ricci in 1829 (and not much favored by Florentine observers today); beyond the pulpit is the exceedingly graceful tomb of the poet and patriot Vittorio Alfieri, done by Antonio Canova (1757–1822) in 1810. Alfieri's tomb was commissioned by his intimate friend Luisa Stolberg, better known as the Countess of Albany (because of her unhappy marriage to the last Stuart

pretender) and the leader of a particularly brilliant literary salon on the Lungarno near Ponte Santa Trinità (see Eric Cochrane, *op. cit.*).

105 The Cathedral of Santa Maria del Fiore, with Giotto's Campanile. Archivi Alinari.

105 Cathedral, interior, facing the altar. Archivi Alinari.

113 Palazzo Vecchio. Scala/Art Resource, New York.

113 Panorama of Florence, in an early-nineteenth century print. Museo di Firenze com' era. "Arnolfo's city" is clearly outlined: to the left, Palazzo Vecchio; at the center, the Cathedral (with Duomo, Campanile, and Baptistery); to the right, Santa Croce. Notice also Ponte alle Grazie, with its little houses, and Ponte Vecchio.

CHAPTER 4

129 Loggia dei Lanzi. Alinari/Art Resource, New York. Originally the Loggia della Signoria, designed around 1376 by Andrea Orcagna; renamed in the sixteenth century after Duke Cosimo's Swiss lancers. Amid the statuary also added then and later, one may make out the *Perseus* of Benvenuto Cellini, front left; Giambologna's *Rape of the Sabines*, front right; and, behind the *Perseus*, the *Rape of Polixena*, by Pio Fede, 1866; in the middle is a statue of Menelaus holding the body of Patroclus, probably a Roman copy of a fourth-century B.C. work, and, to the right, *Hercules Fighting the Centaur Nessus*, by Giambologna, 1599.

134 Bust of Arnolfo di Cambio, by Aristidemo Costeli, 1844. Alinari/Art Resource, New York. This is in the interior of the Duomo.

134 Bust of Filippo Brunelleschi, by his pupil and adopted son Andrea Cavalcanti, called il Buggiano. Alinari/Art Resource, New York. This work, done in 1447, is in the interior of the Duomo, paired with that of Arnolfo.

139 *Giovanni di Bicci*, by Bronzino. Scala/Art Resource, New York. This portrait of the founding figure in the Medici family story, painted posthumously by Agnolo Bronzino, is in the Museo Medici in Florence.

139 *Cosimo the Elder*, by Pontormo. Scala/Art Resource, New York. Pontormo (1494–1556) postdated Cosimo by two generations, but this superb portrait seems to have been made from the life. It hangs in the Uffizi.

139 *Lorenzo de' Medici*, by Vasari. Scala/Art Resource, New York. This posthumous portrait is in the Uffizi.

147 Brunelleschi's Cupola (the Duomo). Alinari/Art Resource, New York.

153 *Brunelleschi Presents His Model of the Church of San Lorenzo*, by Vasari. Scala/Art Resource, New York. In this bit of revisionary pictorial history, Lorenzo is assisted by Ghiberti (crouching next to him) in holding forward a model of the church to the welcoming Cosimo the Elder. The painting is among those on the ceiling of Cosimo's room in Palazzo Vecchio.

153 Church of San Lorenzo, exterior. Archivi Alinari.

154 San Lorenzo: the Old Sacristy. Archivi Alinari.

154 Donatello's Doors, in the Old Sacristy at San Lorenzo. Archivi Alinari.

154 San Lorenzo, interior. Alinari/Art Resource, New York.

157 Piazza Santissima Annunziata. Scala/Art Resource, New York. Brunelleschi's loggia for his Ospedale degli Innocenti is on the right. At the head of the piazza is the portico of Michelozzo's Church of Santissima Annunziata. In mid-piazza, one

sees the equestrian statue of Grand Duke Ferdinando I, by Giambologna (1524–1608), begun in his last years and probably finished by his disciple Pietro Tacca (1577–1640). Tacca's sprightly fountains (transferred from Leghorn in 1643) are visible between two pairs of automobiles on the left.

161 *Jousting on Via Larga*, in front of Palazzo Medici; painted around 1561 by Vasari and Giovanni Stradano (1523–1605). Scala/Art Resource, New York. This picture (which is contained in the Room of Guadralda in Palazzo Vecchio) shows the Palazzo Medici before its enlargement in the eighteenth century. Notice the attached buildings (shops, servants' quarters, etc.), which made part of the original family palazzo.

161 The cloister of San Marco. Alinari/Art Resource, New York.

167 Palazzo Pitti, showing the Boboli Gardens, with the amphitheater and the Fountain of the Artichoke; with the Fortezza di Belvedere, above left. Museo di Firenze com' era. This sketch, by Giusto Utens, an artist of Flemish origin (1558–1609), presented Palazzo Pitti as it was intended to be by Brunelleschi and his followers, before the series of gigantic enlargements in later centuries.

169 The famous view of Florence, known as the "Catena," a form of wood-engraving attributed to Francesco Rosselli and executed in the 1470s. Museo di Firenze com' era.

The "Catena," according to Giovanni Fanelli, "marks a fundamental step in the history of Florentine iconography, and, more, in that of the iconographical typology of the Western city" (*La Città nella storia d'Italia: Firenze*, 1980; p. 77). "It is the first known representation of an entire city," and is the product not of poetic fantasy but of direct observation and controlled perspective.

The vantage point is somewhere on the southwest portion of the city. The reader can make out the various key aspects of Florence: the 1284 wall-circuit, its northern curve balancing the curve of the river; the four bridges and the *pescaie*; Porta Romana at the southernmost point; the Duomo in the very center, with Palazzo Vecchio nearby, along with the Badia and the Bargello; the Palazzo Medici inside the walls to the north and almost in open fields; San Miniato outside the walls on its southern slope. The Oltrarno sector, as Fanelli notes, is somewhat shrunken, but Palazzo Pitti stands out clearly.

CHAPTER 5

173 *The Siege of Florence*, by Vasari and Stradano. Scala/Art Resource, New York. This colorfully dramatic painting in the Room of Clement VII (the second Medici Pope) in Palazzo Vecchio, is among a number of others depicting the 1529–30 war.

173 *Cosimo I*, by Bronzino. Alinari/Art Resource, New York. This portrait, painted around 1540, hangs in the Sala La Tribuna, in the Uffizi.

173 *Eleanora of Toledo*, by Bronzino. Art Resource, New York.

177 The Uffizi, piazza and porticos, by Vasari. Alinari/Art Resource, New York. The Uffizi, generally regarded as Vasari's architectural masterpiece, was begun in 1560. The piazza as designed provides one of the most beautifully composed vistas in Florence, down to the charming archway opening onto the river. The view from the river end, up through the piazza to the edge of Piazza della Signoria, is no less stirring. Twenty-eight marble statues occupy the niches around the piazza,

all commemorating illustrious Tuscans: among them, Dante, Machiavelli, Alberti, Cellini. Immediately on the left is Lorenzo de' Medici and, beyond him, his grandfather Cosimo.

177 *The Mercato Vecchio*—the Old Market—by G. Stradano, c. 1561. Scala/Art Resource, New York. The picture is in the frieze of the Room of Guadralda in Palazzo Vecchio. In this sixteenth-century vista, one perceives the column of Abundance by Donatello (Vasari's handsome Loggia dei Pesce would not be added for a few years); the well; the shops; the display table.

188 Portion of the old wall on the south side, as it looks today. Photograph by Marc Adams; courtesy of the artist.

193 A view of the Florence ghetto, prior to the *sventrimento* (cleaning out) in 1885 and later. Sketch by R. Meacci, Museo di Firenze com' era.

CHAPTER 6

201 Map showing Villa San Francesco di Paola and surroundings, and (below) Via Romana and its area. Composed by Kevin McIntyre; courtesy of the artist. Places and streets mentioned in the text can easily be located: the Torre di Bellosguardo (at this time, the American School), Villa San Francesco di Paola, Via Villani, Piazza Tasso, Viale Petrarca (leading from Porta Romana to Piazza Tasso), Via dei Serragli, Via Maggio (leading to Ponte Santa Trinità) and Via Guicciardini (leading to Ponte Vecchio), Via Romana, Casa Guidi, Piazza and Palazzo Pitti, the Boboli Gardens.

205 Boboli Gardens, with the Fountain of the Artichoke. Alinari/Art Resource, New York.

205 Porta Romana, sketched by Kevin McIntyre; courtesy of the artist.

215 Villa San Francesco di Paola. Photographs by Harry Brewster; courtesy of Mr. Brewster.

220 Duke Francesco I, by Vasari. Scala/Art Resource, New York. The painting (which in complete form includes Pope Clement VIII) is in the Palazzo Vecchio.

220 *Bianca Cappello*, by Alessandro Allori (1535–1607). Alinari/Art Resource, New York. The portrait, done in 1578, is in the Sala La Tribuna in the Uffizi.

237 Montepulciano, panorama. Archivi Alinari.

237 An Etruscan funerary urn, in the museum at Chiusi. Archivi Alinari. A trio of scenes of slaughter can be seen, perhaps deriving from the Oresteia saga.

CHAPTER 7

247 Map of the Borgo Ognissanti area, composed by Kevin McIntyre. Courtesy of the artist. Harry's Bar has been pinpointed by the artist, with other neighborhood features, such as the railroad station of Santa Maria Novella. The Vespucci, Carraia, and Trinità bridges are in evidence, from left to right. Borgo Ognissanti, on which we resided in the 1987 summer, is seen running from left to Piazza Goldoni. Notice also Via dei Fossi, Via della Vigna Nuova, and Via Tornabuoni.

250 Madonna of Mercy protecting the Vespucci family, by Domenico Ghirlandaio; about 1474. Scala/Art Resource, New York.

This painting, in the church of Ognissanti, is described by Vasari in his *Lives*:

"[Ghirlandaio's] first paintings were in the chapel of the Vespucci at Ognissanti, representing a dead Christ and some saints [in a panel above the present painting], and a Misericordia over an arch, containing Amerigo Vespucci, who navigated the Indies." The kneeling elderly man in the red cloak is probably the head of the family, and the elderly woman in the dark coat and white head cover his wife. Near the latter figure is a younger woman, possibly their daughter, with plaited hair well back on her forehead, as was the fashion of the time. Amerigo, kneeling between the two women, seems intense and clear-eyed, though he is still a round-faced child.

253 Piazza Santa Maria Novella: a chariot race; by Giuseppe Zocchi (see note to the picture of Piazza Santa Trinità, in the prologue). Courtesy of Horace Gibson.

259 Portrait of Lucrezia Panciatichi, by Bronzino, about 1540. Alinari/Art Resource, New York. Of this portrait, in the Sala La Tribuna in the Uffizi, Eve Borsook says acutely that it and the companion portrait by Bronzino of Lucrezia's husband, Bartolomeo, "are psychological studies where the pose of a hand and the disposition of the setting are as telling as the analysis of the features of the face." The Panciatichis were a well-known Pistoia family, and Bartolomeo served as emissary for Duke Cosimo I.

263 *Villa Castellani*, by Frank Duveneck (1848–1919); from *Unsuspected Genius*, by Robert Neuhaus (Bedford Press, 1987). Duveneck moved his group of art students— "Duveneck's boys" (John Alexander among them)—down from Munich to Italy in 1879, with winters now spent in Florence. Villa Castellani, also known as Villa Mercedes, looks onto the piazza at Bellosguardo, high above the south bank. Duveneck came to know the villa when it was occupied by the American composer Francis Boott and his daughter, Lizzie. Duveneck and Lizzie Boott were married in 1886, and after her death two years later (and before returning to America, to make his home in Cincinnati) Duveneck created one of his finest works: a memorial tomb for Lizzie, in the Allori cemetery south of the city. Villa Castellani was also known to Henry James, who drew upon it for his description of Gilbert Osmond's villa in *The Portrait of a Lady*.

263 Another view of Villa Castellani (also known as Villa Mercedes). From *Le Strade di Firenze*, courtesy of Casa Editrice Bonechi. Villa Castellani figures in Henry James's *The Portrait of a Lady* as the Florentine home of the American expatriate Gilbert Osmond. The narrator describes it in words that reflect its occupant: "This ancient, solid, weather-worn, yet imposing front had a somewhat incommunicative character. It was the mask of a house; it was not its face." But the narrator adds a different perspective, more like that in the Duveneck painting which precedes this picture: "The house in reality . . . looked off behind, into splendid openness and the range of the afternoon light."

CHAPTER 8

275 Map of the Santa Croce *quartiere*, by Kevin McIntyre; courtesy of the artist. Running east from the piazza, to the left of the church, are Via San Giuseppe and Via dei Malcontenti. Also to the east, we see the *viale*, created in the days of *Firenze Capitale*, curving around through Piazza Beccaria and Piazzale Donatello (with its English Cemetery). Via de' Benci is visible, running from the river to

the piazza, where it becomes Via Verdi, the latter ending in Piazza Salvemini.

Streets going from Piazza Salvemini toward the Duomo can be detected: Via San Egidio and Via dell' Oriuolo. There is Via Palmieri descending to Via delle Stinche; and one sees the little parallel streets heading over to Piazza San Firenze and, beyond it, to Piazza della Signoria. The artist has also scattered about images of some of the monuments in the area, among them the Badia and the Bargello, Palazzo Vecchio and the Loggia dei Lanzi, and the symbol of the great *gelateria* Vivoli.

275 Map of the area around Via della Fornace, by Kevin McIntyre; courtesy of the artist.

281 Piazza Santa Croce: jousting on horseback, by Vasari and G. Stradano. Scala/Art Resource, New York. The scene is among other views of games and celebrations in the frieze of the Room of Guadralda, in Palazzo Vecchio.

281 Piazza Santa Croce: preparation for a game of football (*calcio*), by Giuseppe Zocchi. Courtesy of Horace Gibson. The piazza has changed relatively little since the making of this sketch 250 years ago. Palazzo dell' Antella with its struts stands out clearly on the right-hand side, between two other buildings; the six smaller windows, top right, became ours. The church of course is without any ornate facade and, in the opinion of many, looked more impressive in the eighteenth century than it does today.

282 Piazza Santa Croce; photograph by Nancy Lewis. Palazzo dell' Antella is on the right in the picture; the top-floor-right windows are those of our apartment.

282 Piazza Santa Croce: marker of "midfield" for soccer games in the piazza. Photograph by Nancy Lewis.

282 Piazza Santa Croce: automobile doing somersault. From *La Nazione*, October 11, 1992; courtesy of *La Nazione*. This, as described in the text, was the climax of the live TV show, *Scommetiamo Che?*

285 Church of Santa Croce, with the Pazzi Chapel. Archivi Alinari.

285 Santa Croce, Bardi Chapel: *The Death of Saint Francis*, by Giotto. Archivi Alinari. The walls of the little Bardi Chapel (to the right of the altar) are covered with *The Stories of Saint Francis*, painted by Giotto in c. 1315–20, and perhaps his supreme artistic achievement. *The Death of Saint Francis*, with the dramatic arrangement of the gently, deeply grieving followers, has influenced the rendering of similar scenes through the ages, from Masaccio to Benjamin West. Though partly spoiled by time and flood, it remains one of the ultimate masterpieces.

303 Friends and resources in the Santa Croce neighborhood, mostly to be found on Via dei Neri. Photographs by Nancy Lewis. (*Top left*) The family at the Gastronomia Giuliana: Giuliano; his wife, Luigina; their son, Mario; and a friend, Giovanna. (*Middle left*) Some characteristic offerings in the *pizzicheria*. (*Top right*) The bakery, run by Renato Zanetti and his mother, Signora Zanetti. (*Middle right*) The fruit-and-vegetable shop of Andrea and Massimo Zoccali, with samples of their stock. (*Bottom*): Gino Noci, chef and owner of the restaurant I Che C'e C'e (on Via Megalotta), with Emma and Sophie Lewis.

Some Scholarly and Literary Sources

A. KEY SOURCES

Piero Bargellini and Ennio Guarnieri, *Le strade di Firenze*. Florence: Casa Editrice Bonechi, 1977; expanded and reissued in six volumes, 1986. A unique assemblage of information about Florence by means of a historical account of virtually every street in the city, listed alphabetically. Scores of streets in Florence are named for some significant historical figure, and *Le strade* gives an excellent biography of each one. To this great compilation I am indebted many times over.

Giovanni Fanelli, *Firenze: Architectura e città*. 2 volumes. Florence: Vallechi Editore, 1973. Professor Fanelli has also provided an abridged version of this book: *Firenze* (Rome: Editore Laterza, 1980, 1985), in the series *Le città nella storia d'Italia* (edited by Cesare di Seta).

Firenze: Architectura e città is a masterpiece: urban and cultural history raised to the level of high art. It traces the evolution of the *city*, via its architecture, from the beginnings through the great epoch (1250–1500), down through the centuries of the Grand Duchy, to modern and contemporary Florence. The focus is on the changing configuration of the city and the sources thereof, but every variety of urban history (population, cultural activity, internal strife, and so on) is taken into account. Several of the paeans to Florence that I have drawn upon—by Leonardo Bruni and others—can be found in Fanelli's pages. For me in this book, Giovanni Fanelli's *Firenze* has been, by all odds, the major and pervasive influence.

Mention should also be made of Professor Fanelli's handsomely illustrated text *Brunelleschi* (Florence: Becocci Editore, 1977), essentially the long section on Brunelleschi in the original *Firenze*.

Finally, I am happy to acknowledge Professor Fanelli's great kindness to Nancy Lewis and me during several of our Florence stays, when he escorted us to special cultural events and conversed freely with us about the history of the city and the region. On these occasions and others, Rosalia Fanelli (formerly of New

Haven, Connecticut) also provided enjoyable companionship and offered useful advice.

B. OTHER VALUABLE SOURCES

Harold Acton and Edward Chaney, editors, *Florence: A Traveller's Companion.* London: Constable and Company, 1986. An extremely useful and readable collection of pieces about Florence, its sites and monuments, and major events drawn from fourteenth-century chronicles, and reports of later visits by such "moderns" as John Ruskin and Henry James.

Luciano Berti, *Florence: The City and Its Art.* Florence: Saverio Becocci, 1979. Preface by Harold Acton.

Maurizio Bossi and Lucia Tonini, *L'idea di Firenze.* Florence: Centro Di, 1989.

Gene Brucker, editor, *The Society of Renaissance Florence: A Documentary Study.* New York: Harper Torchbooks, 1971. Descriptions of economic conditions, family life, communities, violence and crime, the *popolo minuto*, and other aspects of the urban scene, drawn skillfully from original documents by a leading scholar of Florentine history.

Eric Cochrane, *Florence in the Forgotten Centuries, 1527–1800.* Chicago: University of Chicago Press, 1973. A truly distinguished work of historical narrative. See comments in Chapter 5.

Christopher Hibbert, *The Rise and Fall of the House of Medici.* New York: Allan Lane, 1974; New York: Penguin Books, 1979. Mr. Hibbert's *Florence: The Biography of a City* (New York: Norton, 1993), appeared too late for me to draw upon its undoubtedly distinguished account.

Marcello Jacorossi, *Introduction to Florence.* Trans. Paul Garvin. Florence: Bonechi Editore, 1976. Italian title: *Incontro con Firenze.*

Mary McCarthy, *The Stones of Florence.* New York: Harcourt Brace, 1959 (paperback 1963). Beautifully written portrait of the city by a sophisticated outsider.

Ugo Pesce, *Firenze Capitale (1865–1870).* Florence: R. Bemporad e Figlio, 1904. The original text (with its subtitle, in English, "From the notes of an ex-reporter"), recently reprinted by Giunti.

Cecil Roth, *The History of the Jews of Italy.* The Jewish publication society of America, 1946.

Marcello Vannucci, *Storia di Firenze.* Rome: Newton Compton, 1986. A lively and loving, if also, at times, ironically critical account of the city: in its own subtitle (in translation), "From 59 B.C. to 1966, the two thousand years of a city unique in the world, which has enacted over the centuries a style of life all its own."

Giorgio Vasari, *The Lives of the Most Eminent Painters, Sculptors and Architects.* Trans. G. and C. de Vere. 10 volumes. London-New York, 1912.

Giovanni Villani, *Villani's Chronicles.* Trans. Rose E. Selfe, ed. Philip E. Wicksteed. London, 1906.

C. LITERARY VISITORS AND VISIONS

Clara Louise Dentler, *Famous Foreigners in Florence, 1400–1900.* Florence: Bemporad Marzocco, 1964. Exceedingly valuable checklist of several hundred visitors to

Florence over five centuries, with pictures of most of them and, at the back, a brief bibliography of each. A typical entry reads: "John Singleton Copley, painter. July 3, 1738, Boston–September 9, 1815, London"; followed by a page of biographical narrative, telling us that Copley came to Florence in 1774, the second American painter (after Benjamin West) to do so; that he spent two years in the city, giving "his whole attention to portraiture: and to Titian and Correggio as the masters whom he studied devotedly."

Olive Hamilton, *Paradise of Exiles: Tuscany and the British*. London: Andre Deutsch, 1974. English visitors from Sir John Hawkwood in the 1360s down through Byron and Landor, Browning and the Trollopes, to D. H. Lawrence and the Sitwells, with a final word on the 1966 flood.

William Dean Howells, *Tuscan Cities*. Boston, 1886. *Indian Summer*. Boston, 1886. See also James L. Woodress, *Howells & Italy* (Durham, N.C.: Duke University Press, 1952), an excellent and unusual study.

Henry James, *Italian Hours*. One recent edition: Century Classics, London, 1986. See also Bonney MacDonald, *Henry James's Italian Hours: Revelatory and Resistant Impressions* (in *Studies in Modern Literature*, A. Walton Litz, editor). Ann Arbor: UMI Research Press, 1990.

Giuseppe Prezzolini, *Come gli Americani scoprirono l'Italia*. Milan, 1933. American visitors to Italy before 1850; a landmark work.

John Ruskin, *Mornings in Florence*. Orpington, 1875–77. A masterpiece of sorts; hypnotically readable even when it is mind-bogglingly wrongheaded.

Giuliana Artom Trevès, *The Golden Ring: The Anglo-Florentines 1847–1862*. Trans. Sylvia Sprigge. London: Longman Greens, 1956. English and American visitors and residents in Florence, primarily during the "Browning era." A charming and informative study.

Nathalia Wright, *American Novelists in Italy. The Discoverers: Allston to James*. Philadelphia: University of Pennsylvania Press, 1965; paperback, 1974. A superior work which exactly carries out its title and subtitle.

D. RETROSPECTIVES

Florence observers continue to look back searchingly into their urban past, recent and relatively far-gone, and to re-create it in pictures and language. The following are among the texts of this kind that I drew upon:

Piero Bargellini, *Com' era Firenze cento anni fa* (*What Florence Was Like a Hundred Years Ago*). Florence: Casa Editrice Bonechi, 1977. The city in the 1860s, as it became the capital of the Kingdom of Italy and underwent transformations.

Piero Magi, *Firenze d'una volta*. Florence: Casa Editrice Bonechi, 1973. Florence in the eighteenth century and later: in paintings and designs from the Museo di Firenze com' era (Zocchi and others). A lovely volume.

Franco Nencini, *Firenze: I giorni del diluvio*. Florence: Sansoni, November 1966. Photographs taken during the great flood and published three weeks later.

Piero Pieroni, *Firenze: Gli anni terribili, dal 1940 all' emergenza*. Florence: Casa Editrice Bonechi, 1969. Florence during the Second World War, with emphasis on the final and terrible phases in the summer of 1944.

Some Scholarly and Literary Sources

E. ON TRANSLATIONS OF DANTE

My choice of the John Ciardi translation of the *Divina Commedia* reflects a personal preference rather than a scholarly and aesthetic judgment. I myself first read the *Commedia*—stray parts of it—in the famous 1805–14 English blank verse translation by H. F. Cary. The version I kept at hand when I read the *Commedia* straight through in college was the widely circulated Temple Classics edition, translated by P. H. Wicksteed. This edition carried the Italian on the lefthand side and the closely approximating prose translation on the right.

Later I became acquainted with the superb verse-translation of Laurence Binyon (completed 1943), which, all things considered, may be the most satisfying English version yet produced, its supple and flexible triple rhyming keeping pace with Dante's. I have also enjoyed the strong prose translation (1939–46) by J. D. Sinclair, and read through much of it when Nancy Lewis was taking part in a two-year seminar on the *Divina Commedia* (every word of it), brilliantly conducted in New Haven by Bianca Calabresi. Dorothy Sayers's *terza rima* rendering (finished 1962) appealed in part because of my deep addiction to her mystery novels.

For purposes of quotation, I do favor the verse translations (though, sometimes, to get the full inner sense of a passage, a prose version is necessary); and for the purposes of this book, I could certainly have drawn on the Binyon work. I chose John Ciardi's text—it was finished in 1970 and published by the New American Library in New York—partly because the ingenuity of its language choice and its rhyming appeals to me, or, perhaps I should say, to my American ear. Ciardi's verse form is *aba cdc*, as in the passage quoted in Chapter 1:

> And curse or custom so transforms all men
> who live there in that miserable valley [the Casentino]
> one would believe they fed in Circe's pen.
>
> It sets its first weak course among sour swine,
> indecent beasts more fit to grub and grunt
> for acorns than to sit at bread and wine.

Dudley Fitts, one of this country's most accomplished translators, says the Ciardi version "has given us . . . a credible, passionate *persona* of the poet," and is "strong and noble in utterance."

Beyond that, I felt a sort of personal involvement with this translation. I talked about it many times with the translator, on visits with him in Rome and New Jersey, and even made a modest hint of a suggestion here and there. My choice of the Ciardi *Commedia* is a belated salute to a dear friend.

F. DICTIONARIES

John Fleming, Hugh Honour, and Nikolaus Pevsner, *Dictionary of Architecture*. London: Penguin Books, 1966 (4th ed., 1991). A major resource for anyone dealing in cultural history. See my Chapter 6 for mention of our enjoyable visits to Messrs. Fleming and Honour at their Tuscan home outside of Lucca.

James Hall, *Dictionary of Subjects and Symbols in Art*. New York: Harper & Row, 1974; rev. ed., 1979. Introduction by Kenneth Clark. The author declares in his own preface, "This book is about the subject-matter of art, about the stories it tells and the people it portrays"; and the volume does exactly that in an engrossing and illuminating way, with "art" understood as referring primarily to Western art.

Edward Lucie-Smith, *The Thames and Hudson Dictionary of Art Terms*. London: Thames and Hudson, 1984 (paperback, 1988, 1991). Excellent reference book, nicely illustrated.

G. SOME INDIVIDUAL STUDIES

Frank Duveneck: Robert Neuhaus, *Unsuspected Genius: The Art and Life of Frank Duveneck*. San Francisco: Bedford Press, 1987.

Ghirlandaio: Emma Micheletti, *Domenico Ghirlandaio*. Trans. Anthony Brierly. Florence: SCALA, 1990.

Michelangelo: Howard Hibbard, *Michelangelo*. New York: Harper & Row, 1974. Sensitive and intelligent critical biography.

Michelozzo: Miranda Ferrara and Francesco Quintero, *Michelozzo di Bartolomeo*. Florence: Salimbeni, 1984. Solidly informative.

Michelucci: *Le Città di Michelucci*. Catalogue of 1976 exhibition, held in Fiesole, of Michelucci's variety of urban designs, especially those for the city of Florence. Copyright by the Commune di Fiesole. A fascinating compilation.

Poggi: *Giuseppe Poggi e Firenze*. Catalogue of 1989–90 exhibition, in the Uffizi, of Poggi's various designs, visionary and practical, for the enlargement and/or improvement of Florence. Copyright ALINEA, Florence, 1989. Mostly impressive, sometimes saddening.

Church of Santissima Annunziata: Francesca Petrucci, *Santissima Annunziata*. Rome: Fratelli Palombi, 1992.

Note: I have also studied with much pleasure and profit the volumes in the Classici dell' Arte series published by Rizzoli in Milan. Each of these offers *l'opera completa* of some individual artist from medieval European times (e.g., Giotto) to the present (e.g., Picasso), in each case supplying a biography, a collection of judgments by the artist's contemporaries, and full notations. Among the artists in this series that are relevant to the present book: Giotto, Simone Martini, Masaccio, Piero della Francesca, Perugino, Leonardo (paintings), Michelangelo (paintings), Titian.

A NOTE ON THE SPELLING OF FLORENTINE NAMES

The spelling of Florentine proper names, both of persons and of places, has been standardized in the past century and a half, but it still remains somewhat eccentric and variable. Even today, you can find a famous name spelled Michelangelo or

Michelangiolo or Michelagnolo. In the same text, you can find a famous old family name referred to as de' Bardi, and the street named for that family as dei Bardi.

Firenze itself could carry an *o*—Fiorenze—up until the modern epoch, and perhaps it still should, to show its origin in the word *fiore* (flower).

My best hope is simply to have been consistent in my choice among the various possible spellings of any given name.

Contemporary Guidances

Eve Borsook, *The Companion Guide to Florence*. London: HarperCollins, 1966 (5th ed., 1988). This is probably the best English-language guide to Florence ever written (and a major entry in the British series to which Hugh Honour contributed his superb *Companion Guide to Venice*). It is a superior mixture of meticulous site-by-site descriptions, searching summaries of Florentine sociopolitical and cultural history, and wise observations drawn from personal experience. It is a book to read, and read in, when one is visiting Florence, and later when one is back home. As my frequent citation of it suggests, Eve Borsook's *Florence* has been as valuable to me in its way as Giovanni Fanelli's *Firenze: Architectura e città*.

    I am also glad to record our appreciation of Ms. Borsook's many kindnesses and her hospitality over more than twenty years. At the Villa I Tatti (where she is a chief staff member), at her attractive home on the hillside near San Miniato, and at various places in town, she herself has been a memorable companion-guide, and one of our most cherished Florentines.

Sheila Hale, *The American Express Pocket Guide to Florence and Tuscany*. New York: Prentice-Hall, 1983. A slim and definitely pocketable (*tascabile*) guidebook, written with wit, vim, discrimination, and, once in a while, arguable opinions.

Alta Macadam, *Blue Guide: Florence*. With street atlas, maps and plans by John Flower. New York: W. W. Norton, 1991. An always dependable volume in a fine series.

Christopher Cowie, *Eating Out in Florence and Vicinity*. Florence: Tower Press, no date given, but apparently 1990. Much the most satisfying introduction to its subject: the restaurants of Florence. The book divides the restaurants into city sections (the Duomo, Piazza Signoria, Santo Spirito, etc.); and there are well-informed, unpretentious discussions of Tuscan food in general and Tuscan wines. Of the two hundred restaurants listed, about forty are treated in some detail, with a profile of the owner and an identification of about a dozen choice items on the characteristic menu.

Edward Hutton, *Florence*. London: Hollis & Carter, 1966. This thoroughly admirable and eminently readable work is a discursive guidebook, leading the reader through site after site and monument after monument. It is the product of a long-time residence in Florence and involvement in its affairs, by the author of thirty-some other books, including three on Florence and Tuscany, plus biographies of Boccaccio and Aretino.

Knopf Guides: Florence. New York: Alfred A. Knopf, 1993. Originally written in French; translated by Cordelia Unger-Hamilton. This is essentially a pictorial guide to the city, with hundreds of pictures amid a flow of text. It is a hefty little package, and appeared too late for me to draw on in this study.

Touring Club Italiano: Firenze e dintorni. Milan, 1922 (6th ed., 1984; others since then). No author given. The indispensable work in Italian.

See also: Touring Club Italiano's volume *Toscana* (Milan, 1922; reprinted regularly). The same high order as the *Firenze* guide, and considerably thicker.

General Index

For the convenience of the reader, a separate index devoted exclusively to Florentine place-names follows the General Index.

Abruzzi, 3, 67

Acton, Harold, 260, 319

Adams, Henry, 110

Adimari family, 93

Alberti, Leon Battista, 29, 38, 43, 72, 129, 145, 169, 256

Albizzi family, 120; Rinaldo, 136–37

Amidei family, 28

Ammannati, Bartolomeo, 30, 174–75; designs Ponte Santa Trinità, 43–44

Ammirato, Scipione, 178

Anderlini, Andrea, 283–84

Andrea del Sarto, 164

Angelico, Fra, 9, 163, 164, 269; *Annunciation*, 9, 163

Antella, Niccolo dell', 276

Apennines, 23

Arezzo, 5, 23, 132

Ariosto, Ludovico, *Orlando Furioso*, 6

Arnolfo di Cambio, 14, 33–34, 52, 57, 84, 92, 94–108, 112, 141, 145, 185, 328; 1284 wall circuit, 94–98; Duomo, 103–5; Orsanmichele, 100; Palazzo Vecchio, 105–7; Santa Croce, 100–2

Artusi, Pellegrini, 311

Assisi, 5

Azeglio, Massimo d', 183

Baccio d'Agnolo, 11–12

Barbigia, Costanza del, 276

Bardi family, 125, 158; Contessina (wife of Cosimo the Elder), 158

Bargellini, Piero, 40, 54, 192, 292, 335

Bartolini, Giovanni, 11–12

Beccaria, Cesare, 293

Bellini, Giovanni, 15

Benci di Cione, 128

Berenson, Bernard, 52

Bibbiena, 23

Boccaccio, Giovanni, 6, 63, 126–28

Bonaventuri, Piero, 218, 221–22

Boott, Elizabeth, 264

Borgese, Giuseppe, 6

Borgia, Lucrezia, 12

Borsook, Eve, 170, 190, 204, 297, 341

Bossi, Maurizio, 260–61, 272, 325

Botticelli, Sandro, 15, 114, 115, 268–69

Bramante, Donato, 11

Brewster family: Christopher (son of Henry), 231; Christopher Starr, 227; Clotilde (Peploe), 226, 232, 324; Harry, 217, 226, 231–32, 324; Henry

Brewster family (*cont.*)
  ("H. B."), 227, 230–31; Kingman, 202, 227n; William, 226
Bronson, Edith, 256
Bronson, Katherine DeKay, 255–56
Bronzino, Agnolo, 15, 175, 258–59
Browning, Elizabeth Barrett, 206–11, 210n; *Casa Guidi Windows*, 207–8, 293–94
Browning, Robert, 206, 209, 210–11, 212n
Brunelleschi, Filippo, 34, 52, 53, 94, 120, 141–58, 159, 166, 330; Duomo, 142–48; Ospedale degli Innocenti, 154–58; Pazzi Chapel, 46, 143; San Lorenzo, 148–51; Santo Spirito, 141–42
Bruni, Leonardo, 7, 102, 132
Buondelmonte de' Buondelmonti, 28
Buontalenti, Bernardo, 174, 212, 219
Burnham, Daniel H., 110

Calabresi, Anne, 275n, 323
Calabresi, Guido, 275n, 323
Campagni, Dino, 21, 27, 54; *Cronaca*, 21
Campaldino (battle of, 1289), 14, 57, 61–63
Cappello, Bianca, 163–64, 212, 218–24
Capponi, Gino, 260
Casa Guidi, 206–7, 211
Casentino, 23, 24, 57–58; Monte Falterona, 58
Cavalcanti, Guido, 240–41
Cavour, Camillo, 209
Cellini, Benvenuto, 115, 116, 175, 258
Cellini, Giovanni, 115–16
Charles V, Emperor, 82, 206
Chirici, Marcello, 233, 237
Chiusi, 235
Ciardi, John, 21–23, 338
Cicero, 7, 98–99
Cimabue, Giovanni, 83; *Crucifixion*, 46; *Madonna*, 293–94
Cinelli family: Delfino, 277; Federica, 277–78, 319, 324
Clark, Eleanor, 15–16, 75; *Rome and a Villa*, 15

Cochrane, Eric, 174, 176
Cole, Thomas, 264
Concini, Concino, 248
Cooper, James Fenimore, 252
Cortona, 234–35
Cowie, Christopher, *Eating Out in Florence*, 307, 341
Crane, Hart, 41, 109

Dante Alighieri, 26, 28–29, 30, 63–64, 93, 124, 284; *Divine Comedy*, 6, 21–23, 60–61, 64, 77, 85–86, 93, 94
Dati, Edoardo, 194
Dati, Goro, 133–34
Dei, Benedetto, 165, 170
della Robbia, Andrea, 78 (La Verna terra-cottas), 156
della Robbia, Luca, 78
Dominicans, 87, 89
Donatello, 102, 143, 151, 184, 234; *Abundance*, 191; *Judith and Holofernes*, 175; *Mary Magdalene*, 47; Old Sacristy doors, 149–51
Donati family, 28
Dori, Eleanora, 248–50
Dostoyevsky, Fyodor, 260
Duke of Athens, 124–25
Duveneck, Frank, 264–65

Edward III (King of England), 125
Eleonora of Toledo, 37, 172, 219, 258
Eliot, T. S., 241; *The Waste Land*, 55, 108–9
Emerson, Ralph Waldo, 8, 12, 111, 261
Empoli, 23

Fanelli, Giovanni, 88–89, 94–95, 145, 170, 184, 194, 335–36
Farinata degli Uberti, 85–86
Ferri, Antonio, 179
Ficino, Marsilio, 72, 162
Fleming, John, 233
Florence:
  HISTORY OF: founding, 23–24; the Roman city, 24; origins of Guelph-Ghibelline conflict, 28–29; *Primo Popolo*, 33, 89–90; formation of the

guilds, 86–87, 92, 94; *Secondo Popolo*, 92–93; division into *quartieri*, 107–8; the Black Death, 126–28; revolt of the *Ciompi*, 129–30; leadership of the Medici (*see* Medici family, esp. Cosimo the Elder); the ducal Medicis, 17ff; House of Lorraine, 180–81; Florence becomes the capital of the Kingdom of Italy, 183–89; destruction of the Mercato Vecchio area, 189–95; German destruction of Florentine bridges (summer 1944), 49–51
WALL-CIRCUITS OF: 1180, 90, 95; 1284, 33–35, 95–98; destruction of the 1284 circuit (1864), 185–89
FLOODS OF: 1177, 41; 1288, 14; 1333, 42–43, 51, 124; 1465, 43; 1557, 51; 1844, 44, 328; 1966, 44–49, 52
SLAVERY IN: 131, 156n
CONTEMPORARY LABOR STRIKES IN: 253–55, 313–14
AMERICAN WRITERS IN: Melville, 12–13; overview of the subject, 261–62; Howells and Henry James, 265–71
Foggini, G. B., 192
Fossi, Nannina Rucellai, 256
Franchetti, Amerigo, 240
Franciscans, 87, 88, 89
Francis of Assisi (Saint), 61, 219–20, 329
Frescobaldi, Lamberto, 33

Gaddi, Agnolo, 284
Gaddi, Taddeo, 35
Galilei, Galileo, 47
Geis, Robert, and family, 247, 324
Ghiberti, Lorenzo, 294; Gates of Paradise, 47, 144n
Ghirlandaio, Domenico, 8, 10, 249–50, 328, 333
Giaccalone, Ida, 200–2
Giambologna, 116, 157, 205, 252
Giano della Bella, 93–94
Gibson, Horace, 242, 324
Giotto, 30, 35, 43, 46, 102, 155; Campanile, 120, 269; *Death of Saint Francis*, 288

Giovanna (Joan) of Austria (wife of Francesco I), 37, 220, 222
Giovanni di San Giovanni, 277
Gonfolina, 23
Gozzoli, Benozzo, 160, 256
Guadralda (wife of Guidoguerra IV), 59–61, 329
Guelph-Ghibelline conflict, 28–29, 61–62, 84–86, 91, 268
Guidi family, 43, 58–61; Francesco, 80; Guido Bevisangue, 58; Guidoguerra I, 59; Guidoguerra IV, 59; Guidonovello, 63; Simone di Battifolle, 61; Telda (Countess), 80

Hale, Sheila, *American Express Guide to Florence and Tuscany*, 245, 284, 341
Harvard University, 6
Haskell, Francis, 261, 271
Hawthorne, Nathaniel, 261
Hazan, Marcella, 237n
Hemingway, Ernest, *Across the River and Into the Trees*, 14n
Henry IV, Emperor, 59
Hibbert, Christopher, 279, 282n
Hitler, Adolf, 50–51
Honour, Hugh, 180, 233
Howells, William Dean, 103–5, 111–12, 182, 251, 260, 261–62, 265–69; *Indian Summer*, 266–67
Hutton, Edward, 219, 224, 341–42

James, Henry, 107, 109–10, 190, 195, 203, 229, 231, 248, 251–52, 255–56, 258–59, 261–64, 311–12; *Italian Hours*, 267, 268–70; *The Portrait of a Lady*, 270–71

Kesselring, Albert, 51

Landino, Cristoforo, 71
Lawrence, D. H., 109, 238–39
Leonardo da Vinci, 6, 26n, 114, 115, 225, 234
Lewis, Beatrix, 200–2
Lewis, Kate, 202
Lewis, Nancy, 8, 258

Licht, Fred, 242, 323–24
Licht, Meg, 242, 323–24
L'idea di Firenze, 271
Lippi, Fra Filippo, 160, 234
Liszt, Franz, 228
Livorno, 23, 132
Longfellow, Henry Wadsworth, 251,
    261
Lorraine, House of, 180; Ferdinando III,
    182; Francesco Stefano, 180; Pietro
    Leopoldo, 163, 180–81, 207, 208–9,
    273
Lowell, James Russell, 12
Lucca, 233

Macaulay, Thomas Babington, 12
Machiavelli, Niccolo, 10, 26n, 102
Magalotti, Lorenzo, 8
Malatesta, Annalena, 203
Manetti, Antonio, 149, 150, 159
Marguerite de Navarre, 6
Mariotti, Enrico (Harry), 14n
Masaccio, 148, 296–97
Matilda, countess of Tuscany, 59
Matthiessen, F. O., 7, 8
McCarthy, Mary, *The Stones of Florence*,
    54, 146
McIntyre, Kevin, 242, 324
Medici family, 134–35; Alessandro, 171–
    72, 276; Bianca, 160; Cosimino, 160;
    Cosimo I (Duke and Grand Duke),
    37, 44, 96, 105, 136, 140, 172–75,
    191, 218, 258; Cosimo II, 179; Co-
    simo III, 179; Cosimo the Elder, 35,
    80, 120, 136–41, 158–62, 168, 171;
    Ferdinando I (formerly Cardinal),
    223, 250; Francesco I, 212, 218–24,
    250; Gian Gastone, 180; Giovanni di
    Bicci, 120, 135–36, 148; Giovanni di
    Cosimo, 160; Giovanni di Lorenzo
    (*see* Popes: Leo X); Giuliano, 71,
    160, 282n; Giulio (*see* Popes: Clem-
    ent VII); Isabella, 219, 222; Loren-
    zaccio, 172; Lorenzo di Giovanni,
    136, 172; Lorenzo the Magnificent,
    72, 139, 160, 163, 171, 217, 225n,
    279, 282; Lucrezia, 160; Maria, 160;

Nannina, 256; Piero di Cosimo
    ("the Gouty"), 160, 164, 171; Piero
    di Lorenzo, 140, 171; Salvestro, 35,
    134
Meiners, Rita, 278, 319
Melville, Herman, 8, 12, 14
Michelangelo Buonarroti, 9, 10, 15, 43,
    84, 102, 288–89; *David*, 9, 112–18,
    175; Laurentian Library staircase,
    176; New Sacristy, 176
Michelozzo, 120, 141, 144, 159–60, 162–
    64
Michelucci, Giovanni, 52–53, 289
Middledorf, Ulrich, 6, 9
Milan, 4
monasteries: Camaldoli, 62, 68, 70–71;
    Camaldoli (hermitage), 69–70; La
    Verna, 62, 71–73, 75–79
Montaigne, Michel de, 252–53
Monte Falterona, 23, 58
Montepulciano, 132, 159, 235–37,
    257
Munich, Matthew, 211

Naples, 4
Nivola, Constantino, 257

Orcagna, Andrea, 9, 128, 206
Origo, Iris, 234, 244
Orsini, Clarice, 282

Panciatichi, Lucrezia, 258–59
Parigi, Alfonso the Elder, 203
Parigi, Alfonso the Younger, 205
Parigi, Giulio, 203, 277, 290, 299
Peruzzi family, 125, 287, 288
Pescara, 5
Petrarch, 7, 243
Piccarda Bueri (wife of Cosimo the
    Elder), 136
Piccini, Giulio (Jarro), 192–94
Piccolomini family: Enea Silvia (Pope
    Pio II), 257, 277; Federica (*see* Ci-
    nelli family); Sallustio, 277
Pico della Mirandola, 163
Piero della Francesca, 284
Pisa, 23, 24, 40, 132

General Index

Pisano family: Andrea, 47; Nicola di, 34

Pitti family, 37; Luca, 166, 168

Poggi, Enrico, 182

Poggi, Giuseppe, 40, 54, 183, 185–89, 295

Poliziano, Angelo, 7, 163, 236

Pontassieve, 23

Popes: Alexander VI, 171; Clement VII, 96, 139, 171; Gregory VII, 59n; Innocent III, 61; Leo X, 139, 171, 206, 217

Poppi, 23, 58, 68–69

Porsena, Lars, 235

Portinari, Beatrice, 290

Portinari, Folco, 290

Pratolini, Vasco, 297

Prezzolini, Giuseppe, 272n

Pulci, Luigi, 280

Raimondi, Livia, 163

Raphael Sanzio, 11

Robinson, Edwin Arlington, 216

Rome (ancient), 98–99

Rome (modern), 3, 4, 5, 12, 15–16

Roscoe, William, 182

Rossellino, Bernardo, 102

Rossi, Ottone, 186

Rubaconte, *podestà* of Florence, 30

Rucellai, Giovanni, 169, 256

Ruskin, John, *Mornings in Florence*, 251, 284, 312

Sabatini, Raffaello, 14n

Sachetti, Franco, 93

Salsi, Renzo, 304–5, 319

Salutati, Coluccio, 132

Salvemini, Gaetano, 6, 289–90

Salzburg Seminar in American Studies, 8

San Francesco di Paola, 213, 217–18, 225n

Sangallo, Giuliano da, 114, 115, 286

San Miniato Tedesco, 23

San Quirico, 257

Savioli, Leopardo, 55

Savonarola, Girolamo, 114, 171

Schauffelen, Irene, 228, 230

Servites, 87

Signorelli, Luca, 15

Silone, Ignazio, 3, 4, 67

Simone di Francesco Talenti, 128

Smyth, Ethel, 229–30

Spencer, Theodore, 6

Spini, Geri degli, 14

Sprigge, Sylvia, 209n

Strozzi family: Alessandro, 224; Filippo, 168–69; Palla, 168

Tacca, Pietro, 157, 174

Taine, Hippolyte, 146, 148

Tasso, Torquato, 212

Tornabuoni, Lucrezia (wife of Piero di Cosimo), 160

Tribaldo de' Rossi, 83–84

Turin, 4

Uberti family, 85–86, 291

Uccello, Paolo, 46

Umiliati, 29, 88, 249

University of Chicago, 6, 8

Val d'Orcia, 257

Vannucci, Marcello, 138, 183, 288, 336

Vasari, Giorgio, 34, 35, 37, 95, 102, 103, 143, 159, 174, 176, 219, 293, 328, 332; Corridor, 37, 44, 52, 174; *Lives of the Most Eminent Painters . . .* , 176; Loggia del Pesce, 191, 194n; Uffizi, 174

Venice, 179–80

Verrocchio, Andrea del, 144

Vespucci family, 249, 250; Amerigo, 249–50, 333

Vieusseux, Gian Pietro, 209, 260

Villani, Giovanni, 30, 41–43, 54, 60, 62–63, 86, 97, 121–22

Virgil, *Aeneid*, 99, 188
Vittorio Emmanuele, King, 181–83, 189, 195
Volterra, 237–38
von Hildebrand, Adolf, 227–29
von Hildebrand, Elizabeth, 231
von Stockhausen, Julia, 227

Warren, Robert Penn, 73–75
Wharton, Edith, 71–73, 244, 256, 261
Woolf, Virginia, 16–17, 109; *Mrs. Dalloway*, 16–17
Woolson, Constance Fenimore, 261
Wright, Nathalia, 272n

Zocchi, Giuseppe, 290, 327

Index of Florentine Place-names

Accademia, 9, 118
American School of Florence, 240–42
Annalena (pensione), 200, 203
Arno, the, 3, 14, 21–56

Baptistery, 9
Bargello, 9, 16, 91, 92n, 95, 121
Bellosguardo, 199, 215, 240, 264–65
Boboli Gardens, 53, 175, 203–5, 269
BORGHI:
    degli Albizzi, 290
    Allegri, 293–94
    dei Greci, 287, 294
    Ognissanti, 246–47
    San Frediano, 29, 54–55, 130
    San Jacopo, 9, 51

CarLies, 305–6
Casa Boccaccio, 199
Cascine, 180, 195
CHURCHES:
    Badia, 88, 91, 92n, 99–100, 121
    Carmine: Brancacci Chapel, 296–97,
      318
    Duomo (Santa Maria del Fiore), 8, 9,
      37, 103–5, 142–48, 252, 269
    Saint James, 318
    San Firenze, 180

San Frediano in Cestello, 179
San Lorenzo, 9, 120; Medici Mauso-
    leum, 178–79; New Sacristy, 176;
    Old Sacristy, 143
San Marco, 9, 119, 162–64; Convent,
    163
San Salvatore al Monte, 189
Santa Croce, 9, 46, 96, 100–2, 184,
    252, 273, 275, 284–86, 329; Giotto's
    frescoes, 46; tombs of illustrious
    Florentines, 284, 286
Santa Maria Novella, 9, 46, 96, 251,
    268
Santa Trinità, 10, 11
Santissima Annunziata, 96, 164
Santo Spirito, 34, 96
Santo Stefano, 51
Costa dei Magnoli, 3

Fiesole, 24
Fortezza da Basso, 186
Fortezza di Belvedere, 188

Gabinetto Vieusseux, 260–61
German Institute, 6
ghetto (in Florence), 172–74, 191

Hospital of Santa Maria Nuova, 290
HOTELS:
  du Nord, 12
  Excelsior, 14n, 306

Isola delle Stinche, 291

Largo Bargellini, 292
Loggia dei Lanzi (formerly della Signo-
  ria), 121, 128–29, 330
Lungarni, 14, 40, 190; Corsini, 179

Medici tombs, 9
Mercato Nuovo, 174
Mercato Vecchio, 190–94, 332
Museo di Firenze com' era, 290, 325

Oltrarno, 26, 34
Orsanmichele, 9, 29, 100, 121, 128
Ospedale degli Innocenti, 119

PALAZZI (palaces):
  dell' Antella, 179, 276–78, 287
  Bartolini-Salimbene, 11–12, 15
  Corsini, 14–15, 16, 179
  Davanzati, 304
  Gondi, 294–95
  Larderel, 11
  della Marescialla, 247
  Medici, 9, 120, 159–62, 331
  Pitti, 9, 37, 50–51, 166–68, 331
  Ricasoli, 16
  Rucellai, 166, 169–170
  Serristori, 286
  Spini, 14–15, 16, 27
  Strozzi, 9, 83–84, 168–70, 260
  Vecchio, 9, 10, 16, 37, 53, 92, 104–10,
    121, 286

Paperback Exchange, 302–3
PIAZZE, PIAZZALE (plazas):
  Beccaria, 186, 293
  della Calza, 204–5
  Carmine, 89
  Donatello, 186; English cemetery, 209
  del Duomo, 55, 297
  della Libertà, 186, 187
  Michelangelo, 35, 107, 189

Peruzzi, 287
Piave, 293
Repubblica, 194–95
Salvemini, 289
San Felice, 206
San Firenze, 180n, 294–95
San Lorenzo, 34
San Marco, 119, 163–64
San Pietro Maggiore, 291
Santa Croce, 89, 185, 278–79
Santa Maria Novella, 89, 184, 251–53
Santa Trinità, 9, 10, 11, 243, 327
Santissima Annunziata, 89, 154–58,
  278, 331
Santo Spirito, 26, 89, 123, 142
della Signoria, 9, 10, 51, 85, 88, 106,
  107, 114; restoration of, 295–96
PONTI (bridges):
  Amerigo Vespucci, 54
  alla Carraia, 27, 29, 34, 54, 88, 96, 97,
    249
  alle Grazie (formerly Rubaconte), 30,
    34, 38, 44, 50, 97, 275
  San Niccolò, 50, 54, 55, 199, 275
  Santa Trinità, 9, 10, 27, 33, 53–54, 84,
    88, 174; *Primavera*, 54
  Vecchio, 5, 9, 27, 28, 29, 35, 38, 50–
    51, 55, 328
  Verrazzano, 54–55
  della Vittoria, 50, 54, 55
PORTE (gates):
  alla Croce, 185, 186
  di Giustizia, 292
  al Pinti, 95, 186
  Romana, 33, 34, 170, 188, 206
  San Frediano, 84
  San Niccolò, 273

QUARTIERI
  Santa Croce, 273–75, 286–95, 298–
    99
  Santa Maria Novella, 251
  Santo Spirito (San Frediano section),
    297–98

railroad station of Florence (Santa Maria
  Novella), 252, 253

Index of Florentine Place-names

RESTAURANTS:
Acquacotta, 304
La Baraonda, 292, 310–11
Cibreo, 292, 310
Dino, 292, 310
Doney's Cafe, 12, 51
Harry's Bar, 10, 14, 311; Leo Vado-
  rini, 10, 14n, 311, 319
I Che C'e C'e, 307–10; Gino Noci,
  chef, 307–8, 309–10, 319
Leland's Tea Room, 10–11, 14
Tavola Calda, 310

Salimbeni (bookstore), 275, 304

Torre della Zecca Vecchia, 293
Torre di Bellosguardo, 240–42

Uffizi, 3, 4, 9, 37, 104, 174, 246; Piazza,
  332

VIE, VIALE (streets); see also BORGHI
Anguillara, 288
dei Bardi, 26, 35, 51
dei Benci, 34, 44, 289
dei Bentaccordi, 288
dei Calzaiuoli, 9, 106
Cavour, 160, 245
dei Colli, 189
G. B. Foggini, 255

della Fornace, 273
de' Fossi, 249
Ghibellina, 38, 289
Guicciardini, 51
Lamarmora, 8, 119
Maggio, 26, 33, 44, 212, 243
dei Malcontenti, 292–93
dei Neri, 299–301
Oriuolo, 184, 290
Palmieri, 275, 291–92
Parione, 10, 14, 185
Pinzochere, 292
Por Santa Maria, 51, 309
Porta Rossa, 185
Proconsolo, 90
Ricasoli, 119
Romana, 170, 200–3, 204–6, 243–44
Sant' Egidio, 290
dei Servi, 158, 309
delle Terme, 12
Tornabuoni, 9, 10, 11, 44, 184
Torta, 288
Verdi, 289
della Vigna Nuova, 9
Villani, 214
Villa Mercedes (formerly Castellani),
  270, 333
Villa San Francesco di Paola, 213, 214,
  217, 228–29, 239–40
Vivoli, 275, 291–92